Randolph Sinks Foster

Studies in Theology

Vol. 5

Randolph Sinks Foster

Studies in Theology
Vol. 5

ISBN/EAN: 9783337815875

Printed in Europe, USA, Canada, Australia, Japan

Cover: Foto ©Andreas Hilbeck / pixelio.de

More available books at **www.hansebooks.com**

WORKS OF RANDOLPH S. FOSTER, LL.D.

Beyond the Grave,	$1 20
Centenary Thoughts for the Pew and Pulpit,	1 50
Christian Purity,	1 35
Objections to Calvinism,	75
Philosophy of Christian Experience,	1 00
Studies in Theology:	
Vol. I. Prolegomena,	3 00
" II. Theism,	3 00
" III. The Supernatural Book,	3 00
" IV. Creation,	3 00
" V. God, Nature and Attributes,	3 00
Union of Episcopal Methodism,	75

Studies in Theology.—V

GOD

NATURE AND ATTRIBUTES

BY

RANDOLPH S. FOSTER, D.D., LL.D.

A Bishop of the Methodist Episcopal Church

ΠΡΟΣ ΤΟ ΦΩΣ

NEW YORK: EATON & MAINS
CINCINNATI: CURTS & JENNINGS
1897

Copyright by
EATON & MAINS,
1897.

EATON & MAINS PRESS,
150 Fifth Avenue, New York.

PREFATORY STATEMENTS.

IN a former treatise by the author, the second volume in the series of *Studies in Theology*, it was shown that the outcome of rational thought is the certainty of the existence of an eternal personal Cause as ground and source of the universe. In that discussion the sole aim was to educe evidence in support of that position. The argument necessarily involved statements and reasonings which in a general way have bearings on the deeper questions of the nature and attributes of that causal Being. The existence of a first cause, and the nature and attributes of the Being who is that first cause, are closely related subjects; but they are also distinct, and require distinct treatment.

The present volume is occupied wholly with the second question. In the former discussion the argument was educed from nature—the cosmos was alone interrogated. In the discussion now to be conducted nature and revelation will jointly furnish the materials of the argument and conclusion; and it will be shown that, while each in its own way contributes its specific material, the two lead to precisely the same finding. What revelation affirms of the nature and attributes of God is found to be implicit in the Creator of the universe.

It will be of service to the reader to reexamine, if within his reach, the treatise on *Cosmic Theism* before taking up the discussions conducted in this volume. The two discussions are so related that neither is complete without the other; but lest it may not be convenient to recur to the former treatise some points of essential bearing are repeated here with sufficient fullness to preserve the completeness of the argument.

The present discussion proceeds upon the conceded grounds that God is not an object of immediate cognition either as to being, nature, or attributes. He does not appear at all, either initially or at any time, as an object of perception. Reason sees him only as he is mediated as ground of phenomena of persons and things. Thus he is discovered by the reason as existing, and thus his attributes become known. Revelation adds its light, but never contradicts these primary outgivings of the intelligence itself.

Cause is as fully known by the effects which it produces as if the Being who is cause were an immediate object of cognition.

Since our knowledge of God concededly comes thus through his works, or through effects of which he is cause, and not by immediate visions, through his works we must arrive at the knowledge of his attributes; but the knowledge thus acquired is no less real than if he were a direct object of vision in his substance and essence. In his works *he is not seen*, but *it is seen that he is the worker*. This knowledge is intuitive, immediate. The work is seen, and is thus known. The worker is not seen, but it is seen that he is, and it is seen that he has inherent in him all the attributes manifested or of necessity required for the work performed.

The quality of a true science has been denied to theology on the ground that it rests on the fact of an infinite and absolute *True science denied to theology.* Being. This, it is said, can never be matter of knowledge, and so the whole superstructure must in the necessity of the case be a superstructure of belief merely, without warrant of reality of any kind. When theologians and

philosophers present a series of definitions, notions, detailed propositions, and dogmas with reference to this world of mystery, in which the existence, personality, and interior nature of the absolute and its relation to the finite world are laid down with a show of systematic precision, and we are asked to accept this as entitled to rank as knowledge beside the sciences of observation and experience, we are informed that the claim cannot be accepted. "Natural Theology," says one eminent scientific authority, " is a science falsely so called. . . . It seeks to weigh the infinite in balances of the finite. . . . It is to the scientific man a delusion, to the religious man a snare." "If," says another, "religion and science are to be reconciled, the basis of reconciliation must be this deepest, widest, and most certain of all facts— that to us the power the universe manifests is utterly inscrutable."*
"We not only learn by the fruitlessness of all our efforts that the reality underlying appearances is totally and forever inconceivable by us, but we also know why from the very nature of our intelligence it must be so." † "The office of theology," a third writer declares, "is now generally recognized as distinct from that of science. It confesses its inability to furnish knowledge with any available data. It restricts itself to the region of faith, and leaves to philosophy and science the region of inquiry." ‡

Now, there is much in this view of the distinctive provinces of science and religion which we may, without giving up anything worth contending for, be ready to admit. If it means merely that the science of religion is not of the same order, dealing with the same class of objects, and reaching its results by the same method as the physical sciences—in other words, that it is an inductive science— this may readily be conceded. For it means no more than this, <small>Distinctive provinces of science and religion.</small>

---

* Spencer, *First Principles*, p. 46.   † *Ibid.*, p. 98.
‡ Lewis, *History of Philosophy*, p. 17.

that the objects of religious knowledge cannot be perceived by the senses or generalized out of the facts and phenomena which sense perceives. It means that God cannot be seen or touched or handled, and that by no mere generalization from the finite could you ever reach the infinite. But if the implied assertion is that human knowledge cannot transcend the objects which exist in space and time, and take cognizance of that which eye hath not seen, nor ear heard, nor imagination in its highest constructive efforts can conceive, and that theology and speculative philosophy, in so far as they pretend to the possession of such knowledge, are fictitious and spurious sciences, this is a view which cannot, without surrender of the most cherished convictions, be surrendered. It may be that the labor of countless thinkers in this province of inquiry has also been labor in vain, that the intellectual instincts which age after age have attracted the highest minds to it have been mere illusions, and that the results they seem to have reached are altogether deceptive and worthless; but if this be so, the very extent and persistency of the delusion demand the most careful scrutiny of the arguments of those who claim to have exposed it.

Of the view to which I have now referred, Caird says: "The limitation of science to things finite, and the impossibility of any such science as theology, or philosophy of religion, while held perhaps in a vague and uncritical way by many, has received its fullest and ablest exposition in the writings of Herbert Spencer; and to his treatment of this subject, resuming, as it does, the arguments of previous writers, and restating them with much freshness of thought and fidelity of illustration, I shall in what follows confine myself. His thesis is that the provinces of science and religion are distinguished from each other as the known from the unknown and unknowable. Science deals with ascertained phenomena, their order and relations, and comprehends all knowledge that is definite and positive. But positive knowledge does not and cannot embrace the whole possibilities of existence. Every addition to the gradually increasing sphere of science does but bring it into wider contact with the sphere of nescience, with the unknown and unknowable background in which lie the origin and explanation of all things, the unascertained something which phenomena imply, but do not reveal. Now, this dark, impenetrable background beyond experience is the possession of religion. But the attitude of mind which alone is possible with respect to this is not intelligence, but silent reverence for the unknowable; and this, Mr. Spencer maintains, is the common essence of all religions, and that which gives to religion the widest and purest sphere of action. The more completely our notion of the unknown reality is purified from earthly analogies, from anthropomorphic conceptions and images—the more, in short, we approximate to the state of simple awe before the altar of the Unknown and Unknowable, the nearer do we come to the perfect ideal of religion.

"The grounds on which this thesis is maintained are twofold. Human intelligence can be proved to be incapable of any absolute knowledge, (1) empirically, by pointing out that every attempt to press our knowledge beyond certain limits, every ultimate conception, religious or scientific, which we try to frame, gives rise to 'alternative impossibilities of thought;' (2) rationally, by an examination of the nature of human intelligence, which issues in a demonstration of the relativity of all human knowledge. The empirical or intuitive proof, however, when closely examined turns on the same principle with, and is resolvable into, the deduction. I shall treat, therefore, mainly of the latter.

"Mr. Spencer here adopts and carries to its logical results the doctrine of the relativity of human knowledge, which, derived, as it is supposed, from Kant, has been reproduced in this country, with special application to theology, by Sir William Hamilton and Mr. Mansel. It is, in substance, this: that inasmuch as to think is to 'condition,' to think or know the 'unconditioned,' or the infinite and absolute, would be simply to think the unthinkable. 'Infinite' and 'absolute' are merely terms expressive of the negation of the conditions under which thought is possible. Take the first of these terms: The very nature of thought implies distinction, and therefore limitation. A thing can only be thought of by being distinguished from other things, defined as possessing what others lack, lacking what others possess. But the infinite cannot be thus limited, and is therefore unthinkable. 'A consciousness of the infinite necessarily involves a self-contradiction, for it implies the recognition by limitation and difference of that which can only be given as unlimited and indifferent.' Take the other term, the absolute, and the same incompetency of thought will be seen to apply to it; for thought is only possible as the relation of the thing thought to the thinker, and an object of thought can only be known or enter into consciousness in relation to the thinking subject. All human knowledge is, therefore, necessarily relative. Things in themselves, as the absolute, or God as he is in himself, we can never know. 'The conception of the absolute thus implies at the same time the presence and absence of the relation by which thought is constituted.' A science of nature, of man, of all that this finite world contains, we may have; but a science of God and things divine is nothing less than a contradiction in terms.

"With this proof of the inherent incapacity of human intelligence to know the absolute Mr. Spencer, however, with what consistency we shall see in the sequel, attempts to combine the assertion that we are constrained to believe in the existence of the absolute, and that we can in a vague manner, not amounting to positive thought, have a certain 'consciousness' of it. 'Though the absolute,' he says, 'cannot in any manner or degree be known in the strict sense of knowing, yet we find that its positive existence is a necessary *datum* of consciousness, and that so long as consciousness continues we cannot for an instant rid it of this *datum*.' * 'Reality, though not capable of being made a thought, properly so called, because not capable of being brought within limits, nevertheless remains as a consciousness that is positive, is not regarded negative by the negation of kinds.' †

"On the foregoing argument I offer the following observations: First, the two elements of the theory are inconceivable. It is impossible to hold at once that human intelligence is limited to the finite and that it is cognizant of an existence beyond the finite; or, otherwise expressed, that all knowledge is relative and yet that we know the *existence* of the absolute. It is, indeed, easy to understand the genesis of this theory, which forced the mind of the author to the combination of two elements which, when closely examined, are seen to be contradictory. The assertion that man's knowledge is limited to the finite and relative would have no meaning save by a tacit reference to an infinite and absolute object to which his knowledge does not extend. When we say that a thing is only a phenomenon or appearance, a quality or attribute, we of course imply that there is something which is not mere appearance, but reality, not a mere quality, but a substance, with whose deeper nature we place the former in contrast. In order to pronounce that we only know phenomena we must needs be aware that there is something other than phenomena; we must know at least of the existence of things in themselves, realities lying behind phenomena, from the knowledge of which, in the full sense of the word, our intelligence is debarred. If we knew no other than finite and phenomenal existences, then we

* Spencer, *First Principles*, p. 29.   † *Essays*. vol. iii, p. 273.

should never know or be able to characterize them as finite and phenomenal. To pronounce, in short, that our knowledge is, in any sense, limited, we must have access to some standard to which that limited knowledge is referred; we must be aware, at least, of the existence of something beyond the limit, which is to our intelligence inaccessible.

"But, while the two elements—consciousness of the limits of human intelligence, and consciousness of that which transcends these limits—are correlative and inseparable, it is impossible, except by a *tour de force*, for a theorist who holds that human knowledge can ever transcend the finite to bring these two elements together. If we start with the assertion that thought is by its necessary conditions subjective and finite, or, on the other hand, that the absolute is only another name for that which is out of relation to thought, we cannot, save by an act of violence, drag in a consciousness, in any sense, of the absolute in order to meet the exigencies of our theory. We cannot, in other words, deny all consciousness of the absolute in order to maintain that human knowledge is limited, and in the same breath assert a consciousness of the absolute in order to justify our cognizance of that limitation. In so far as the lower animals are devoid of reason they are unconscious of their irrationality, and it is only we, in virtue of our rational, intelligent nature, who can discern their lack of it. So, it might be possible for another and higher intelligence, an observer of human nature possessed of absolute knowledge, to pronounce that man's knowledge is purely relative, that there is a region of realities from which human thought is shut out; but it is not possible for one and the same consciousness to be purely relative and conscious of its relativity. Grant the fundamental assumption of the theorist, and it follows that humanity is not only hopelessly ignorant of reality, but absolutely unconscious of its ignorance." *

* Caird, *Philosophy of Religion*, vol. i, pp. 10-18.

SUBJECT AND ATTRIBUTE.

In the discussion conducted in the following pages we shall find occasion to use the term subject, as distinguished from attribute. It is important that we understand precisely what the distinction is. For the term subject other terms are frequently used, as essence, substance, being, nature.

From necessity the mind when it cognizes any object posits being, that is, substance of it. Thought necessitates one who thinks; cognition, one who cognizes and that which is cognized. If the object of thought be simply an idea, the idea necessitates a subject whose idea it is; if it be a feeling, it necessitates the existence of one who feels; if of a force, it necessitates the existence of that which exerts the force.

By subject we always understand a *real being*. By attribute we understand some permanent and essential property or power which cannot be abstracted and the subject retain its identity. The attribute is not the subject, but the subject does not exist without the attribute.

The relations of a subject may change, and it may vary its activities, and the subject may yet retain its identity; but an attribute pertains in such forms to its essence that if it could be obliterated the subject itself would become another and different being or kind of being, or would become extinct. An attribute differs from secondary powers, which may not pertain to a subject, but may be product of habit merely; it differs from quality, which may be superinduced by use of attributes; and it differs from acts, which are results of exerted attributes.

The nature of a being depends upon its attributes, or *vice versâ;* the attributes depend upon the nature and are exponential thereof. The being and attributes do not exist apart, that is, there is not a subject without attributes or attributes without a subject; and yet the attributes are not the subject, nor the subject the attributes, but the subject possesses the attributes, and is not without them; the attributes are in the subject, not by it. The mind cannot conceive pure being, that is, subject simply as such apart from attribute; nor can it conceive pure attribute, that is, attribute apart from subject. To conceive at all, or to propound existence of any kind, it must unite in the conception and predication subject and attribute.

Shedd thus puts it: "The attributes are not part of the essence of which this latter is supposed. The whole essence is in each attribute and the attribute in the essence. We must not conceive of the essence as existing by itself and prior to the attributes, and of the attributes as an addition to it. God is not essence and attributes, but in attributes. The attributes are essential qualities of God. Hence Augustine, the schoolman, Calvin, and Melanchthon say, 'Divinæ virtutes sunt ipsa essentia.' Turretini (iii, 5–7) remarks that 'attributa dei non possunt realiter differere ab essentia, vel inter se tanquam res et res.'" *

That which is not being or substance, by not being a substance is nothing; and of a pure nothing it is not possible to predicate attributes, properties, activities, or modes of any kind. Whenever we affirm existence we predicate of a subject, or of that which implies a subject.

In every case the attributes determine the nature of the subject. Attributes of one kind show a subject of one kind. No subject ever directly shows itself. It appears in some manifes-
<small>Attributes determine the nature of the subject.</small> tation of its attributes. To think the subject we must think it under some manifestation of some attribute, and to describe it we must recite its attributes, or some mode of action of its attributes. This is a universal fact.

<small>* Shedd, *Dogmatic Theology*, vol. i, p. 334.</small>

"Attributes," says Fleming, "are always real qualities, essential and inherent, not only in the nature, but even in the substance of things. 'By this word attribute,' says Descartes, in his letter to Regius, 'is meant something which is immovable and inseparable from the essence of its subject, as that which constitutes it' (by this he did not mean creates it, but that without which it is not), 'and which is thus opposed to *mode*.' Thus unity, identity, and activity are attributes of the soul; for I cannot deny them without at the same time denying the existence of the soul itself. In God there is nothing but attributes, because in God everything is absolute, involved in the substance and unity of the necessary being."*

I quote from Dr. Miley, in his recent excellent work, *Systematic Theology*. No author has written on the subject in hand more luminously:

"In a general sense an attribute is anything which may be affirmed of its subject. This wider sense may include what is accidental as well as what is essential. In the more definite sense an attribute is any quality or property which is intrinsic to the subject, which characterizes and differentiates it, and by virtue of which the subject is what it is.

"Attribute, property, quality, faculty, power are in common use much in the same sense, though mostly with some distinction in application. Thus extension, solidity, divisibility are properties or qualities of body; intellect, sensibility, will are faculties or powers of mind; omniscience, goodness, omnipotence are attributes of God. We do not allege an invariable uniformity in such distinctions of application, yet we think them common. We certainly do not use the term faculty in application to either body or God, while it is the common term in application to the human mind.

"Qualities are neither possible nor thinkable as separate or

---

* Fleming, *Vocabulary of Philosophy*, art. "Attribute."

self-subsisting facts. For both thought and reality body is more than its properties, mind more than its faculties, God more than his attributes. Sensationalism or positivism may, in a helpless agnosticism, be content with the surface of things or with the merest phenomenalism; but for deeper thought, the thought without which there is neither true science nor philosophy, properties, faculties, attributes must have a ground in essential being. The necessity is as absolute as that of a subject to its predicate in a logical proposition.

"Physical properties must have a ground in a material substance. Reason equally determines for the mental faculties a necessary basis in mind. For the divine attributes there must be a ground in essential divine being. Reason is in each case the indisputable authority. The distinctive sense of being in God is that it is the ground of his attributes.

"As there is no empirical grasping of essential being, so there is no such grasping of the connection of attribute and subject. Even reason cannot know the mode of this connection. But reason can and does affirm it to be most intrinsic. The connection is in no sense a loose or separable one. Being is not as a vessel in which attributes may be placed and from which they may be withdrawn; not as a ground on which they may repose as a building upon its foundation or a statue upon its pedestal, and which may remain after their removal. The connection must be most intrinsic, so that neither is nor can be without the other. Being and attribute are separable in abstract thought, but inseparable in reality. Neither can exist without the other. While extension must have a basis in material body, such body must exist in extension. While intellect must have a ground in mind, mind must have the faculty of intelligence. In the present conditioning relation of a nervous organism to the activities of the mental powers their normal working may be interrupted or temporarily suspended, but they must ever exist potentially in mind, because necessary to the very notion of mind. In the very being of God are all his attributes. Without them he would not be God.

"While attribute and being are correlatives of thought and inseparable in fact, they are separable in abstract thought, and for clearness of view must be so separated. Only thus can we attain to the truer notion of attribute and subject respectively, and in the unity of being." *

MATTER AND SPIRIT.

Attributes determine the nature of the subject, but they do not preexist and create the subject. They coexist with and in the essence of the subject. There are two classes of subjects in existence, and but two. They are of divers natures, differentiable and determined by dissimilar and unassimilable attributes, matter and spirit. The two have nothing in common but existence.

"The two substances, matter and spirit, are wholly diverse, and have nothing in common, except that each is the base of certain properties and the ground of certain phenomena. These properties and phenomena, being different in kind, prove that material substance and spiritual substance differ specifically and absolutely. Matter cannot think, and mind cannot be burned. Spiritual substance is known by its qualities and effects. In this respect it is like material substance, which is cognized only by its qualities and effects. Neither matter nor mind can be known apart from and back of its properties. That these are two substances and that each has its own peculiarity is a common belief of man." †

If we define subject or substance, as Plato does, as "that

---

* Miley, *Systematic Theology*, vol. i, p. 159, *et al.*
† Shedd, *Dogmatic Theology*, p. 160.

which possesses any sort of powers to affect another or to be affected by another," or as "that which has the power of doing and suffering in relation to some other existing thing," which seems to reduce the idea of substance to that of power, which in fact he says it is, we do not get clear of the idea that substance is something which exists and has the property of being—of a that which has power and acts. Indeed, there is no escape from the idea of a subject so long as we predicate of a power, or an act, or a possibility merely. Entity underlies all, and entity underlies even the idea itself of power, for the idea does not and cannot exist without an entity which has it.

We are so accustomed to think of substance as something that is solid, tangible, visible, figured, that to most minds unaccustomed to close and critical thinking it is difficult to conceive of substance, or real being of any kind, which does not manifest itself in these forms. Positivism, or "dirt philosophy," boldly declares that that which does not disclose itself to the senses directly is nothing. It is admitted that spirit substance does not so disclose itself, cannot. It is therefore, according to this philosophy, nothing. Even matter itself, reduced to its ultimate, the atom, becomes invisible and intangible, and ceases to manifest itself in any way to sense by any aid in our reach. Aggregation reveals it, and discloses the fact that extension is fundamental to it; it is a substance of which extension is an inseparable attribute; but which neither in the atom nor in any aggregation or composition discovers intelligence or self-determination as belonging to itself. There are those who doubt the existence of any such substance—idealists; but the doubt is possible only to a few minds.

Like matter reduced to its primary forms, spirit is a substance which is not cognizable by any sense; but unlike matter there is no process by which it can become cognizable to sense, and unlike matter it is a substance which discloses itself as existing, but not as extended, but as intelligent and self-determined, by effects which it produces and by self-consciousness. The proof of its real existence is more direct and conclusive than the proof of the existence of matter, if it be possible that there are degrees in the strength of proofs which alike compel conviction.

Dr. Shedd has well remarked on this point: "The Westminster Confession" (and so do all Christian creeds) "defines God to be a most pure Spirit, without body, parts, or passions." These qualifying clauses define, so far as is possible, the idea of spiritual substance. The invisibility of spirit, as previously remarked, would not itself differentiate it from matter and material nature. The forces of gravity, the chemical forces, electricity, magnetism, and the like, are as invisible as God himself or the soul of man. Heat, according to the ancient theory, is the invisible motion of invisible molecules. There is an invisible ground of the visible and tangible. Back of the world of ponderable physics, which we apprehend by the five senses, there is an unseen world which is natural still, not moral; physical still, not spiritual. Who ever saw, or ever will see, that principle of life of which outward and material nature is but the embodiment or manifestation? When we have stripped the visible world of its visibility and ponderability, and have resolved it into unseen forces, we have not reached any higher sphere than that of nature and matter." *

In saying that God is a pure Spirit, and is "without body, parts, or passions," a definite conception is conveyed by which spirit and matter are sharply distinguished; not because one is invisible or unapproachable by sense, but because matter may have bodily form and be divisible, and be wrought on by other

* Shedd, *Dogmatic Theology*, vol. i, pp. 163, 164.

ponderables. But none of these characteristics can belong to God or any spirit ; the predicables of the one case never, under any circumstances, become the predicables of the other ; there is an absolute and immutable difference between the attributes of the two natures.

A most fundamental distinction between spirit and matter is noted by Cudworth, in his great discussion, *The True Intellectual System of the Universe.* "There are," he says, "two kinds of substance in nature : the first, extension or magnitude, really existing without (that is, exterior to) the mind, which is a thing which hath no self-unity at all in it, but is infinite alterity and divisibility, as it were mere outside and outwardness, it having nothing within, nor any other action belonging to it, but only locally to move when it is moved ; the second, life and mind, or the self-active, cognitive nature, an inside being, whose action is not local motion, but an internal energy within the substance or essence of the thinker himself or in the inside of him." Dr. Shedd, from whom I take quotation, adds with great pertinence : " Material substance is moved *ab extra ;* spiritual substance is moved *ab intra,* that is, is self-moved. This is, perhaps, the most important distinction between mind and matter. Mind moves voluntarily ; matter is moved mechanically." *

Clearly nothing is more plain than that the two positions taken are correct, namely, that there is invincible ground for the distinction between subject and attribute, and that two kinds of subjects or substances are known to us which are fundamentally different, neither possessing any attribute which is possessed by the other.

"As the notion of essential being is conditioned on some knowledge of properties, so the notion of a distinction of subjects must be through some known distinction of properties. As an attribute requires a subject, so it requires a subject

---

* Shedd, *Dogmatic Theology,* vol. i, p. 168.

answering in kind to its own distinctive quality. The latter requirement is as absolute as the former. For the two kinds of facts classed as the properties of body and the faculties of mind reason must imperatively determine essentially distinct and different subjects. Empirical science can allege nothing of any weight against this position. It may gratuitously deny any real distinction between the two classes of facts or assert the identity of the mental with the physical; or it may pronounce for agnosticism in respect to the nature of matter, and then by the covert assumption of a most pretentious gnosticism proclaim a new face of matter which accounts for the facts of mind. No assumption could be more gratuitous, no assertion more groundless. It is a dogmatizing which would shame the method of the most positive theology. Reason is still the decisive authority. While a material ground can answer for the properties of body, only a spiritual ground can answer for the faculties of mind. The divine attributes must have their ground in spiritual being."

Though there is a real distinction between subject and attribute, the human mind has no power to discern pure subject; it can only see the subject by way of its attributes. The attribute, like the essence, does not appear to any sense, but becomes known to reason by external signs of its presence, and by the same signs discovers the existence of the subject; it does not even know itself as subject, except through its attributes in visible manifestation in effects. Pure being is not subject of pure cognition. It cannot even be conceived. To bring any object *en rapport* with our finite faculties it must report itself in some mode of phenomena— some attribute or property or quality must project itself upon us in effects. Thus the object or subject becomes known and takes form in thought. It is a law of mind, that is, an absolute necessity, that when brought into contact with phenomena of any kind it should posit some underlying subject. It is

<small>Subject only discernible through attributes.</small>

compelled to assert that the phenomena are phenomena of something.

Through the phenomena the mind reaches the idea of substance, and proceeds to determine the kind of substance. Dr. Pope says truly: "What is true of all the objects of our knowledge is true also of the Highest. Save in his qualities and attributes God is not revealed to his creatures. The Eternal unclothed in these is not a definite object of thought at all. On the other hand, the entire divine essence is made known in his qualities predicated of it." * The truth of this position will appear if we consider how we became aware of any existence. We know as a fact that we are conversant with phenomena. The phenomena which we discover are phenomena of the self and of the not self. Of the self the phenomena are those of feeling, thought, volition. These are caused in us by the impingement upon us in some form of objects which are of the not self. Those objects do not discover themselves to us in their essence, but in their phenomena. The immediate result is self-consciousness, which gives us the knowledge of the self, or is self-cognition. The knowledge so acquired is that we who are so affected have essential being. We are compelled to posit ourselves as affected. But we are no more compelled to posit ourselves, as real beings, than we are compelled to posit that behind the phenomena which affect us there is real substance. This arises from a law of mind.

But now how do those phenomena of self and not self discover to us another Being of which they are not phenomena? <small>How do phenomena discover God?</small> We say of which they are not phenomena, for the phenomena of the self and of the not self are not phenomena of God's essence or being. There are no phenomena of these. God's essence never appears, not even the essence of

* *Com. of Theology*, vol. i, p. 287.

the self or not self, but is simply a predicative of the reason as a necessary implication of the phenomena. God certainly does not appear as the subject of the phenomena which we behold; that is, the phenomena of the sensible object and of the self are not phenomena of God. In them he does not appear as subject. How then do we arrive at the knowledge of him through these phenomena? The answer is that we are compelled to posit a cause of the existence of the self and of the not self. This is a demand of the reason as absolute and universal as the demand that phenomena shall have a subject as their ground. Thus God emerges as *cause* of the self and not self. The phenomena which do appear show him as cause of the things whose phenomena affect us, that is, as the cause of the self and not self. He does not emerge in our knowledge as an immediate object of cognition, either as to his essence or attributes, any more than the self and not self so emerged, but he emerges in the reason as cause of the entire effect. But if he does not appear in his essence he must appear in his attributes, which are employed in producing the effect. What are the attributes which appear in the effect? Reason compels the answer (*a*) that as phenomena point to a real substance, so cause points to a real Being; (*b*) that the real Being who is cause of all must himself be eternal and uncaused; (*c*) that as causation implies power he must be a Being in whom power inheres; (*d*) that as the effect shows knowledge and wisdom he must be a Being that is wise and knowing; (*e*) that as the effect shows ethical quality he must be a moral Being. Thus the attributes which emerge in the effect compel us, by the same law of mind which compels us to posit substance behind phenomena, to posit substance behind these attributes which appear in the effect. As the self and the not self are substantial beings manifested by phenomena, God is also a substantial Being who manifests himself in effects.

The effects, in showing his attributes, show us what kind of a Being he is.

CREATORSHIP.

In revelation creatorship is ascribed to God. The universe furnishes in itself proof that it was created. Revelation declares what kind of a being God is, and points out certain attributes which inhere in his nature and are of his essence. The universe declares to reason that the Being who created it must, in nature and attributes, be identical with the Being thus posited in revelation.

It is quite important that we fix the meaning of the term create. Creation differs from emanation.* Emanation means to flow from, an effluence from a substance, and involves similarity of essence. According to several systems of philosophy and religion which have gained greater or less prevalence, all the beings of which the universe is composed, whether matter or spirit, have proceeded from and are parts of the divine Being or substance. This doctrine of emanation found expression in the systems of Zoroaster, the Gnostics, and Neoplatonists. It still exists in modified form in modern pantheistic thought.

Creation differs from evolution, which, in its absolute form, supposes the universe to be evolved from eternally existing matter and inhering forces, but in a modified form allows that possibly evolution is a mode of creation—a method in which God produced and is still modifying cosmic facts. It is admitted by those who hold the theory that it may be either atheistic or theistic. It is the popular fancy of a class of scientists.

"Creation is not production from any previously extant substance. It is not a modification of an eternal material substance.

---

* See *Creation: God in Time and Space*, by the author.

"The old theologians distinguished between the first and second acts of creation: the first, the creation from nothing, indicated in Gen. i, 1, 2; the second, the work of the six days, bringing all into shape and order, and implying, what is perhaps correct, a distinction between the creation of the prime material and its specific arrangement and organization."*

Pantheism has assumed two forms, both and equally contradictive of the Scripture idea of creation: (*a*) that there was a primordial condition of eternally existing matter which unconsciously grew into cosmic order and developed into consciousness; (*b*) that spirit, not matter, is primitive, but spirit was unconscious and unintelligent, containing tendencies merely—a sort of impersonal or semipersonal affections, longings, uneasinesses—which developed matter and the material universe without intending it; and with a growing intelligence in itself there came orderly forms, and finally intelligence and self-consciousness.†

Creation denies the eternity of the universe, whether cosmic or atomic. "The cosmic form of the theory as anciently held taught that the cosmos itself, that is, the organized world, with all its phenomena as to form, order, relation, law, and influence which we now behold, had existed from eternity. There never has been chaos or noncosmos. This view is attributed to Aristotle. He, indeed, like Plato, speaks of unformed matter; but according to his fundamental principle this could only exist in conception, never in fact."‡

Over against all these and all other possible theories of the origin of the universe creationism affirms that a personal God, who alone is eternal, by an exercise of power raised all things

---

* Smith, *System of Christian Theology*, p. 92.
† See Lord's *Christian Theology*, p. 206.
‡ See Lord's *Christian Theology*, p. 204; also Dollinger's *Gentile and Jew*, vol. i, p. 334; also Shedd's *Dogmatic Theology*, vol. i, pp. 462-526, the entire chapter—exhaustive and valuable.

into existence. This is the biblical theory.* It is also the theory to which reason is compelled to come. It matters nothing that we cannot conceive how power can create; we are compelled to assent that it has created. The instrumental forces with which we are familiar, by which changes are wrought, have no such power. The direct force or power of which we are the conscious possessors is inadequate to any such result. But that the Eternal by a volition raised out of non-existence all things we are under a rational necessity to admit. He not only raised the structure of the universe, inorganic and organic, from foundation to finial, but he created the substance itself. "He spake, and it was done; he commanded, and it stood fast."

The properly creative act was the production of the substances of the universe. The formation of matter into various collocations is sometimes and very properly styled a secondary creation, not simply because it is subsequent, but because it is in great measure effected by instrumental or secondary causes concreted in the created substances, or exerted in them—called material forces or agents, but really divine energizings. It is sometimes affirmed that proper primary creation as here defined is impossible, as implying a contradiction of the ancient and, properly understood, impregnable maxim, *Ex nihilo nihil fit;* but this arises from a misinterpretation of the maxim. It assumes the meaning of the maxim to be that there is no power which can confer existence. Were that true it would necessarily follow, indeed, it would in effect be the direct affirmation, that whatever is must be eternal. The meaning of the maxim is not that; but it is this, that from nothing it is impossible anything should come; that is, had there once been nothing in existence there never could have been any existence. The

---

* Gen. i, 1; Col. i, 16; John i, 3; Heb. xi, 3; Psalm xix, 1; cxxiv, 8; Heb. iii, 4; Acts xvii, 24.

maxim so understood is impregnable. But given a Being of infinite power, creation is not causeless effect. If it were true that creation is impossible, the assumption of it and inferences derived from it as to the nature of the cause would be groundless. It is necessary, therefore, to clear the point before passing to the argument.

The doctrine of creation *ex nihilo* is not only clearly the doctrine of the Jewish and Christian Scriptures, but it is original to them. It was either unknown or directly contradicted by all the ancient cosmogonies. The eternal existence, or chaos of matter, was the common foundation of all their theories. Plato, Aristotle, Philo, and all the schools of philosophy held substantially this view. When they seemed to affirm creation it was always a *creatio mediata, ex præexistente materia*, and not *immediata*. They did not believe in the production of matter itself from nothing. God, with them, was merely a builder, not the creator, of the world.*

<small>Creation *ex nihilo*.</small>

The germs of modern evolutionism are transmitted from these ancient sources, and without improvement in their more scientific form. If they do not wholly dispense with God, they construct the universe by the operation of natural forces, and in their most objectionable forms as completely displace him as did the older materialists, reducing him to a mere demiurge, or possible factor in and with matter, rather than a creator. Development theories, spontaneous generation, pantheistic conception, and kindred fancies have the same origin or remote parentage—of eternal matter with a possible copartner in the formation of the cosmos. Absolute creation, if not formally denied, finds no necessary place in any of them, and is in effect left out as a working idea.

The Bible alone presents the doctrine of creation *ex nihilo*.

---

* Vide Knapp, *Christian Theology*, chap. ii, sec. 47 ; also Shedd, *Dogmatic Theology*, vol. i, p. 464.

Its account of origins is succinctly expressed in a single phrase, which has the majesty of a maxim and also the impregnability of a primary truth of reason: "In the beginning God created the heaven and the earth." That the creation here predicated refers to the material substance of the entire universe is found in the fact that the detailed account of the process goes on to show that the fashioning of the substance into an orderly cosmos follows the creative act, and is not called a creation, but a making up or arrangement. He first created, then arranged. This is a most important and surprisingly delicate discrimination, considering the brevity of the statement. Both acts are ascribed to God, but they are not only different, but imply radically discriminate modes of action which have come to be of great and fundamental significance.

The primal act was the creation of the material substance of the universe, that is, the causing it to exist, the only proper idea of creation. In the creative act nothing comes between the effect and the cause. The effect is product of an immediate exercise of the power of the cause. There is not a subject in which, or, in any way, by means of which, the creative power is exercise, deffecting a change of some kind, but the creative power produces the subject itself.

The precise posture of the case is that until the Creator acted he alone existed. There was not a something else for him to act on, or in, or by, or through, but, as the direct result of his act, another order of substance, or kind of being, was raised into existence. After the exertion of his power there were two kinds of being in existence—Creator and created; any further action of the Creator must consist in working changes in the thing created. This mode of action would be radically different from that which preceded, and might be by mediate or secondary causation vested in, the thing created; that is, the thing created might now become a factor in effects of change and construction, as, in fact, it is; but not by its own power, but by a power vested in it, or of which it is media.

To see the full significance of the foregoing statement we must linger yet for a further expansion. We have said that the creative act gave existence to the material substance of the universe, that is, to matter. We find matter existing in vast masses—worlds. If we should understand by matter these vast aggregations and collocations, as they are now found, and thence infer that the creative act which gave matter its existence gave it existence in mass or masses as we find it, which is no doubt the popular idea, and if we should impute that idea to the Bible, we must soon discern that both ourselves and the Bible become entangled in inextricable difficulties.

Masses of matter are not created as masses; that is, the man is not created in collocation. Matter is reducible to the atom, invisible and impalpable, but an entity, or something which has real substance of being. Masses, all worlds, are compounded of these infinitesimal atoms; the universe is built of these invisible and impalpable constituents. The atoms are differentiable among themselves. They are innumerable. They are impersonal. They are indestructible, save by the power which created them. They are centers of force. Each atom is vested in its essence with a definite power of interaction on all related or contiguous atoms. Strictly speaking, the forces which are manifest in matter are not entities created, but modes of divine efficiency immanent in matter. The essence of the atom and its definite force, which is inseparable from its essence, the force not acting without the atom nor the atom existing without the force, are unchangeable and incapable of disruption. The forces of all the atoms interacting according to fixed and immutable laws produce collocations and masses. Neither the essence of the atom nor the force inherent is personal or intelligent, but the atom and the force alike are outcomes of the action of a person, and the action of atoms upon each other is declarative of an intelligence and person whose force it is; the force is not a person, but it is of a person, personal. If they are to be viewed as agents they can only be viewed in a secondary sense. No atom or force, however impersonal, is so removed from the personal agency in and present with it as to enable it to exist for a moment or achieve anything which is not under the direction and control of personality. Both the creation of the atom and the collocations effected by it are traceable to the immediate or mediate agency of God. *Qui facit per alium facit per se.**

If the ground held by creationists as here defined be true there are certain implications which must also be accepted as true, and it is wise to take note of them, to see whether they can rationally be accepted. Every theory must be answerable for all that is implied in it.

Of the maxim, *Ex nihilo nihil fit,* Shedd says: " It is true in the sense that nothing comes from nothing, (*a*) by finite power; (*b*) as the material out of which something is produced; (*c*) by the mode of emanation, generation, or evolution, because this supposes existing matter. Lucretius lays down the position (i, 151), *Nullam rem e nihilo gigni divinitus unquam.* The reason which he gives why even by divine power (*divinitus*) nothing can be produced from nothing is, that in this case there could be no need of a seed or egg; and that, consequently, everything might be produced out of everything; men could be originated out of the sea, and fishes and birds out of the earth. Lucretius does not conceive of the seed or the egg as created, but as eternal. His reasoning is valid against pseudo-evolution or evolution defined as 'the transmutation of

---

* See *Cosmic Theism,* by the author, pp. 162–226, 255–284.

the homogeneous into the heterogeneous.' Everything may be originated out of everything upon this theory. The homogeneous vegetable may develop into the heterogeneous animal, the homogeneous animal into the heterogeneous man. And the process may be downward as well as upward, because either process is alike the transmutation of a homogeneous substance into a heterogeneous one. If it were possible by the operation of merely natural law to convert the inorganic mineral into the organic vegetable, it would be possible by the same method to convert the organic vegetable into the inorganic mineral. The rule would work in both ways. As plausible an argument might be constructed out of the deterioration and degradation of some of the human family, to prove that man may be evolved downward into an anthropoid ape, as that which has been constructed to prove that he has been evolved upward from one.

" Spinoza's definition of 'substance' was intended to exclude the doctrine of creation *ex nihilo*. He defines substance as 'that which exists of itself;' that is, the conception of which does not require the conception of anything else. But the conception of a creature is the conception of a substance that requires another substance to account for it. A *created* substance, consequently, is precluded by Spinoza's definition of substance. Descartes had previously defined the *absolute* and *primary* substance as 'that which so exists that it needs nothing else for its existence.' But Descartes added a definition of *created* or *secondary* substance, as 'that which requires the concurrence—*concursus*—of God for its existence.' . . . Fichte says that 'the assumption of a creation is the fundamental error of all false metaphysics and philosophy.' Hegel explains the universe of matter and spirit as an 'immanent process of God, a material efflux out from the absolute which is retracted again as an immaterial spirit.' . . . Kant, on the other hand, asserts that 'the proposition that God, or the universal first cause, is the cause of the existence of substance, can never be given up without at the same time giving up the notion of God as the Being of all beings, and thereby giving up his all-sufficiency, on which everything in theology depends.'" *

The maxim, *Ex nihilo nihil fit*, is false in reference to the supernatural and omnipotent power of God. The Supreme Being can originate entity from nonentity. The following are the characteristics of creation from nothing: 1. Creation had a beginning. It is not eternal emanation of an eternal substance, or the eternal evolution of an eternal germ. 2. Creation is optional, not necessary, for God. It proceeds from free will, and is expressed by fiat. 3. Creation originates another new substance; but emanation and evolution produce only modifications of an old and existing substance.

Creation *ex nihilo* is the only true idea of creation, but the arranging and building of the universe into an orderly cosmos is no less ascribable to the immediate power and wisdom of God than the creation of the substances of which it is built. If not properly a creative act, it is nevertheless a divine act. The employment of natural forces primarily created to that end makes God not only the cause, but the sole cause. It is he that originates the forces and that determines their effects. They do not exist without him. They are not accidental properties of the substances which he creates, which proceed to evolve collocations and organisms, either fortuitously or intelligently, but they do precisely what he made them to do, and are powerless to any other effects. The cosmos is his product in all stages of its development, as really as it would be were each effect the result of his immediate agency without the atom. The forces are not natural in the sense of springing from created substances themselves, but are so simply because he has **vested**

* *Dogmatic Theology*, vol. i, p. 467.

them, or better yet exerts them, through the creative substance as a permanent mode in which he works out predetermined ends. Throughout he is the worker. He is immanent in the created substances, and they have no existence and no power apart from him, while they are not parts or modes of his being.

The formation of the universe is properly called a mediate creation or a secondary process in the creative scheme. The account of creation uniformly set forth in the Scriptures, beginning with the Genesis story, recognizes this fact. There is an immediate and mediate creation. How completely the universe was formed by the divine fiat at once does not appear. The nebular hypothesis, which has much plausibility, makes nothing against that account. For aught that appears, God having primarily created the atoms and stored them with forces to that end, the worlds were built through their instrumentality in infinite ages; but whether or not, he was the great builder.

The popular theory that the work was immediately completed, the inorganic and organic alike, the text does not require, and science discredits it. That there have been other immediate creations than the substances of matter and without the instrumental agency of forces working in matter, is not only clearly taught in the Bible, but is rationally certain.

Whatever life is, it is an immediate product of divine agency in its beginnings. This is the *dictum* of science through its most accredited representatives. Life is not a spontaneity of mere matter. It appeared ages removed from the creation of material substance. Immediate divine agency is necessary to its production.

Later still the entity of human spirits has required a direct creation. This is required, whichever theory of the origin of souls, creationism or traducianism, be adopted.

The original mass of matter cannot be accounted for on the theory of evolution. The mass was created without the mediation of material forces.

The organic universe was at first instituted by direct divine power, and now exists through divine agency exerted. But no act of immediate creation is now necessary to its continuance. The world of life is renewed and carried forward through established instrumentalities, but by the creative agent. Each new organism is a secondary creation, but it could not have been so at the first. Nor must it be supposed that this established order runs itself or in any way disconnects God as direct cause from each individual life. Intermediates are not causes, but instruments merely. There is one Cause of all things, even though his agency reaches effects through a thousand various channels.

The great fact stands that the universe was devised, when it was not, by an infinite mind; and that when it was not, it was created from no existing substance, and is being sustained and carried forward by the same power which created the substance of matter and spirit which are found in it.

The doctrine of creation, immediate and mediate, or primary and secondary, is as ancient as any Christian dogma. It appears early in theological writings, and continues throughout all the controversies which have existed. Augustine clearly made the distinction in substance. He says: "God created a chaotic matter that was next to nothing, that is, the most tenuous and imponderable form of matter. This form of matter was made from nothing before all days; that is, in that given period marked by the words 'in the beginning.' This chaotic unformed matter was subsequently formed and arranged."

"Creation is divided into prima or immediate, or secunda or

mediate. The immediate creation is that which took place when God first gave existence to all the variety of things, when before there was nothing. The mediate creation is that which is seen since the original creation was completed, in the production of plants, the generation of animate creations, and the whole natural propagation of the various kinds of beings. God works since the creation is completed, not immediately, but generally by means of the powers of nature which he himself has bestowed and regulated." *

On the subject of mediate and immediate creation Dr. Hodge says: "While it has forever been the doctrine of the Church that God created the universe out of nothing by the word of his power, which creation was instantaneous and immediate, that is, without the intervention of any second causes, yet it has generally been admitted that this is to be understood only of the original call of matter into existence. Theologians have, therefore, distinguished between first and second, or immediate and mediate creation. The one was instantaneous, the other gradual; the one precludes the idea of any preexisting substance and of cooperation; the other admits and implies both. There is evident ground for this distinction in the Mosaic account of creation." †

Creation as an effect includes all existences, all beings, and all cosmic laws and arrangements, both in the spiritual and material universe. The biblical formulation is, "the heaven and the earth." "In the beginning God created the heaven and the earth." The phrase is intended to comprehend all existence: "the heaven"—all celestial bodies, and all inhabitants thereof; "the earth"—the globe and all organic beings dwelling upon it—all things wherein is life. In many different phraseologies all existence is ascribed to God. It is im-

---

* Knapp, *Christian Theology*, chap. ii, sec. 47.
† Hodge, *Systematic Theology*, vol. i, p. 556.

possible to conceive of any existence without him. The signs of creaturehood are upon all, from the primitive atom to the highest organism—mutation and change. God only is eternal.

The thing made declares the maker—not only that he is, but also shows what he is. There is no other way by which we can know him than through his works and any word revelation he may have given of himself.

TABLE OF CONTENTS.

	PAGE
PREFATORY STATEMENTS	v
GOD IS A SPIRIT	3
UNITY OF GOD	8
ETERNITY OF GOD	12
GOD IS ABSOLUTE, UNCONDITIONED BEING	23
GOD IS A PERSON	37
FREEDOM OF GOD	48
MORAL NATURE OF GOD	72
DIVINE ATTRIBUTES	81
OMNIPRESENCE OF GOD	120
OMNIPOTENCE OF GOD	132
OMNISCIENCE OF GOD	145
GOODNESS OF GOD	220
JUSTICE OF GOD	265
TRUTH A DIVINE ATTRIBUTE	274

NATURE AND ATTRIBUTES OF GOD.

NATURE OF GOD.

GOD IS A SPIRIT.

As seen in the pages immediately preceding, attributes imply a substance or subject. Though subject and attribute are inseparable in fact, neither existing without the other, they are not identical. In thought and in logical order, though not in being, the subject is precedent and conditioning to the attribute—underlies it.

We have seen that there are two kinds of substance, and but two, matter and spirit. All attributes are attributes of one or the other of these subjects, substances or essences or natures, by whatever term the being is designated.

Of the two, we postulate, God, in nature and substance, is spirit, not matter. This is the categorical statement of the Bible: "God is a Spirit." The position is affirmed in every possible form, by implication and assertion, throughout the Scriptures. No one who has any knowledge of the Bible doubts that it is the doctrine of the inspired volume. As this is an undisputed point there is no occasion for supporting it by adducing further proof. The fact that it is a doctrine of the Bible may not prove to some minds that it is a true doctrine. That, therefore, remains to be proved.

We now, therefore, affirm that what is thus taught in the Scriptures is the necessary outcome of rational thought. This will appear as we examine the attributes which are requisite to, and exhibited in, the creation and government of the universe. The attributes determine the nature of the subject, and the attributes discoverable in the existence and constitution of the universe declare that its Creator is a spiritual being.

The spirituality of God is denied only by materialists—atheists, who deny his existence; and pantheists, who identify him with the universe of matter and take from him personality. For the refutation of these theories the reader is referred to *Cosmic Theism*, by the author, where the subject is fully discussed and the theories shown to be, not simply unsupported, but absolutely irrational, self-subversive, and involving contradictory implications which it is impossible should be true.

That God is spirit without body, pure spirit without participation in matter, is proved by the following considerations:

1. He is intelligent. Intelligence is an attribute, not of matter, but of spirit. This has been disputed by pure volition, not by reason. No one pretends that there is any proof that matter has either power to know or will. The proof is positive that it has no such power. To pretend that it has is irrational. But there is a subject which manifests these powers and therefore possesses them. We know of the existence of such a subject, for we are conscious that we ourselves are such a subject. We are conscious of power to think and know and will. The universe is proof that God is such a subject. For anyone to doubt that He who created the universe, with its wondrous adaptations and manifold evidences of design, together with the minds which are found in it, is himself intelligent, borders so nearly on self-stultification as to render argument inapplicable. Creation implies three things: (*a*) The existence of the being who creates; (*b*) An archetypal idea of the thing to be created; (*c*) Free self-determined forthputting of power by which the effect is produced—each of which is proof absolute that the Creator is a spiritual being. The effect is impossible without such a cause. On this point the

Bible is explicit; it not only categorically and without exception affirms that he is spirit, but it also expressly denies to him any of the properties of matter, and most explicitly that which is the absolutely fundamental property, without which matter cannot exist—the property of extension or form. Anthropomorphic and anthropopathic ascriptions to him of organs, as eyes and ears, and hands and feet and wings, and other things likening him to man, are well known to be figurative and in accommodation. Rational thought harmonizes with revelation, in absolutely refusing to him any of the properties of matter. Difficult as it is to think a subject without extension, mind finds itself compelled to affirm such a subject when it thinks of the Creator of the universe.

2. There is an ethical nature in God. He will do nothing which his moral nature does not approve. His wisdom and omnipotence must forever do homage to his holiness and work in its service. Love of the right and the good sits on the throne and holds empire over the ineffable perfections. He determines all, but determines nothing but at the instigation of love; all divine choices and all divine efficiencies wait the bidding or have their inherent sources in love. The ethical nature of God proves that he is a spiritual being. Matter is unethical. Try to think of an atom feeling moral obligation or differentiating between right and wrong. The perfect knowledge of the right and good is an inherence of the essential, that is, of the eternal omniscience of God; the choice of it, and the efficient determination of himself to it, is a free choice of his will, and constitutes the perfect and changeless holiness of his nature. The standard of the perfectly right and good is not something objective to him, but is an inherence of his perfect knowledge and infinite love—is subjective in him. Here, as in every other respect, he is unconditioned and absolute.

The ethical can only be predicated of the spiritual nature, and is inseparable from personality. Let anyone attempt to affirm any moral quality of an impersonal substance, and the absurdity appears. Let him attempt to eliminate ethics from the universe, and his conscience and reason at once raise a protest which it is impossible to silence. There are moral laws and moral beings. Conscience is witness to the former; consciousness affirms the latter. Their existence demonstrates the ethical nature of God, in whom they have their sources. The inevitable outcome is that God is purely a spiritual being.

The differentiation between matter and spirit is so absolute that neither has anything in common with the other, and neither can by possibility acquire anything belonging to the other; alike they are incapable of transmutation or assimilation. Spirit is invisible and impalpable; matter is visible and tangible. Spirit is formless; matter has necessary extension. Spirit is self-determining; matter can only act as acted upon. Spirit is intelligent; matter is unintelligent. Spirit thinks, wills, feels; matter does nothing, but is so made as to have and exhibit color, weight, form. Spirit is simple, indivisible, uncompoundable; matter is various, divisible, and compoundable. Spirit is personal and responsible; matter is impersonal and irresponsible. Spirit has the power of growth, increase, perfectibility; matter is inert, dead, and incapable of self-improvement. Spirit has hope, aspiration, and endeavor; matter is impassive, unaspiring, and incapable of desire. Spirit loves, appreciates, approves; matter is attracted, combined, molded. Spirit is conscious of worthiness, dignity, power; matter can make no such distinction. Spirit feels shame, remorse, sorrow, grief, despair, desert of punishment, joy, gladness, rapture, delight, ecstasy, desert of reward; matter can experience no emotion of any kind. Spirit discerns truth, beauty, virtue, has insight, discrimination, seeks out hidden secrets, invents, subordinates nature to its service, builds laws, governments, institutions, learnings, civilizations, religions; matter is a servant, drudge, slave. Spirit may degenerate, be degraded, debased, become a slave to passion and vice, but it can never change its nature so as to be mere matter; matter cannot debase or refine itself, nor be refined so as to become spirit. Thus there is an absolutely impassable gulf between the two substances. There is not a single point of union between them. They have relations, but no common qualities or properties. The relations are those of creator and created, superior and inferior, master and servant. The gulf can neither be filled up nor bridged; the separation has the diameter of infinity—absolute otherness.

UNITY OF GOD.

THE next implication is that God is one. If there be proof that God exists, that he is a spirit, that he is a person, and if reason or revelation requires that we should so think him, the same reason and revelation require that we should think him one. By unity is meant that (*a*) in his nature is essential unity—he is not complex or divisible; (*b*) there is but one being who possesses the attributes which constitute Godhead; (*c*) he is so one that it is impossible there ever should be another being of the same kind. His unity is absolute, necessary, and eternal. Other spirits are one in simplicity of essence, but there are many of the same kind. He alone is so one that it is impossible even to himself that there should be a duplicate— eternity, necessary existence, independence, underived infinite perfection were not participated by a plurality of distinct essences originally, but belonged to a single being, and as there was originally but one eternal, there never could be another by creation. The original perfections are not communicable. This glory of exclusive Godhead can never be alienated or shared. "The primary law of thought that predicates the infinite and the absolute of the divine Being demands his eternal unity as a necessary postulate." * "In God there is absolute soleness, *soleitas*, though what lies hidden in the mystery of this *essential oneness* we know but partially." †

This doctrine excludes polytheism and dualism—the doctrine of many gods, and the doctrine of two eternal beings or principles. God is the sole unitary ground of all existence. Revelation is explicit: "Hear, O Israel: The Lord our God is one

---
* Pope, *Christian Theology*, vol. i, p. 253.   † *Idem.*

Lord" (Deut. vi, 4). "Know therefore this day, and consider it in thine heart, that the Lord he is God in heaven above, and upon the earth beneath: there is none else" (Deut. iv, 39). "Is there a God besides me? yea, there is no God; I know not any" (Isa. xliv, 8). "We know that an idol is nothing in the world, and that there is none other God but one" (1 Cor. viii, 4). "I am the Lord, and there is none else. I form the light, and create darkness" (Isa. xlv, 6, 7). See also Deut. xxxii, 39, 40; Isa. xliv, 24; Rev. i, 17; Isa. xliv, 6; John xvii, 3–5; Matt. xxviii, 19. There is nothing in revelation to oppose to these unequivocal statements—no incidental allusion or implication. The doctrines are in accord with it. It is everywhere assumed and implied, when unexpressed. There is no possibility of mistake on this point. Only one God is known to the Bible, either in the more ancient or recent books. There is not a hint either of polytheism, or tritheism, or dualism, or pantheism, or atheistic monism, but the unvarying assertion of one God, who is an infinite spirit and an adorable person or persons.

Is there anything in the realm of nature—the cosmic facts—to oppose to the doctrine? That there is *one God* has been shown to be the inevitable outcome of reason applied to evidence. He cannot be thought away and rationality be maintained. Nature is full of one God. He so permeates it that were it possible to withdraw him nature could not only not be intelligible, but it would lapse into nonexistence. All this has been established by many and circumstantial proofs.

What we now assert is that nature contains no hint of a plurality of gods. "Unity is stamped on the entire creation so clearly that the whole system of science is based upon this presupposition; its latest conclusions pointing to some one primitive and central force, which some in their blind enthusiasm almost deify as the unknown God. And as it is in earthly things, so it is in things spiritual and heavenly. There is one conscience in man, suggesting one law and Lawgiver. There is evil and there is good; but they both pay homage to the supreme will behind them, which is their equal standard. Hence the erring philosophy of the world, in the better tendencies, has seldom been polytheistic or dualistic; its animal tendency toward pantheism declares its indestructible conviction of the unity of God. This has been its snare, to carry the principle to the extreme of denying all personality or creaturely existence outside of the One and All." *

"It is, perhaps, a more decisive fact that all the demands of reason are met by the conception of one God. An infinite first cause, reached by whatever form of the argument, precludes all need of any other such cause, if, indeed, the supposition of any such other is not unphilosophical and absurd."† If it should be assumed that there are many gods, that is, many eternal, self-existing personal beings, or more than one, and the proof should be demanded, it is impossible to adduce a single proof or even hint. Everything that we know anything about may be traced to one cause. There is no hint of multiplicity or plurality. The supposition of plurality is groundless, and rational thinking therefore excludes it. In the absence of all proof it can have no other ground than imagination, or mere irrational fancy. The gods of the Pantheon are human fictions. Let us keep steadfastly in our minds the difference between the ground for the admission of one God and of many gods; and also the difference between the grounds for the denial of one God and of many gods. It furnishes no proof, or intimation even, of more than one. One God must be thought as a necessity; more than one has no ground but imagination. The denial of one God is the absurdity of supposing the uni-

---

* Pope, *Christian Theology*, vol. i, p. 259.
† Lord, *Christian Theology*, p. 128.

verse to exist without a cause. The denial of many gods is the rational act of denying that of which there is no proof whatever, and against which there is much proof. The one God who alone is God manifests himself in all things that have being. He confronts us which way soever we turn. He pervades us; he presses himself upon our consciousness, our intuitions, our rational thinking, our conscience. We can no more escape him than we can escape ourselves.

The mythological divinities, whether of classic or uncultured peoples and ages, furnish no other proofs of their existence than the dreams of those who invented them—sometimes beautiful, more times grotesque and hideous, always the figments of fancy.

The great biblical truth of the unity of God is also the great and ultimate truth of reason. For rational thought not less than for Christian faith the world ground is one, and that ineffable One is a self-conscious Spirit acting with intelligence and purpose—a personal God. To think other is to think without reason, against reason.

ETERNITY OF GOD.

If we find ourselves obliged to think of the world ground as one, and that one an infinite Spirit, we are likewise compelled to think him eternal.

What do we mean by eternal? It is impossible to form an abstract idea of eternity. It is strictly predicative and requires a subject. It signifies that which has permanent existence without beginning or end, and therefore without succession. That which exists, not from moment to moment, but in whose existence all moments are embraced, and whose existence cannot be divided into, or measured by, aggregation of separate parts, and of whom it cannot be said that he *was* in some past time, or is in the present time, in any sense in which he is not also now existing in all past time and in all future time. The term thus describes a mode of existence. "I am" is God's own definition of the mode of his existence. He only is the "I am." The predicate applies to no other being. It is a predicate of mode, and must be forever exclusive. When predicated of a being it means one whose existence is necessary—to whom nonexistence is impossible. It is a term of infinitude. Necessary existence is existence which precludes the possibility of nonexistence, and must fill all duration. It is in strict contrast with the terms time and temporal. Time denotes measurable duration. It is predicable only of existence which begins. The essence of the terms eternal and eternity is unbeginningness and unendingness. The essence of the terms time and temporal is beginningness and endingness. Both are predicables of existence—the one of limitless existence, the other of limited existence; the one of underived, necessary existence, the other of derived, dependent existence.

God is eternal. All other existence is temporal. He alone never began and can never end. All other being began and will end, or at any period of its existence, even though it may never cease to exist, will be measurable. They can never rise out of the temporal into the eternal, even though they should be immortal. They must forever continue to be beings who once were not, who began to be, and the quantity of whose existence is limited between the date of their beginning and the present moment, which period must forever be divisible into a definite number of years or moments. The existence of the Eternal is not divisible into moments or computable by years. The predicate is greater than our comprehension, but it is a necessity of thought. There must be such a being, or there could never have been any being. It is sometimes said that "time is a part of eternity," "a fragment broken off at both ends," and that "eternity is time indefinitely extended." These are misleading conceptions. The only true way of thinking them is to keep the essence of each term in mind and note their radical contrast. Moments make time. Moments do not make eternity.

Time can be comprehended; eternity cannot. There is an exact measure of actual time. It is included between the two points now and that point in the remote past when the first thing which had beginning began. There necessarily was such a moment. That moment was the birth of time. Before that there was nothing temporal—no time. If it were possible to suppose that that first event, the birth of the time order of being, was the creation of a world, which immediately commenced a diurnal revolution of twenty-four of our hours, and which it has continued without intermission until this day; and if we could suppose a self-registering chronometer indicating each revolution, we should be able to determine the exact number of days and seconds of actual time, or the exact period in which all temporal things have existed. There is just as exact a measure of time as that, and there is no more time than that. Behind that is the Eternal—the Unbegun; a term in which, more or less, minutes or days or years or cycles have no meaning, because we have passed out of the temporal order into the eternal, and He who alone remains, or is, gives to himself the name " I AM."

If we keep in mind the significance of the term time, or temporal, namely, that it denotes duration, from a point of beginning, through a period of successive moments, measurable and limited, we should see at once that it cannot apply to anything in the being or perfections of God; for in them there is no beginning and no progress or change or succession of any kind. In respect of these he is immutable. He is never more nor less. He does not become what he was not. He does not pass from what he was into something else that he was not. There is nothing to denote succession. He does not add cycles to his existence. In all respects in which he is eternal he is strictly changeless.

Is there, then, no past or future in God? If the term past denote something which is gone from him, and if the term future denote something which is yet to come to him, we must answer, No. All that he was or will be he now is. There is no was or will be that is not now with him, as to himself. By the passage of time which increases the life of the creature there is no addition to the life of God. He becomes neither wiser nor older by the coming and going of centuries or æons.

What do we mean when we predicate of anything that it is not eternal? We might answer, We mean that it is a thing of time; but the answer is simply tautological—mere repetition—that which is not eternal is not eternal. We do in fact have a definite meaning, and it is not difficult to state it. When we affirm noneternity of an object we simply affirm, as a first thought, that it did not always exist, or, what is the same thing, that it began to be; there was a time when it was not. The idea is plain and intelligible. We predicate it with perfect confidence of its truth, and with the certainty that we have a clear meaning in its use as applied to all the objects we behold and all the events of which we have experience. Thus, the earth itself once was not, it began to be; we ourselves were not, we began to be; to-day was not, it began to be; all things come under the same category. But we have more in our meaning than this; we mean, as a second thought, that it exists in an order of succession—moment by moment.

The result formulates itself into the statement that all the objects with which we are acquainted exist in this mode—they are things of time; so many moments tell how long they have existed, and point to a moment behind which they did not exist. The moments they have existed may amount to millions, but the mode of their existence is such that they have had but a moment in their possession during the whole process—successively they have possessed each moment in transition. All temporal existence is in this mode. It is a universal predicate of all the things we know and of all persons, except one. How, once nonexistent, they came to be, we may not be able to explain; but we do not doubt the fact; we know it is so. The transitive mode of this existence we know. Time is the term which describes the fact and the mode. Yesterday was and is not. To-morrow is not, but will be. Now is, and is all of time that is. There have been vast measures of time, and will be ages to come; but time, all time, is the simple aggregate of successive nows. Things register their ages, and of some we are able to read the record. If we had a perfect record, and could translate it, we could read backward the history of creation to the beginning of all. We should find thousands of events arising in the same moment and disappearing with it. Time is thus simply a flow of consecutive events—denotes a mode of successive existence and experience, or a duration measurable by adding successive moments together. We use the words past, present, and future to denote the relation of the events to each other or to our mode of thinking them. They exist in time, and can only be thought in this form. They do not coexist, and they are not permanent, and under this law we must think them. The general and universal fact is that all individual things existing under the mode of time have a limited and measurable existence; and the same is true of the whole aggregate. Time, as comprising all succession or all things which exist in the mode of succession, is finite. Time is not an entity or substance. It is but a name indicating a mode or order of events. Some events have been—we use the term past to denote that fact; some events are now transpiring—we use the term present to denote that fact; some events will be—we use the word future to denote that fact. The term time simply denotes the order of succession. Were there no succession the several terms past, present, future, and time would be meaningless—would indicate nothing. There would be no mode of existence requiring their use.

The so-called river of time denotes not an entity, but a simple succession of events. Let us suppose the succession to begin by the creation of the world, and that its flow represents millions of years as marked by millions of successive revolutions of our earth. Now let us suppose God to be a being who exists without succession at every point along the banks of this flowing river. We will have as the result the entire millions of years permanently under his gaze, as it is. Let us take some one spirit, who commenced his existence at that point a million years ago, and who has continued from that point until now, and whose experience has been marked by some new thought or feeling or act each interval as denoted by hours along the whole line; we shall have as the result simple succession of events, and an observer who has a perfect view of all the incidents from the starting point to the end. The whole line will always be present to him, as it is, beginning, middle, and end. Add all possible millions to it, and the same will be true. The events succeed each other and do not co-exist in the same moment. This we know is a fact which it is impossible to change.

But, then, is there no change in the thoughts, feelings, and acts of God, growing out of these changes in the line of events? So it has been sometimes affirmed, but we are compelled, both on rational and scriptural grounds, to dissent. That which is true is; as to attribute and being there is no change. These belong to his essential nature and are strictly eternal. The same is true of the ethical quality of his nature. It changes not. There is here no modification. He is the eternally good and holy. His principles remain the same forever and ever; but the changes which emerge in the creature, and in the order of events, will affect his feeling and actions. These are not eternal. Let us find an illustration. Let it be that of a soul's life. At a point in the series of events he beholds a soul emerging into existence. We will designate it as A. A is a being who passes through moral changes. God observes these changes in A. When A is a sinner he feels toward him the appropriate ethical sentiment of disapproval and condemnation; when he repents he feels toward him the appropriate sentiment of forgiveness; when he is a holy saint he feels toward him the appropriate sentiment of approval and complaisance. But these different conditions or states of A are not coexistent in time, but are in succession. The same must be true of the feelings and sentiments of God toward him. This is precisely what is taught in the Scriptures, and to suppose it otherwise would be to deëthicalize God.

We must, therefore, conclude that the unchangeable with respect to being and essential attributes is not unchangeable with respect to feelings and administrative acts. His immutability here issues in modification there. He eternally hates, condemns, and punishes sin. He eternally loves and rewards holiness. Man changes from holiness to sin or from sin to holiness. These changes in the creature issue in changed relations to his Maker, and because the ethical nature of his Maker changes not, the change in the creature issues in a change of feeling and administration toward him by the altered conditions.

On this point I quote from a recent author, who has taken the rank of a standard among us. He says: "But the perfect idea of eternity, as it is in the human mind, cannot tolerate deviation or succession of thoughts as necessary to divine consciousness. And this is the deep perplexity of our human intellect, which, however, must accept the profound meaning of the name 'I AM,' as teaching an eternal now enfolding and surrounding the successive existences of time. The personal Jehovah once, and only once, declared his pure eternity. His name is the only word which human language affords in its poverty to express that thought; such terms as eternal and everlasting have temporal notions clinging to them; and all our phrases go no further than those that the Supreme fills all space and time, that he was before them, the very word carrying duration with it. But 'I AM'—before time or space was, 'I AM'—has in it all the strength of eternity. It is literally the assertion of pure existence, without distinction of past and present and future; that is, of past and present and future as measured in time and regulated by motion in space. We must accept this doctrine of God in all its incomprehensibleness, as the only one that satisfies the mind. The Eternal in himself knows no succession of time any more than he knows circumscription of space; and when he created all things his being remains as independent of duration as it is independent of locality. No attribute, however, has given rise to more discussion than this. The deepest thinkers of all ages have consented to annihilate in the divine essence all that we mean by time and succession of thought. They have agreed to think of a *duratio tota simul,* of an *æternitas* in which *"fuisse" et "futurum esse" non est, sed solum "esse."* And the name Jehovah—the name of God, and of each of the three Persons in the Godhead—demands and sanctions this. It is utterly vain to attempt to penetrate this abyss of mystery; it is equally fruitless either to fight against it or to illustrate it.

"Opponents of this truth deny that there can be duration without succession; but duration is succession; both words are equally inappropriate to the Eternal, who simply *is*. They insist also that to take from a personal being the act and operation of successive thinking is to destroy its personality. But this is simply arguing from our finite nature—which cannot think but under conditions of time and space—to the infinite, which by the very definition knows no such limits. The only answer possible to all such objections is the common apology required everywhere by this subject; we cannot search out the divine being unto perfection, though the perfection in which we are lost allows no past to recede before God and no future to rise before him. When the argument takes another form, and we are pointed to the tenor of scriptural representations that speak of the Eternal as having purposes which have been fulfilled and are in course of fulfillment, our reply must be cautiously and yet boldly given. Time is the creation of the eternal God, who *made the ages*. It is, with all its endless phenomena and laws, a reality to Him who brought it into being; and all its succession unfolds in his presence as past and present and future. Our only difficulty is to hold fast the truth that he sustains two relations to time. As the abiding eternal One he views it in his place, himself absolutely unconnected with it. As the God who works out for the creature and with the creature his own purposes he beholds, directs, and controls all things as under the law of time. This is, of course, a deep mystery to human thoughts; that is, to conceive of eternal willing* and temporal acting, of a timeless and successionless agent, working out and watching the evolution of his plans. But the mystery, such as it is, is only that of the incarnation anticipated; and as we receive this we may receive that. We may dare to say that the Eternal inhabits eternity, and yet that in the Son, the firstborn before every creature, he inhabits time also. As in the incarnation God is manifest in the flesh, so in the creation God is manifest in time. And as God will be forever manifest in his incarnate Son, so will he forever have in and through his Son, the vicegerent of created things, a manifestation in time; that is to say, in plain words, eternity and time will henceforth coexist. Something pertaining to time will cease—its changes and probation and opportunity. In this sense, χρόνος οὐκέτι ἔσται; but in no other sense." †

To the same effect Dr. Hodge says: "The infinitude of God relatively to space is in his immensity or omnipresence; relatively to time it is his eternity. As he is free from all limitations in space, so he is exalted above all limitations of time. As he is not more in one place than in another, but in every place equally present, so he does not exist during one

---

* There can be no eternal willing in the sense of executive or causational volitions, but there may be eternal willing in the sense of purposing to put forth causational efficiency. God's purposes are eternal, but the carrying of them out is and must be in succession and in time.

† Pope, *Christian Theology*, vol. i, pp. 297-299.

period of duration more than another. With him there is no distinction between the present, past, and future; but all things are always present to him. . . . He is, and always has been, and always will be; to him there is neither past nor future; the past and future are always and equally present to him." *

When it is said that "God inhabits eternity" the meaning can be nothing other than that he exists in the mode of eternity, not in the mode of time—his name "I AM" implies this. Eternity is in him, not in parts, for it is not divisible. It is in its illimitable wholeness in him, and he is in it. The distinction between him and temporal being is this: temporal being inhabits a *passing instant, called now*. No temporal being ever exists save in the passing moment. It did exist in moments past, it does not now exist in them. It will exist in future moments. It does not now exist in them. It never can have more than the moment. The time that it has existed and does exist and will exist embraces all the moments through which it has passed, is passing, and will pass, and is always measurable, but it can never have more than a moment in its possession. Its home is a movable point—a floating, transient instant. Can this be said of God? Does he exist only in the passing moment? Either this, or his mode of existence differs entirely from the mode of existence of any temporal being. God lives in all years. His now is not a movable point, but is the all-inclusive eternity— an all-embracing now. The past is still with him and in him, not as thought, but as reality, and the future is with him, and in him, as much as it will ever be, not in *posse*, but in *esse* or reality. From eternity to eternity, which only means eternally, all things are with him. As to temporal being, there is a coming and a vanishing; not so with the Eternal. Here there is an abiding, stable, immutable I AM. He does not exist moment by moment, transferring himself from one moment to another,

---

* Hodge, *Systematic Theology*, vol. i, pp. 386, 387.

losing the last when he enters into the next ensuing, thus coming along to our time from some remote eternity. The forever is in him always in all its fullness, "the same, yesterday, to-day, and forever." The eternity of God is the infinite reservoir, exhaustless, changeless. Time is the divine energizing flowing forth, in creation and administrative acts, fertilizing the ages of finite existence. The river issues from the reservoir, but is not the reservoir. Pantheism turns the river back into the sea from which it flows, and the finite becomes lost again in the indistinguishable infinite. Theism makes the flow perpetual, but leaves the infinite sea stationary and undiminished, while it forever pours itself into advancing, deepening, and widening river, every atom and increment of which it gives. The flowing atoms make the river, but do not measure or make the sea.

GOD IS ABSOLUTE, UNCONDITIONED BEING.

God is absolute, infinite, unconditioned being. These terms need explanation. They play so important a part in discussions concerning God that they cannot be omitted. Only one of the terms is ever employed to indicate an attribute of God. They are predicates of his nature or being rather than of attributes which inhere in his essence, or of both. Both absolute and unconditioned indicate a mode of existence out of conditions and relations. To predicate them of God is simply to say that his being as such is unconditioned and independent of all relations.

His being is absolute—out of all relations. This does not mean that God sustains no relations to other beings. This would be to deny that he is the creator and governor of the universe, for these acts relate him to everything that exists. But this fact of creatorship, which brings him into such intimate relationship to all being, is proof positive that his being in itself is absolute and out of all relations. Creatorship necessitates that he should have existed in the perfection of his being when no other being existed. His being then was absolute and out of all relations, for there was nothing in existence with which relations could obtain. There can be no relations to the nonexistent, for that would be relations to nothing. The fact of his creating other beings and thus creating relations with them, prior to which no relations could exist, does not prove that his being is not absolute, but rather that it is absolute; yea, that of necessity it must be; for by the very terms of the proposition he existed alone. If it should be said that the idea of the universe must have existed with him from eternity, and thus he was in eternal relation to it, we answer, this does not interfere with the absoluteness of his being, which means out of all relations with other being, but not out of relations with himself. His idea of a universe to be, and even his purpose to create, were not a relation to *it*, for it was not; it was but a relation to his own thought and purpose, and left his being as purely absolute as if the thought and purpose did not exist. God exists in relations, but they are relations which he creates, and not relations coeval with his being, or of his being as such. Voluntarily created relations are not necessary relations; as he once existed out of them he might have existed out of them forever and his being been unimpaired.

"The absolute, taken in its etymological sense, may be explained as that which is free from all necessary relations; which exists in and by itself, and does not require the prior or simultaneous existence of anything else. The unconditioned, in like manner, is that which is subject to no law or condition of being, which exists, therefore, in and by itself, and does not require the prior or simultaneous existence of anything else. The absolute and unconditioned are also identical with the real (not all real is absolute and unconditioned, but all absolute and unconditioned must be real), for relation is but a phenomenon requiring and depending on the prior existence of things relative, while the true real (primary real) is unrelated.

"Mr. Calderwood defines the absolute, which he rightly identifies with the infinite, as 'that which is free from all necessary relations;' it may exist in relation, provided that relation be not a necessary condition of its existence. Hence he holds that the absolute may exist in the relation of consciousness, and in that relation be apprehended, though imperfectly, by man.

"According to Sir William Hamilton, 'The unconditioned denotes the genus of which the infinite and absolute are the species.' According to Kant, and Sir William Hamilton agrees with him, the absolute and unconditioned is not an object of knowledge, but its notion is a regulative principle of the mind itself—is more than mere negation of the conditions. According to Schelling, it is cognizable, but not conceivable; it can be known by sinking back into identity with the absolute, but is incomprehensible by consciousness and reflection, which are only of the relative and the different. According to Cousin, it is cognizable and conceivable by consciousness and reflection, under relation, difference, and plurality. Instead of saying that God is absolute and infinite, Krause and his admirer, Tiberghien, ascribe to him sèité (selbheit) and totality. Totality, or the infinite, manifests itself everywhere in nature. Nature is made up of wholes, and all these constitute one whole. In spirit everything manifests itself under the character of spontaneity or sèité. Spirit is always what it is by its own individual efforts."

This citation shows how difficult it is for the most philosophic minds to attain to clearness of idea and expression when they deal with the infinite and absolute; but it shows also that the existence of the incomprehensible infinite and absolute is a necessity of thought. Behind the finite related and conditioned is discerned as inevitable the infinite, absolute, and unconditioned. The finite thinks in terms of phenomena, but it is certain of underlying substance, though it can only express the essence in terms of attribute or quality. The attributes come to manifestation in phenomena, but they can only exist in the infinite and absolute. God comes to knowledge only as related to the finite, but his existence is discerned to be antecedent to the finite, and so is itself not to be conditioned by the finite. God is unconditioned as to his existence. The term unconditioned differs but little in its essential meaning from the term absolute. The latter, as we have seen, means that which is free from all necessary relations; which exists and has its whole being in and by it itself, and does not require the prior or simultaneous existence of anything else. The former, unconditioned, is that which is subject to no conditioning law or conditioning ground of being, which exists therefore in and by itself, and does not imply anything else to condition its existence. For a being to be conditioned it must be in the matter of his existence or in respect of his nature and attributes. To be conditioned in any of these respects there must be some other being to impose the conditions, or something in the nature of things. Now, since God is the only eternal and his being dates back of all other existence, it does not appear how he could be conditioned. There was nothing to condition him; he could not even condition himself, as to his nature and attributes; and nothing can possibly exist in time that can condition him in these respects. As it was impossible that he should be conditioned as to his being, which was unoriginated, so also he was unconditioned as to his creative acts, except as his own nature imposed conditions upon him. Nor can it ever be possible for the creature to impose conditions upon the Creator as to the manner of his dealing with it; any conditions that may arise, under the exigencies of administration, to influence or determine him must still be self-imposed; administration, as much as creation, must forever be his purely personal acts. As by creating the universe he created relations of himself to it and so brought himself personally into relations with the thing created without affecting the fact as to the absoluteness of his being, so any conditioning of his acts arising from the exigencies of administration is not a conditioning of his being. It might even be admitted that subsequent acts of God to the great original act of creation are conditioned without at all affecting the question as to whether his nature and essential attributes are conditioned. The position held is one and simple, that God is, and is what he is, wholly without exterior conditioning and without interior conditions. No other existence conditions his existence, and he does not condition his own existence; as he is uncaused, so he is unconditioned. The sum of which is that relationship and conditionedness are terms which arise with creature existence and have no meaning whatever as applied to the uncreated.

It thus appears that as to existence and all that is comprised in the mere fact of being God is a pure spirit, intelligent, self-conscious, and self-determined, absolute and unconditioned, existing as he is from eternity and of necessity, there being no cause of his being, no cause in any way conditioning or modifying it. It also thus appears that he is a person and not a thing, or abstract force, or mere idea, or impersonal substance evolving itself.

The true character of this amazing being remains to be elicited by further pointing out several predicates of him as he has discovered himself to us. His being and his several modes of manifestation implicate qualities and attributes. Himself is invisible; no eye has ever seen him; no sense has ever discerned him; but reason discovers him in every visible and invisible object; and in his own word he declares himself; incomprehensible, he is yet apprehensible.

While it is an absolute necessity that the Eternal cannot be conditioned, the one term excluding the other, it is just as necessary that each specific act of the Eternal should be conditioned, otherwise we introduce into his acts absolute fatalism. But his acts can only be conditioned by himself. He must absolutely determine himself and cannot be determined by another, since he alone exists. His self-determined acts are not like his nature, eternal. The nature originates them; he is the true cause, not of himself, for himself being eternal cannot be caused, but of every objective expression or forthputting of his nature. Every such act falls within time, has a beginning. Creation and governance of the universe in all its incidents forever and ever are acts of this kind. They are not inherences of the unconditioned and eternal nature, but are free expressions by the eternal nature, self-determined and differentiable from the self, as the acts of free mind are differentiable from and dependent on the mind which put them forth. This we consider a most important position.

Let us see to what conclusion the principle here enunciated leads us. The principle is that God, as to being and attributes, is necessary, eternal, and unconditioned; that as to objective acts, that is, acts not included in his subjective nature and necessary to it, acts of self-consciousness, he is free to determine, first, what such acts shall be, and, second, to cause them. In both cases he is sole and self-conditioned cause; not even his nature necessitates them, but only makes them possible, and he as a person determines and executes them. Until he thus personally acts they do not exist. If his acts were necessary outcomes of his being we should have sheer and absolute fatalism; but even then the acts would not be eternal, but must exist under time order or in succession, which is time. The principle of necessity introduced into the divine nature as to such modes of action destroys the divine personality.

God is infinite. This, like the terms absolute and unconditioned, is a predicate both of his nature and attributes. The three terms are affinitive, but not identical. Each has a shade of meaning not contained in the other. The term absolute, as we have seen, signifies that which exists apart from any necessary relations; which is were there nothing else; which requires nothing else in order to its complete being; that which has fullness of being in itself. Unconditioned signifies that the existence of which depends upon no conditions; which has the entire ground of being in itself, and does not need anything else to the full realization of itself. It is what it is in absolute independence of any other existence or law of any kind. The two terms as applied to God signify that his being is so above all, so complete in itself, that nothing can add anything to him or subtract anything from him. He conditions all, but is conditioned by none. The term infinite is of the same general import, but with a difference. It is the antithesis of the term finite or limited. It means, therefore, not simply the absolute and unconditioned, but also the unlimited, He to whose perfections there are no bounds. Absolute and unconditioned are terms of being without reference to quality. Infinite is a term of perfection describing not only unconditioned existence, but limitless perfection.

The plausible objections to the infinitude of God are (a) that we can form no conception of the term; (b) that it includes other being and reduces to monism; (c) that it renders personality impossible. To the first we answer, it is true we cannot comprehend infinity, or picture it in thought, but it is not true that the term conveys no idea. Though unpicturable we know that we do have a distinct meaning when we predicate infinity of an object, and we have the unalterable conviction that the affirmation is true, as of eternity, power, knowledge, truth, goodness. The term simply means that there is neither limit nor defect. It is the equivalent of absolute perfection. We have the unalterable conviction when we predicate infinitude of the divine perfections that it has a true meaning and is a truth. As in the former case, we can fix no limit to them, nor conceive of a possible limit. To conceive the possibility of a limit of his duration, for example, we must be able to form the idea of a time when he did not exist; but this collides with his necessary existence, and excludes the possibility of accounting for his existence at all; in fact, precludes the possibility of any existence, since if once there had been nothing it would be impossible there ever should be anything. Thus existence of any kind compels the thought of unbegun existence, which is infinitude. The same is true of other ineffable perfections of the divine nature. We conceive that to be to which we can assign no limit, and which we know in fact has no limit.

To the second objection we answer, the infinite does not necessarily include the all. The existence of some beings who once were not does not hinder the existence of one being who always was. The finiteness of the one does not take from the infinitude of the other, or in any way affect it. The finite may be and is a product of the Infinite. He does not thereby limit himself and become less or other. His infinitude is the ground and support of the other being. If some creatures can know some things this does not prevent him from knowing all things; their possession of limited powers does not prevent him from having all power, if the power they possess is his gift and is in dependence upon him. The infinite is not the all, but the ground of the all. He was once the only. There is now a universe which is other to him. But this does not detract from him or impose limits upon him, but simply manifests him. There is nothing in it which is not of him, as source. It is but an expression, of which he is the expressor; it cannot therefore diminish him. He is and must be forever still the infinite cause. Nothing that is bounds him, fetters him, transcends him, takes from him, diminishes him, defies him, is without him, either as causing or permitting it or not choosing to prevent it. He transcends all, is before all, limits all, governs all, is independent of all—could, if he chose, abolish all by a volition. No limits can be fixed for him except those which he imposes on himself by a free exercise of his own choice. He cannot grow or develop into something greater than he is. Neither time nor eternity can increase him; nor can the mind conceive of enlargement or improvement of any perfection of his nature.

To the third objection we answer that, if personality means a being who is one, a self-conscious, intelligent, and volitional being, and, it may be added, a free moral being, it is impossible to prove that infinitude precludes this. The thesis requires us to think of an eternal being of this description. What shall hinder? It is answered that such a being could not exist, because self-consciousness would be impossible in such a case. Why impossible? It is answered, because self-consciousness demands as its ground a not self—a ground of differentiation. This cannot be proved, and is a groundless assumption. Suppose, as we are compelled to admit, there were an eternal self-existing and sole-existing being, who possessed all knowledge of himself and of all possible things, and who had all power to produce all possible things, and who to produce must volitionally act, and who was perfectly free to act according to his own pleasure, and whose pleasure could only be to act according to certain ideas which we call ideas of right and goodness and wisdom, what would hinder that such a being should be self-conscious—a true personal being? Could he not know his own knowledge and himself as possessing it? And would not this be self-consciousness, and consciousness of himself as a person? And would not here be the absolute, infinite in self-conscious and solitary existence? Would the fact that his knowledge was a knowledge of possible things, and of himself as a possible cause, be a limit to his infinitude or detract from his absoluteness? Would he not still be the only being, out of all relations except personal relations to himself? Could the knowledge of himself and of the possibilities in himself be pleaded as a bar to his absoluteness and infinitude? It is answered that the supposition itself gives, as a necessary ground of self-consciousness, the supposable other, known as possible, and therefore is a limitation or condition; and so God would thus know himself as conditioned and limited, and not as infinite and absolute. We answer, the knowing would be simply self-knowing—the consciousness of himself and what was possible to himself. He would know himself in fact, and necessarily, as the only being, as a person possessing infinite attributes. At the same time knowing himself, he would know all possible but nonexistent things, which he could make real and which according to his own pleasure he would make real. The known nonexistent possible is no more a limitation than the known actual. The possible has no existence as possible even but by him. He bounds it; it does not bound him. It proves his perfection, does not limit it. To know it is simply to know himself. In self-consciousness the mind is subject-object—it knows itself and knows its states and subjective acts. In self-consciousness God from eternity, when nothing but himself existed, knew himself as subject-object, as possessing power for the production of the nonexisting things, as proposing to make them or not make them; but this does not limit him, while it does prove him to be an eternally self-conscious being or person. Personality is a necessity as much as existence is. He never had power to be anything else but what he is—a personal being. But does not that lack of power set limits to him, and prove that after all he is not infinite? We answer, No. It proves no limitation of power that an eternal being should not be able to make himself noneternal, since infinite power cannot work a contradiction. There is almost an inevitable tendency of mind, in studying the infinity of the divine being, to confound infinity with the all of being, and immensity with unlimited extension, and eternity with continuity. Now the all does not express the infinite, nor does unlimited extension express the omnipresence, nor does continuity express the eternal.

The ideas of time and space add to the bewilderment. Let us affirm that as ordinarily understood there is neither time nor space; they are subjective forms of thought merely which arise from perceiving succession and extension among things. Take away the order of existence which has being moment by moment, and the idea of acts which begin, and you remove the possibility of the idea of time. There is nothing left to create or answer to the idea. When the mind moves on beyond creative existence and creative acts it finds no ground for the time idea, simply because successions and beginnings have disappeared. So take away objects which are extended and figured, and you remove the space idea; the term loses its significance. God is not an infinitely extended being. The predication of infinite extension is a contradiction; all extension is of necessity finite. This is axiomatic, as much so as, "The whole is greater than any one of its fractions." We reach the idea of God's infinitude of presence when we find his presence with all being, and his potential presence with any other being that he may create. When it is said extended being occupies space, what is meant is that extended being has measurable size. Extension is predicable of material substances, and not of spirit and personality. Extension is not a predicate of the infinite, but is a predicate of the finite. It denotes a limited and bounded existence. Every possible extension admits of more. Nothing that ends, or is bounded, can be infinite. For the same reason infinite number is an absurdity and self-subversive; infinite extension is a contradiction and impossible. No number of atoms of time can make eternity, and no number of extended particles can make an infinite mass. Succession and extension must forever be finite. It is strictly impossible for the human mind to think or form a concept or idea of the utterly non-existent. All thought must be composed of what is given in reality. From the elements given in knowledge of real things unreal things may be formulated in thought, but they must be composed out of the elements given in knowledge; thus we can never think entirely away from reality—cannot create an object of thought which is made out of elements which do not exist—cannot think such elements. All human thinking must therefore enter and revolve within the realm of the known. To conceive of a being at all it must have qualities of something known, and cannot have implications utterly outside of the known, and therefore inconceivable. The concept may be of some real being, and will have strict correspondence with reality, or it may be of some unreal being, and have no correspondence with reality in the composition of its parts; but in this case the parts must have correspondence with known reality somewhere, in order that it may be conceived. The nonexistent is not reached in any of the elements, but only in the composition of the concept.

As we cannot form a concept of the utterly nonexistent, so it is possible there may be kinds of existence of which we have no knowledge—kinds of existence utterly unlike the realities we know of; but if there be such we have no power to conceive of it—it cannot be represented in our thought. To reach the concept of it we should have to be other kinds of beings from what we are—should have some faculty unlike our present faculties, or exist in conditions unlike our present conditions, of which in both cases we are at present unable to conceive, lying, as they do, wholly outside of experience.

Thus, in order that the idea of God may exist in our minds at all it must either be a creation of our minds out of elements of our knowledge of reality, and thus be a picture of the imagination—an unreal composition out of known elements—or it must be an idea of real being having qualities analogous to those which we know. We must think him, if we form any concept at all, in these qualities; we have no power to think him at all in any others. He must come to our thought through the faculties we possess, but these faculties cannot give being or thought of being separate from what we have known, or beyond what we know in some form of reality. We have no power to abolish the idea of some real existence; for that would require us to abolish the idea of our own existence. We cannot think there was a time when there was or might possibly have been no existence, for that would require us to think there is no existence now; that is, that we ourselves do not exist; for the fact of present existence necessitates the idea of eternal existence, since it is impossible for us to think even that if there had been once no existence there ever could be any existence; that is, that something could come out of nothing, or that nothing could create something.

We must think of existence with him as analogous to our knowledge of existence. The term can have no new meaning —it is actual being or reality. We must think him as having materiality, that is, the qualities of existence which we find in matter, or as not having them. If we think these qualities away we must then think him either a figment, having no existence, and of which we can have no other idea than pure nonexistence, or we must think of him as a being who, apart from any material components, thinks, wills, exerts power, is as real as if he were material, but wholly destitute of material qualities. Still, we can posit in him no qualities except such as we know. He must emerge in our thoughts through our faculties, which can form no concepts of anything wholly unlike what has been given in experience of consciousness. All the predications we make of him must come under this law, for we have no power to rise above it.

Do we predicate that he is a pure spirit? What is the concept? We can only answer, "It is that kind of being whom we know as a being who has power of knowing, feeling, and willing. We can form no other concept or thought of it that is not germane in these attributes. Do we predicate of him that he is eternal? What do we mean by it? We mean simply that he is without beginning. This includes the idea that he is not dependent or derived. This we know to be a logical necessity, but we can form no proper thought of it; it is a simple negation of what we find in other beings, together with the idea of existence—the "I am" of the Bible. When we predicate of him infinitude we mean simply that to his attributes there are no limits. Again, we do not form a proper thought, for we can only think within limits. But we do conceive of his attributes and know what the predicate means—he knows, he wills, he feels, he is. We fail to be able to measure him by our thought, though we are able to think him as being, and to think his attributes as to kind. When we predicate the infinitude of his knowledge we do not mean that there are no other beings that have some knowledge, but simply that he knows all. When we predicate that he is omnipotent we do not mean that there are no other beings that have some power, but we do mean that he can do all that is possible to power, and that all finite power is imparted by his infinite power. His infinity does not exclude innumerable finites. When we predicate of the infinitude of his being we do not mean that there are not other beings. He would be what he is if they were all removed. They neither add to nor take from him, nor in any way limit his being. He is forever the all-knowing and all-powerful source of all other existence, but not all other existence. He was the only, he originated the many, but he does not by originating the many limit himself, or reduce himself from infinitude to finitude. That which he makes does not impart something to him which he did not have before, or make him something which he was not before.

GOD IS A PERSON.

THE term person is of frequent occurrence and of great significance in theological polemics, and not less so in psychology and ethics. The universe is divided into two hemispheres by a strict and invariable line, on one side of which lie impersonal, and on the other side personal, existence. There is no possibility on the part of either, by any process of transmutation or evolution or degeneration, to pass over to the other. The impersonal can never become personal, and the personal, however it may degenerate, can never become impersonal. The difference is a radical difference of substance and attributes. In the impersonal realm the substance is some modification of matter and inhering forces operated under a law of necessity or automatism, or some semispiritual substance which can never be raised to self-consciousness or ethical quality, however it may be possessed of a mimicry of reason. Throughout, from the merest brute matter to the highest animalism, it remains simply a thing, and will admit of no other treatment than that of a thing, but with a difference demanded by the difference which exists between a sensate and insensate thing—between a clod and a life. But life is not personality, whether in the lower form of the vegetable or the highest form of the merely animal.

In the personal realm the substance is pure spirit, though sometimes allied to and conditioned by matter. The person has an individualized existence—is a real being. He is invisible and intangible. He has a real life of his own. He knows himself. He is self-conscious of a distinct existence apart from every other being. He has power of self-direction. In a word, personality as predicable of a created being involves four things: (*a*) A being whose substance is spirit; (*b*) a being endowed with rational powers; (*c*) a being who is self-knowing or self-conscious; (*d*) a being who has power of self-determination, or who is endowed with freedom of choice.

Personality as predicated of God includes these things: (*a*) The existence of God as an individualized real being; (*b*) that he is a pure spirit; (*c*) that he is self-conscious; (*d*) that he has infinite knowledge, power, and eternity; (*e*) that he has an ethical nature which distinguishes the ought and ought not; (*f*) that he has complete power of self-determination—is absolutely free. There are other predicates of him, but these are essentials of his personality, and having these the supreme Author and Ruler of the universe is a personal Being, and were he not such the universe itself could not exist. Personality is thus seen not to be a development, but a form, of existence. Supreme personality belongs to God and is the eternal and primary form of existence. Finite personality is being created in his image and answerable to him for the use of conferred existence and powers. Impersonal being is a divine creation for the service of the finite personal universe or individual created personalities. On this point Dr. Miley, in his *Systematic Theology*, says:

"There are mighty forces in physical nature; but they can act only on the proper adjustment or collocation of material things, and thereon must necessarily act. Their action is without consciousness or aim as well as under a law of necessity. Such forces, however great in potency or wonderful in operation, can have no quality of personality. Life, with its marvelous agency in the vegetable kingdom, still makes no advance beyond the purely physical realm toward any intrinsic personal quality.

"In the animal orders, notably in those of the higher grades, there are instinctive impulses toward ends, and a voluntary power for their attainment, but no evidence of other essential requisites of personality. We cannot study the psychology of animals as we can that of minds like our own, because we cannot place the facts of the former in the light of our own consciousness as we can the facts of the latter. Yet strong instinctive impulses and strong voluntary power are manifest facts in animal life. But there is no evidence of such rational intelligence in the conception of ends and such freedom in the choice of ends as must combine in the constitution of personality.

"Pure intellect, intellect without any form of sensibility, however great, could not constitute personality. Conceptually, such an intellect is a possibility, though its sphere of knowledge could not be universal. A deeper analysis must find in the sensibilities a necessary element of knowledge in many spheres. Such a mind might have great intuitive power and a clear insight into the abstract sciences, but it could have no interest in their study. Neither could there be for it any eligibility of ends. For such a mind the mightiest potentiality of will would be useless for the want of all motive or reason of use. The only possible action would be purposeless and purely spontaneous. Personality is intrinsically a free rational agency. This is impossible in pure intellect, however great—impossible even with the complement of a will potentially very strong.

"Rational or moral motives are a necessity to personal agency, and therefore to personality. Such motives are not mere instinctive impulses toward action, but forms of conscious interest in ends of action, which may be taken up into reflection and judgment. Motives are possible only with a capacity for conscious interest in ends. This capacity is broader and deeper than can well be expressed by the term sensibility. The profounder motives arise from the rational and moral nature rather than from what we usually designate as the feelings. There can be for us no eligibility of ends, and therefore no rational choice, except through motives arising in some form of conscious interest in ends. But rational choice is the central fact of rational agency, and the only difference between rational agency and personal agency is a difference of verbal expression. With the power of personal agency there is personality. It follows that for the constitution of personality an emotional nature, with a capacity for rational interest in ends, must combine with rational intelligence.

"Will is the central power of personal agency, and therefore a necessary constituent of personality. Without the will there could be no voluntary use or direction of the mental faculties, no voluntary action of any kind. In such a state man would be as incapable of personal agency as an animal or even as any force of physical nature.

"The result of the previous analysis is that rational intelligence, sensibility, and will are essential requisites of personality. But such a complex of faculties does not in itself complete the idea of personality. There must also be the freedom of personal agency. Such agency means, not merely the freedom of external action, but specially the free rational choice of the ends of action. The freedom of external action requires simply the freedom of the bodily organism from interior impotence and exterior restraint, and may be as complete in an animal as a man. The bodily organism is merely instrumental to the external action, and can be free only as a freely usable instrument. The mere freedom of external action can have no higher sense. The true freedom must lie back of this in the personal agency, and must consist in the power of free rational choice. With this there is true personality.

"There is still a profound question which vitally concerns the reality of personality. It is the question of the relation of motive to choice, or, more properly here, the decision of the mind with respect to an end—more properly, because whether such decision be a choice or not depends upon the relation of the motive to the mental action. That motive is a necessary condition of choice is a plain truth—so plain that the maintenance of a liberty of indifference may well seem strange. Any voluntary decision in a state of indifference must be a purely arbitrary volition, and therefore cannot be a choice. Choice in the very nature of it is the rational election of an end. For its rationality there must be a motive. But what is the action of the motive upon the elective decision? This is the question which vitally concerns the reality of personality. If the motive is simply a solicitation or inducement which may be taken up into reflection and weighed in the judgment, personality is secure. But if the motive is a causal efficience which determines the decision to the end, then there is no choice, nor the possibility of one, and personality sinks with personal agency beneath an absolute law of determinism.

"Only as rational intelligence, sensibility, and will combine in the constitution of free personal agency is there the reality of personality. There must be rational intelligence for the conception of ends, sensibility as the source of motives with respect to ends, and will in combination with intelligence and sensibility as the complement of power in choosing between ends. With these facts there is personality. Our own personality is in this complex of powers.

"With moral reason and a capacity for moral motives, motives sufficient for the choice of the good against the evil, there is a moral personality. Conceptually, there might be a rational personality without the necessary powers of a moral personality. These powers might be an original omission, or the rational might remain after the moral were sunken beneath a law of necessitation. Moral personality must sink under a moral necessity to evil, just as rational personality must sink in the want of its essential requisites. There is no deeper moral necessity, none more exclusive of moral personality, than an incapacity for the motives necessary to the choice of the good. For complete moral personality there must be free moral agency.

"There can be neither human nor angelic personality, nor even a divine personality, without this complex of essential requisites. There is no need and no purpose of asserting a complete parallelism in all personalities. There is no such implication. As we ascend through the orders of higher intelligences, angels and archangels, even up to God himself, there may be, and in the divine must be, large variations from such a parallelism. The variations may be not only in the grade of faculties, reaching to the infinite in the divine, and particularly in the forms of sensibility, but there may be other powers, now wholly unknown to us. The position is that the complex of requisites in our own personality is a necessity for all personality. Neither angel nor archangel is or can be a person in the true, deep sense of the term without these powers, whatever their grade in such higher intelligences, whatever variation in the forms of sensibility, or whatever other powers they may possess. The same law of requisites must hold for the divine personality. But this application must be treated under a distinct heading.

"Any conception of the divine personality irrespective of our own is for us impossible. It does not follow that our own must be the measure of the divine. We have previously disclaimed any necessary complete parallelism between human and angelic personalities, and pointed out how profoundly this is true as between our own and the divine. Still, there may be a likeness between the former, with its finite powers, and the latter, with its infinite perfections, which is greatly helpful toward a truer and clearer notion of the divine. There is a deep truth in our creation in the image of God. With the revelation of this truth there is no rashness in looking into our own personality for the likeness of the divine. Nor is it, after a recognition of the difference in the grade of powers and the forms of sensibility between the two, open to the reprehension, 'Thou thoughtest that I was altogether such a one as thyself.' Personality is the deepest truth of our likeness to God. Our vision of his personality is in the reflection of his image in our own.

"There must be in God the three forms of power which constitute personality in us. In the lack of any one he could not be a person. Such perfections as omniscience, omnipotence, and immutability, in however complete a synthesis, could not of themselves constitute a divine personality. There must be even for God the eligibility of ends and freedom in the choice of ends. These are the absolute requirement of personal agency, which is the central fact of personality. But, as we have previously seen, the eligibility of ends can arise only with some form of conscious interest in them. This conscious interest cannot arise either from pure intelligence or from the will—not even from an infinite intelligence or an omnipotent will. There must be motivities of the divine nature, as in distinction from intellect and will—rational and moral motivities as the necessary ground of interest in ends. With the powers of intellect, sensibility, and will, and the freedom of rational and moral self-determination with respect to ends, there is a divine personality." *

The same proofs which establish that God is spirit establish that he is a person. Mind is self-conscious. In knowing he must know himself as knowing—know that he knows. Knowledge implies subject and object and includes both.

* Vol. i, pp. 166-170.

This is self-consciousness. If now we add self-determination, that is, power in the subject to determine his own acts, we have personality—a free self-governing and self-knowing being. As neither of these is possible to matter, it follows that the subject in which they inhere is not matter, but spirit, and it also follows that a being of pure materiality cannot be a person, or ever attain, to personality. Matter, which has no power of self-determination, but which acts only as acted in or upon, can of itself account for nothing; throughout all its realm the law of dependence and necessitation reigns; whenever and wherever it exists, but especially in conditions and under forms and relations which indicate ends, purposes, designs, it demonstrates coexistence with it and antecedence to it of another subject, an intelligent, self-conscious, and self-determining personal being.

The inevitable implication is that God is a person, or personal being. We do not reach the limit of our power to think him when we reach the idea that he is a being. If we attempt to think him impersonal we find it impossible. The reason rebels against the suggestion that he is an impersonal force. It is a necessity of rational thought that we clothe him with personality. Person or personality stands for a thinking, intelligent being that has reason and reflection. The seat of intellect is a person. "This has been the uniform and constant sense as to this matter. Personality cannot then exist apart from, but is constituted of and consists in, a rational nature and faculties. Men never call an inanimate thing or creature a person. A person is a being which has intellect, which exercises thought, volition, and affection, and acts in freedom; and whoever has these attributes and puts forth these exercises is a person. These things constitute and therefore form personality. God is a living, conscious, infinite person, not a mere unconscious influence, force, or law." *

The attempt of agnosticism to discredit the great truth of reason, so adroitly championed by Spencer, Mansel, Hamilton, and others, must prove a failure until they shall be able to prove that the order of the universe is timeless, or that originated processes which are packed with thought do not imply a mind. All scientific research up to date tends the other way. For order there must be an intelligent cause, and for a beginning there must be a free cause, and a free cause must be self-conscious—must, knowing its power, consciously exert it to a chosen end. These constitute personality.

With this teaching of reason the word agrees. As reason demands that reason should think God a person, the revelation represents him. The grand psalm of creation opens with the assertion of his personality: "God said, Let there be light: and there was light." "Let us make man in our image, after our likeness." Thenceforth on every page he is represented as the almighty and infinitely wise Governor of the universe, the universal Father, the loving guide and friend. He sees, hears, speaks, commands, approves, condemns, loves, hates, judges, plans, executes, acts in all respects as a person. That the God of the Bible is a person no one has ever had the temerity to deny. But that he can be thought as a person has been denied on several grounds by those who admit that he is so represented in the Scriptures, and even in reason. That is, while it is admitted that he must be supposed to possess the attributes of personality, and that they are invariably ascribed to him, it is frequently contended that it is inconceivable to thought. The grounds of the allegation are that it is impossible to conceive how the infinite and absolute can be self-conscious, which

* Lord, *Christian Theology*, p. 127.

is a necessity to personality. If the allegation were true it would not sustain the conclusion that he is not a person, or that he may not be so thought. There may be, and is, a necessity that he should be so thought, even though we should not be able to remove the apparent contradiction. The evidence is paramount, whatever may be the difficulties in the case. The farthest possible point to which the objection can be carried is that we are not able to conceive fully how it can be. Our inability cannot be disproof—works nothing against the overwhelming support of the position. The evidence must dominate us, rather than our weakness of comprehension.

Thus the manner in which we are compelled to think God is opposed to materialism on the one hand and to pantheism on the other. Rational thinking excludes these ideas as certainly as does revelation itself. To give either one or the other a standing the laws of thought must be ignored. Nature and revelation are both theistic. While the laws of though remain unchanged all attempts to unsettle this corner stone of the theological structure must prove abortive. An impersonal God is no God. The one term excludes the other. The idea of an impersonal force as the world ground has been shown to be as irrational as it is certainly antibiblical. That which acts is. That which acts rationally is rational. That which is rational is a person. The universe is replete with proofs that a rational being forms and sustains it. To think otherwise is to think against the first dictate of reason, namely, that where thought and purposes are plainly in the effect they must exist in the cause—must have their ground in a thinking and purposing agent. A being that knows knows that he knows; a being that purposes knows that he purposes; a being that produces according to a purpose knows that he fulfills his purpose in producing. The last result is inconceivable without the preceding. We know that the universe expresses thought as well as we know that our acts express thought, and we are compelled to put an intelligent being behind the one as much as we are behind the other. However incomprehensible the fact is we are thus shut up to the necessity of thinking that the world ground is a personal Being—knowing himself, knowing his own thoughts, acting with a purpose, and self-consciously carrying forward the cosmic order in all its marvelous details and still more marvelous homogeneity, from the beginning to its highest completion.

FREEDOM OF GOD

The term "will" plays so important a part in both philosophy and theology that it becomes quite necessary that we have a definite idea as to its meaning. It would sometimes seem, from the use made of it, to represent a thing in itself, instead of an attribute or faculty or mode or capability of a being—a sort of despotic master which enslaves a person, instead of a subjective quality or attribute of the person himself.

Personality means a being who has capacities which manifest himself to himself and to other beings of the same kind in three forms. These are: (*a*) He has the power of intelligence, that is, power to think, to know, to understand, to reason, to remember, to imagine, and of self-identification and differentiation from other objects—self-consciousness. These several terms represent modes of activity of the person. It is he who thinks, knows, and does all these things. (*b*) Capacities or capabilities of sensibility or feeling; that is, power or ability to be impressed by external objects, and to experience subjective feelings, as joy or sorrow, love or hate, delight or disgust, pleasure or pain, sense of right or wrong, feeling of obligation, fear, dread, hope, and the almost innumerable emotions of which the person is conscious. All these are simple forms of personal experience which arise under appropriate conditions. (*c*) Capacity of self-determination in certain forms of activity. This capacity takes the name of will. Rightly understood, the term simply means the power the person has over himself. It is not the will that wills and determines the person. It is the person who wills and determines himself. The act of will is his act of self-determination. It differs both from feeling and knowing, as they differ either from the other, but it is conditioned by them. To know is one phase of personal experience; to feel is another form; to will or determine the self to a given end is still another; but in each case it is the person who acts or has the experience.

The law of the soul, which is only another name for the person, is that it should (*a*) act as intelligent; some object must first, either by external impingement or internal reflection, memory, or imagination, be present to it as a cognition or conception. (*b*) The object being present awakens, or is accompanied by, some kind of feeling. (*c*) The knowledge of the object and the feeling become the occasion of some kind of self-determination, or some action of the person with respect to the object. The will has thus, though itself always remaining inactive until an object, conceptive or actual, has been presented and a feeling created, been called the active power of the mind—the power by which the person determines himself to or against the object which is presented and which has awakened feeling of some kind. The object and the feeling which have possession of the mind, and on occasion of which the person determines himself either to or against, has taken the name of the motive or mover or instigator to the person to act. So far all is plain, and there is no dispute. But here a vexed question emerges, which has filled the ages with wrangle and debate, both in the philosophic and theological ranks, but with the greatest vehemence in the theological. That question is whether the motive determines the man, or the man determines himself; whether his will-act is free or necessitated; or, perhaps, what presents the real issue better, whether, all the circumstances considered, the man when he determines himself one way could at the same time have determined himself the other; in a word, whether when he sins he might have avoided it.

If the view we have presented be correct—and we do not see

how it can be escaped—the world ground must be, for rational thinking, an eternal Being, therefore having necessary existence, therefore independent and self-sufficient, to account for all other existences. He must possess infinite wisdom and almighty power; must pervade all with his presence, and include all in his knowledge—be omnipotent and omniscient. There must be no limit to his energy, or decay of his power, or abatement of his interest. So much is necessary to him as eternal and as cause of the material cosmos. Nor would even these endowments suffice to account for material nature alone. Going no further, we should have to add the highest sign of personality—*self-determination*. The world ground must have necessary existence; but to it, that is, to the effect, he must also be free—free not simply from outward constraint, but also from inherent necessity —must be able to determine his own act, and select the manner and end of his energizing. It is impossible that he should be constrained from without, since there is nothing in existence besides himself to constrain him. It is impossible to suppose immanent necessity, since that would require that the creative act should be eternal, since any necessity inherent in his existence enforcing creative activity must have been eternally inherent, and the necessity must always have existed; the act therefore must also be eternal, for if necessary it could not not be, which is a contradiction, since any creative activity must of necessity have a beginning, as it is in the very nature of an effect that it is the coming to pass of that which was not in existence; and, also, it is contrary to demonstrable facts. The world ground must therefore be, to rational thinking, a free cause. In this absolute freedom is found not only the soul source of causational activity, but also the basis of his eternal nature and personality. The universe of which he is the sole cause and free cause is throughout what he, self-moved and freely, chose to make it. All the reasons for its existence are in himself, freely acting thereto; and the same freedom which was exercised in its creation is exercised in its entire ordering and ongoing. It is impossible that he who has the ground of all existence in himself should ever come under the law of necessity or constraint of any kind. He must forever be self-determined. Thus absolute freedom is eternally integral to the nature of God. Herein is found the essential and necessary condition of true causality. There can be no true ultimate causality without a free personality. Thus we come again by a necessity of thought upon the great discovery that the world ground is a personal Being.

We dwell for a moment upon the point here made, that causality necessitates absolute freedom in the cause. To cause is to begin action. *Eternal causation is a contradiction.* The eternal Being has the power to become cause, but not the power to be an eternal *de facto* cause; that is, the causal act must have a beginning, antecedent to which it was not performed. This we have already shown to be among the necessary truths. But if a causal act must have a beginning, he himself who originates it must be free, and must also be eternal.

When we predicate freedom of God it will at once be perceived that, being eternal, *his existence* cannot be a matter of choice or a thing with relation to which he is free. That would involve absurdity. And as his *essential attributes* are inseparable from his being the same is true of them. The sphere of freedom relates, not to being or perfections, but to the manner of handling himself. He does not choose to be eternal, self-existent; he is so. He does not choose to have infinite wisdom; he has it. He does not choose to be omnipotent; he is omnipotent. He does not choose to have power of self-determination; he has it. He does choose *how* he will use his wisdom and omnipotence. Herein is the proof that among his perfections is that of a will, or power of willing—of volitionation—and herein is the sphere of his freedom. Necessary, not necessitated, as to his being, he governs his acts volitionally, and is without restraint or constraint, either internal or external.

If it should be asked, What determines him to choose as he does? the answer is already given: He determines himself, not under the law of necessity, but under the law of freedom. The principles which furnish the grounds of his self-determinations, not the necessitation of them, are his essential perfections of wisdom and love, and he freely chooses to obey their behests. The free cause of the universe uses his power in creating and ordering it according to the dictates of infinite love and wisdom.

Might he use his power otherwise than the dictates of wisdom and love prescribe, or might he decline to use it according to their dictates? If he could not so employ it, or if he might not decline to use it at all, wherein is his freedom? If he might so employ it, or refuse to employ it, what becomes of his wisdom and love? The only possible answer to the apparent dilemma must be that if we suppose him to have a moral nature at all he must be free, and, if free, must have ability to the alternative of acting according to the dictates of his eternal attributes, or adversely—must be able to renounce himself or revolutionize his own eternal perfections. That he remains loyal to himself must be a free self-determination, else God himself and the universe are bound up in mere fate.

Will he so use his freedom? The answer is: His will, by his own free self-determination, immutably follows the dictates of his infinite wisdom and love, but does so in absolute freedom. His wisdom and love are among his eternal perfections, and cannot change, since that which is eternal has the quality of necessary existence. His will-acts, whatever may be his power to the contrary, are immutably certain to honor these ineffable perfections. "I am the Lord, I change not," is the testimony he gives of himself.

The intelligibles or thoughts of the Infinite are necessary inherences of his eternal nature. They are not acquired, but exist; not growth of knowledge, but infinite knowing. Such of these eternal intelligibles as he chooses are transformed into objectified realities by self-originated volitional activity, and are the concrete cosmic order, or phenomenal world. The volitional activity is under form of time and space, which have no existence apart from it. It is permanent in all objective reality as the ground of its existence. It may be questioned —as it is, with great learning, in Professor Bowne's recent books, and by many other able thinkers—whether the objective reality is anything else than a mode of volitional energizing. Thus the Infinite is forever present with and immanent in all cosmic phenomena, and it is a perpetual rendering of his own eternal thought; it is forever known to him in all its multiform and ever-changing history. Omnipresence and omniscience are necessary concomitants of the divine will. As will, he can never act except in the presence of these attributes and with reference to the ends which they furnish.

If now we ask why he acts with reference to the objects, giving reality to some rather than others, we answer, not simply because he chooses so to do, but because there is in him the ethical sense that that which is the highest ideal of wisdom and love ought to be, or has a right to be. These ideals are the abstract conceptions of right, or they are the rule of right, for all ethical being forever. As right, he wills their actualization immutably. This constitutes his eternal righteousness, or his righteousness is the immutable coexistence in him of these ideals, and a free determination of himself to their actualization. The free and immutable purpose that they should be is a permanent state of his will, and his will becomes causational of them when and as he continues forever to put forth volitional energy, thereby giving them objective existence or realizing to himself all cosmic phenomena.

It emerges as a necessity of rational thinking that the world ground should be conceived as an ethical being. Translating or interpreting him from our own self-consciousness, which furnished the only key by which we can interpret him at all, we are compelled to impute to him moral feelings and motives. They alone explain the working of his power. For the purpose of translation we have to begin with his work and read backward to the motive. The concept of an end, and the conscious power to realize it, are not adequate to solve the problem. Another factor is needed. There must be found something in the nature of the eternal being to explain why he shall work at all, and why he should work to one end rather than another. The choice of the end reveals the deepest fundamenta of his nature—the bottom and governing principles, the principles which subordinate power and wisdom itself.

The motives to creative and providential activity in every form lie in the region of ethical sensibility. Were there not an ethic in the world ground there could be no world. The logical order for thought is: (*a*) An eternal mind; (*b*) the conception of a world order; (*c*) the intuition of power to create; (*d*) motive or some form of desire to induce the exercise of creative power; (*e*) the volitional determination or choice; (*f*) the executive act of will by which power is exerted and effect produced; (*g*) for an end proposed; (*h*) freedom to the end; (*i*) a motive in ethical sensibility; (*j*) executive or creative volition. It is the final member of the series that dominates the whole, and so furnished the highest expression of the ineffable nature underlying all cosmic phenomena. There could be no creative volition without a motive. There could be no motive without a sensibility to be moved. The sensibility could not be moved without an end, first in the perception, and second in the sensibilities. There could be no such end without a perceiving or knowing mind. There could be no effect without power. There could be none of the series without being.

With respect to the will of God, by which we mean his power to determine his own acts—first, to choose what he will do; second, to realize his choices by a volitional exercise of energy to that end—this is the sum of our findings:

1. God is an eternal being possessed of the eternal inhering perfections of omnipotence, omniscience, wisdom, and goodness, with absolute freedom of will as to his choices and executive volitions.

2. While absolutely free in the exercise of will, the *ground*, not the necessitation, of every act of will lies in his perfections of wisdom and goodness—his rational and ethical sensibility. He cannot act at all volitionally without motives drawn from the logically antecedent, but really coincident, action of these perfections; though being free, he possesses the power to act adversely thereto.

3. His will-acts, like his nature, are immutable and irreversible; what he chooses once he chooses forever; what he condemns once he always condemns, and what he approves once he forever approves; but this does not mean that changes of character in creatures do not work changes of feeling and action toward them, but the very opposite. The immutability of the principles on which he determines his will-acts is the very ground of change of attitude toward creatures who change. The change in the creature brings it into new relations to the unchangeable will.

4. The divine will is the organ of divine energizing. Omnipotence is simply a mode of volitional action. What he wills is effectuated simply by the willing. The act of creation ascribed to God can be explained in no other way and on no other principle than the exertion of energy directly by simple

volition; the same is true of the upholding and ongoing of the universe.

5. Acts of will must be differentiated from more permanent states of disposition, inclination, desire, pleasure. God would have every man to be saved; it would be pleasing to him; he is favorably disposed to it; but he wills only the salvation of those who can be saved on immutable ethical principles. No will-act of God can ever override or abolish what is immutable in his nature. There is a strict propriety in the phrase, "He wills as he pleases," which is to say that whatever his volitional act, whether of choice or executive energizing, he is pleased to do; but this is not the equivalent of denying that if the circumstances were different it would be pleasing to him. His pleasure may arise from the obligations of righteousness eternally recognized by him, or from delight in well-being. He would have, that is, it would delight him to have, universal happiness; but he cannot will, that is, choose or efficiently cause, the same happiness to attend sin as he causes to attend virtuous obedience.

6. God's will, that is, that which he wills, constitutes his essential righteousness—his perfect holiness. Did he will differently his moral character would be wholly changed. The perfect conforming of his will to the dictates of his infallible wisdom and immutable love of the good constitutes the guarantee of right, or absolutely just, dealing with the universe, and is the crown and glory of his moral nature.

There are some things or facts of the finite self over which it is certain the person has no power—with respect to which he neither does nor can act as a will or determine himself. With regard to them he exists under the strict law of necessity—neither consenting nor dissenting, nor in any way exercising any self-determination. This includes a large class of personal experiences and activities.

It is quite common to make the distinction between persons and impersonal things that the former implies freedom and the latter necessity or necessitation ; a thing has no power over itself or over its relations to other things, a person has perfect power of self-determination, or power over his acts. The distinction is too broad and leads to error.

There are experiences over which a person has no more power of self-determination than a thing has. In some respects the personal being is as much under the law of necessity as is a clod or a stone.

It will be of service to call attention to the matters in which personalities exist under the strict law of necessity, with respect to which they do not at all act in the form of willing. These are : (*a*) In the matter of existence. The person does not determine himself to exist; he cannot determine himself not to exist. It is impossible for him to exercise himself as a will on the subject. It transcends his choice ; it cannot be effected by his volition ; in fact, he has not the power to volitionate at all about it. He may determine to destroy his body, and may so do ; he may determine to misuse his powers and pervert his own being, but he has no power to abrogate or annihilate himself, any more than to create himself. (*b*) The same thing is true with regard to many of his mental acts and states, such as perception, or when an object is before the mind, as thoughts, feelings, memories. These are purely involuntary states with respect to which the person has no power. (*c*) The same thing is true with regard to instinctive and natural feelings, as pleasure when an object is present which excites it, or disgust, or love, or hate, or joy, or sorrow, or fear, dismay, terror, and such like. Over such the person has no power ; they are not subject to the will. The same is true of self-consciousness in general. (*d*) The same is true of hereditary tempers, dispositions, all natural and instinctive desires and preferences.

These are given with existence, or fall under the law of necessitation and impersonal states and conditions. As such they involve nothing of moral or ethical character. (*e*) The same is true of all physical traits, inherent lusts, and tendencies. They are not products of the will, nor subject to the will. Over all this realm necessity reigns, and with regard to it there is and can be no personal responsibility or ground of merit or demerit any more than there is for hunger or thirst, or any other inevitable state or condition. They are never made the subject of command or prohibition. They belong to the nature of things which God has established as much as the tides or gravitation.

What, then, is the sphere of the will? To this we answer: The sphere of the will is that of personal self-control or self-determination with respect to ends to which the person is free, whether ethical or unethical. Not all self-determinations are ethical, but only those which relate to duty or right. A man determines to walk instead of ride, to sit instead of stand, to speak or be silent. There is nothing ethical in such determinations in themselves considered, but there is proper will action. The sphere is strict and limited to those things with respect to which the person has power of self-determination.

While the person acts in the mode of a will with respect to things which have no ethical significance, all ethical requirements or moral laws have respect to those things only which are subject to or under the power of self-control, and are addressed to and imposed upon the person as a will. The seat of moral character is strictly the person acting as a free will— neither the understanding nor the sensibilities as such, nor anything but the will. The will determines moral character, and yet the moral character does not leave out the understanding or the affections. We have said that certain mental states and activities exist wholly irrespective of the will, and as such have no ethical significance—mean nothing morally—as perception, self-consciousness, and memory, and such like. We now say that this does not mean that the person, as a will, has no function with respect to these uses of the mind. It is found that he, while he cannot help but perceive when the object of perception is present, nevertheless has large will power over the states and acts of the mind, as he can determine, and does determine, whether he will keep himself aloof from low and vile imaginings, or will seek to banish these and bring before his thought better things; whether he will be studious or idle; whether he will busy himself with high or debasing subjects of meditation and contemplation. There is a sphere for self-determination, and so he may and does come under the law of freedom and ethical obligation with respect to the condition and action of the mind; that is, of himself in matters that pertain to the mind. The same is true with regard to his feelings. He can have no direct power over them, but as a will he has power over those feelings which are discovered to be evil and wrong; if not immediately to banish them or prevent their existence, he has power to disapprove them, to restrain them, to seek deliverance from them, to refuse action to which they prompt, and thus to deliver himself from the evil of them, and the still better power to seek forgiveness of them when they have been indulged, and by grace to have them purged away. So far as they are natural, such as pleasure and pain under certain conditions, he can have no power over them; so far as they are improper he can correct them; so far as they influence the will and come under the law of morality he can refuse to indulge them; so far as they are polluting he can avail himself of divine power to purge them by regeneration.

It is not an uncommon thing in writers on the will to represent the will as being involved in states of the mind and of the affections which exist wholly irrespective of it, and over which the person has no control at all, as disposition and preference.

To prefer a thing or be favorably disposed to it is considered an act of the will. What is meant by this? A man prefers pleasure to pain, one odor to another, beauty to deformity. Is the will involved in such preferences? Who will pretend it? The preference means simply that one thing is more agreeable than another. If the object be a moral object, the preference of an evil to good discovers a debased state of the affections. Inherited depravity may be the source of such a condition; in that case the will has nothing to do with its existence; but it becomes involved in its indulgence and continuance, if a remedy be within its power. A bias to evil, an inclination, a predisposition is found to be natural to fallen and hereditarily depraved human beings. As natural and inherited the will has nothing to do with such states any more than it has with hereditary physical disease, and there is no more guilt in the one case than in the other.

The sphere of the will is strictly limited to matters which are under the control of the person, or with respect to which he has power of self-determination. Now, what are these matters? The correct answer to this question is of the utmost moment. We discover by self-consciousness two forms of will action, or power in us to govern our actions of self-determination in two ways, and the will-act is always purely subjective. It relates often, indeed generally, to some external object, but itself is entirely internal. The two forms in which we act as will are choice of an end, that is, objects are before the mind which awaken in us a sense of obligation to act with reference to them in a given way, or which awaken a desire, or which furnish the opportunity merely for some personal act with regard to them; the possible or suggested act may be ethical or indifferent. The primary act of the will or the person is an act of choice—not of preference, which is not an act, but a state antecedent to choice, which itself may not suppose any antecedent will-act; an act of choice by which the person elects an end—determines himself to that end. The next act of the will is the putting forth of energy, an executive volition to realize the end chosen. Both these forms of act are subjective, but both have an end which is objective. The first act chooses the objective end, the second effectuates it. This is the complete account of the will. The primary act may be a general one, or it may be specific. In the first place the person deliberately determines to a general course of conduct, without reference to any particular thing. He decides, that is, chooses, say, to give himself up to a life of lust, of sinful indulgence, to deny himself no pleasure; to disregard all restraints of conscience; to live as he lists. This choice is fundamental and radical. As such it involves the total overthrow of all virtue and the utter ruin of character. It is not necessary that there should be a single act of choice of some specific wrong to involve him in utter guilt. But in point of fact this self-determination to a general course of sin is followed by specific acts of choice when specific opportunities of indulgence arise. He chooses in each case the indulgence to which by a general choice he has already determined himself. There is not a single case in which he does not put forth a choice; and not a single case when there is not an executive volition to carry out to its end the thing chosen, the fair opportunity being given. His will attitude is that simply of waiting the opportunity and of readiness to embrace it on all occasions when possible.

With respect to all such acts the person is free cause both in the first and second form—free to choose and free to execute, that is, so far as the subjective act is concerned. Hindrances external may prevent the carrying out of the executive volition —such as want of opportunity, physical inability, fear of consequences—a thousand things—but the will has acted in the fixed determination and choice, and is in the attitude to put forth power to the end when opportunity offers.

With regard to all such acts the person is free, that is, does not act under necessity—has power to choose or not choose. The act is his own, and not that of some constraining force external to himself.

Choice is always preceded by conditions. To choose there must be an object of choice. The will does not instigate action without an end. A perceived object does not become instigator simply as object. If it be totally devoid of interest to the mind, it passes out of observation as a thing indifferent, demanding no action and leaving no impression. To elicit any determination of the self with respect to it, it must have power in some way to move the mind—must be a motive. There are a thousand ways in which a perceived object becomes a motive. It is pleasing to the taste, or inviting to the passions, or offers gain, or awakens a sense of duty, or creates desire, or excites disgust, or fear, or shame; attracts or repels; falls in with inclination, preference, disposition; the mind is impressed—moved; the influence is strong or weak. The mind must act one way or another with respect to it; must accept or reject it. There is absolutely no escape from action. There is no necessity more absolute. One can no more refuse to know what is known, or feel what is felt, than it can refuse to act as will in such a case. It must choose for or against, or postpone decision for the present, which is an action of the will. The question remaining is, Is it free in the matter of its final decision? To this we answer: If by freedom be meant a total absence of all influence, both internal and external, impelling, attracting, inclining, repelling, then there is no free being in the universe—neither God, man, nor angel. It is no more certain that matter under all circumstances is under the dominion of necessity than it is that mind under all circumstances acts under influences subjective or objective. As there is no motion in matter without a mover, so in mind there is no action without a motive. Perception is excited by an object; self-consciousness is awakened by something which stirs the mind to think or feel; feeling has a cause; so every act of will must have an occasional cause in some internal or external influence.

If by freedom be meant unembarrassed action, or equal ease of action one way or the other, then again there is no such thing as freedom in the universe. Necessity is always equal. Any necessity is just as strong in every respect as any other necessity, and always implies the absolute impossibility of the opposite; on the other hand, freedom does not imply equal ease of action one way or the other, or, if it be supposed to mean that, freedom does not exist. Matter acts only as acted upon—its reaction is always fixed and determined by law; it can do no otherwise. Will acts directly toward an end, and is impotent without an end. Choice is choice of something. Executive volition is to realize something. Freedom of will signifies the power of a person to determine himself to or from any object of choice, under whatever pressure of influence one way or the other, either internal or external.

When the power does not exist, no difference from what cause, the choice or action of the will comes under the law of necessity, and the act ceases to have ethical significance. Up to the point when influence is converted into necessity responsibility continues. At the point where necessity begins responsibility ends, or the remaining responsibility is for antecedent abuses which resulted in loss of freedom. So long as the person has power over his acts, responsibility may be proportional to the difficulty; the greater the difficulty the higher the obligation and the more meritorious the free act.

There can be no moral being where freedom does not exist; no obligation where there is not corresponding power; no desert of praise or blame for acts over which the person has no determining control, and none where the mind has no means of knowing the right or wrong in the case. Free choices of ends which are indifferent—that is, neither right nor wrong—have no moral significance, and neither indicate nor affect moral character. Every act in which the mind supposes the quality of right or wrong to exist, whether or not the act has the quality imputed, is a moral act and reflects moral character. Worthiness or unworthiness, or moral character, depends on the intention of the person acting, on his absolute freedom to the act performed, and on the worthiness of the end chosen. These principles are of universal application in the moral universe.

To determine the moral character of a moral being, environments must be considered, not as absolutely causative, but as in a degree modificative. It is, indeed, the being who acts and who is sole cause, and the moral quality of the act is found in the purpose of the actor; but environment must be taken into the account as showing the pressure under which the purpose is formed and executed. The same act and the same motive do not determine that the moral quality of the action is precisely identical in worthiness. Under one set of environments the act would be easy and natural, and its performance does not show that the performer has such a quality of moral integrity as would endure a great strain of temptation to the opposite, or as would overcome or persist if beset with actual and severe trial. The quality of character is good, but possibly not strong.

Great inducements to a wrong act addressing the person on every side, and great embarrassments, hindrances, and sufferings of one kind and another lying in the way of the right act, were the right still adhered to would prove a higher quality of character and a correspondingly superior degree of worthiness than if the circumstances were precisely opposite. Environment, including in the term internal and external facts, must be taken into the account in fixing the moral quality, if not the moral status, of the actor.

Freedom is the indispensable condition, but other things have relative bearings. As there may be a perfectly free being and perfectly free acts which are totally void of significance, because void of every moral intention and required by no law, so there may be moral acts which, under some circumstances, have less moral significance than the same acts would have under another set of circumstances.

All moral goodness—and the same is true of moral badness—does not determine that the actors are equal in good or bad character, however they may determine that they belong to the one class or the other. Not every wrongdoer is a devil, nor every rightdoer a saint or a hero; or, may we say, possessed of power to be so. To be possessed of a moral character at all he must be free, and have power over his acts or choices, in the circumstances in which he is placed; but this does not imply that he could lead a forlorn hope in a moral struggle, under the greatest possible strain, in which the greatest issues are involved. This we deem a point of great importance. Free beings are responsible only when their power equals the strain put upon them. They are responsible to that limit.

We come now still further to apply this principle as related to the Infinite and the finite. As applied to God: What is it that determines the infinite holiness of God? The answer is: He determines it himself, by choosing from among all possibles the absolutely best. It is that free self-determination which is his essential and perfect holiness.

For a clearer understanding of this, recur for a moment to all the circumstances of the case. These are: (*a*) We have before us the only Being in existence—there is as yet no universe, no single creature, but God alone. (*b*) This solitary Being is a Being of infinite wisdom and power and freedom; that is, he can do as he pleases or whatever he chooses to do. By his infinite wisdom he knows innumerable possible things. Among these are all sorts of harmful or evil things, all sorts of good, better, and best things. His power is equal to the creation of any of them, for there is nothing impossible to it—it is infinite.

Which among these known possibilities shall he make real? It is obvious that he alone must answer that question, for there is none other even to counsel, much less determine, him. It must be determined by his own free will. He has power to this or that or the other. Which shall it be? Just that which he chooses. What shall determine his choice? He alone must determine it. Is it said, No, his own eternal perfections will determine it. We answer: His eternal perfections are only another name for himself. What they determine is himself determining.

But then it is said, In any event if he determines himself, then either whatever is is best, or he shows himself to prefer that which is not the best; but then he cannot be absolutely good. We answer: Whatever he *chooses* and *does* is best; but this does not prove that whatever is is best. He is not the only being. There are other beings who have introduced marring and evil into the perfect system of good, or the best possible which he made. But is it said, Why, then, did he make beings who could mar his creation, or why did he not prevent them? We answer: It could be for no other reason than that it was a part of the best possible system that there should be beings who could introduce evil. Well, then, evil must be best. Not at all. The existence of a being who might cause evil might be the highest possible proof of goodness, but that would not prove that the evil he caused was the best; but, on the contrary, it would be proof of the ideal best which might have been but for his marring. The real best possible required the existence of the finite personal existence, despite the evil which might thereby find entrance into the universe.

The term love is the all-inclusive term. "God is love." To reach its full content it must be analyzed into the several forms of its manifestation, and it must appear that it is a necessity to rational thinking that the world ground be clothed with this attribute. Revelation is full of it, but does the problem of being require it in order to its solution? Were revelation closed up, should we still find the need of it? It cannot be pretended that by mere insight it would be possible to develop a complete idea of the nature of the Infinite, any more than that we are able to comprehend it when it is made known by revelation. But may we not find evidence on the point in question? This is a question for rational thought. The precise thesis we lay down is: God is a Being of infinite goodness. This attribute is inherent and eternal. It is not elicited by created being, but it is itself the deepest fountain of created being.

It is a necessity of thought that the Eternal be conceived as once existing alone. The concept leads us into a region dark with mystery. Why did the Infinite not continue to dwell alone? We have said that it is impossible that he should have been moved by some ab-extra necessity, or even some ab-intra necessity; and yet he must have acted from some motive under some powerful impulse. The possible motive to rational thinking must have been one or several of the following: either (*a*) he was moved by mere caprice; or (*b*) he was moved by purely selfish considerations; or (*c*) he was moved by a purpose of pure malignity; or (*d*) he was moved by a mixture of malevolence and benevolence; or (*e*) he was moved by infinite and unmixed benignity. Every other conceivable motive is resolvable into one or other of these. The result and his own testimony in the premises must interpret him. How are we compelled to think him from these composite sources of evidences? We shall not be able to get all the evidence, and our faculties will not rise to the height of the problem; but we are able to go far enough in the solution to reach a conclusion which, for rational thinking, will be satisfactory.

It is of no small value as a determining factor that even before the investigation begins we instinctively reach a conclusion. Corporate with our rational existence is an invincible conviction, sometimes obscured, but in the end asserting itself. The soul of man may be debauched by superstitions and perverted by sin, may miss its way and lose hold of its Maker and Eternal Father, and may come under self-accusings and sink into despair, but it will still in its deepest self be loyal to the instinct that God is good, that somehow he is infinite love. Driven about by the scourges of self-conscious guilt, and loaded down with fear and dread and dismay, it still feels that the fault is within itself. No sophistries, however plausible or ingeniously wrought, can rub out of the heart the sense of the Eternal Fatherhood. The prodigal amid the swine—hungry, naked, forsaken, friendless—has still, amid the embers of a wasted and wicked life, the instinct of home and the love that reigns there. Amid the moral ruins of the most abject heathenism there are evidences that something of the thought and feeling of this deep truth still remains. Obscured, distorted, almost obliterated, still in the soul of man archaic memorials remain impelling to worship and a feeling after the lost treasure. All seeking after God comes from the dim feeling that his favor may be found and his love secured.

But there are difficulties. No one can dispute it. Perhaps they cannot be explained. Suppose we admit it. Will there, then, be no rational alternative but doubt of the infinite love? May we not rather think of our insufficiency to measure the meaning of a plan which so transcends us in every respect? What are the difficulties? Are they inherent in the idea itself?

Is there intrinsic absurdity in the affirmation, God is love? So some have thought. If it could be made to appear to reason it would forever close the discussion, and only a dumb, irrational instinct could survive, which would make an intelligent faith impossible. Under the force of such a demonstration religion would perish from the earth.

What are the inclusions of the idea, God is love? They are these: That He who made the world was moved thereto by a principle of benevolence; that is, that (*a*) there was in his nature a feeling of good will toward the creatures which he made; (*b*) that before he made them, when they as yet were only in his thought, he was moved to make them real, simply out of good will toward them; (*c*) that he so made them as that they should receive good from him; (*d*) that in their good he finds enjoyment; and (*e*) that he continues forever to take interest in their welfare—that a loving heart, as well as an omnipotent will and omniscient mind, is at the foundation of the universe; that they coexist with the thought of the universe, which we have found must have been coexistent with the eternity of his own being and an inherence thereof. To this benevolent impulse toward creation and to this impulse of good will, as fundamental as either omnipotence or omniscience, the universe owes its existence. This is God's own account of it. Is there anything in the conception intrinsically absurd or contradictory to right reason?

Having now found that God is a Spirit, and as such a personal being, we are prepared to consider the question, What may we predicate of him? There is a difference between predicates and attributes. We have seen that attribute is some quality which inheres in the very essence of a subject, without which the essence does not exist. The essence does not create it, but includes it; thus figure is a necessary inclusion of matter, and intelligence, a necessary inclusion of spirit; each absolutely requiring its respective subject; there is nothing with form that is not material, and nothing material that has not figure.

But while an attribute is inseparable from a subject and an inherence of its essence, it is found also that any subject must have modes of existence of some kind—cannot exist without a mode of some kind; but while mode is a necessity, and even a given mode is a necessity to a given subject, and peculiar to it, mode cannot be considered an attribute, but is simply a predicate—possibly an invariable and peculiar predicate, denoting and characterizing the subject as really as an essential attribute does. For illustration, an atom is matter; it is the minutest particle of matter, but minuteness does not enter into its essence; it is simply a mode or predicate of it; thought is a fact of mind, but it is not an attribute, but an exercise. Not every predicate of God, even when it is a necessary predicate, and entirely peculiar to him, denotes an attribute. God is, but existence is not an attribute; God is a spirit, but spirit is not an attribute of him; both are true predicates, but neither denotes an attribute. The same is true of other predicates, as: God is one, God is a trinity, God is unconditioned, God is absolute, God is self-existent, God is independent, God is necessary being, God is a person. These are all true predicates, but not one of them denotes an attribute. They each and severally point either to modes or facts of his existence, but not to attributes of his being; but all of them have been treated as attributes. The explanation is simple. Many writers and thinkers fall into the blunder of supposing that whatever can be truthfully affirmed of a subject imports an attribute of it, and especially if it can be affirmed of no other being. It is descriptive; it is attributed; this leads to the idea that it is an inherence of the essence. Even acts are thus raised by some into the eligibility of attributes. Creation has been styled an attribute of God, because he alone creates. No mere mode or exercise, or fact originated in or by a subject, however descriptive of it, can be ranked as an attribute of it, but may be declarative or predicative. It is even questionable whether eternity can be classed properly as an attribute of God, though he is eternal, and the only Eternal.

MORAL NATURE OF GOD.

THE same considerations which prove the spirituality of God are in proof of his moral nature. Mentality primarily distinguishes spirit from matter. Where mental phenomena are spirit is. Mentality is the necessary condition of morality or of an ethical nature. The prime quality of an ethical nature is sensibility; mentality is its conditioning antecedent. The sense of a good and the feeling of obligation thereto are the complete proof of an ethical subject. Freedom or power of self-determination—a *will*—lies implicit in obligation and the sense of it. Where these facts exist, the facts of mentality, sensibility to the good and the feeling of obligation thereto, and the power of self-determination, we have a perfect idea of a spiritual subject and of a moral nature. The proofs that these coexist in God are abundant.

If the material universe, by its order and manifold harmonies, compels us to impute power guided by wisdom to him, the conscience within us (1) which makes the distinction of right and wrong, or evil and good, and enforces the obligation of the one and prohibits the other, compels us to impute moral ideas and sensibilities to him. The moral law is as universal and regnant in the spiritual realm as gravitation in the material. The presence and permanence of the law can be explained only by its presence, not only in idea, but in fact, in the nature of its Author as an original inherence. It would be forever impossible for him to act as a will choosing an end were there not motive in him to act. The motive must be inherent. There can be no motive where there is no sensibility. When the end chosen is always the good of being, the proof is that the author is himself pleased with the good and averse to its opposite. Thus love, justice, holiness are as much shown to be qualities of God as power, wisdom, and eternity.

The sense of right and the feeling of obligation thereto in us necessitates its presence in the Author of our being. The law which imperates the right can be viewed as nothing else than an expression of his will. If he wills the right, and enforces it with high sanctions, there can be no higher proof of his moral nature and of its absolute perfection. That he does will it is in proof both in his revealed law and in conscience. The history of moral beings is a history of moral administration over them, that is, an administration which is based on moral ideas and feelings. The sovereign thus proves that he is governed by moral ideas and feelings.

We have found that God is a Spirit; that he has absolute and unconditioned being; that in nature and perfection he is infinite; that he is one; that he is a person.

These predications we have made of him as terms of being rather than as designating attributes—terms which are applicable in common to his attributes rather than themselves names of specific attributes. They are sometimes classed as attributes. We prefer to use the term predications of being. This seems to be the view taken by the elder Hodge. He says: "To the divine essence, which in itself is infinite, eternal, and unchangeable, belong certain perfections revealed to us in the constitution of nature and in the word of God. These divine perfections are called attributes, as essential to the nature of the divine Being, and necessarily involved in our idea of God."*

Dr. Shedd says: "The divine attributes are of two classes, according as they denote a passive relation of the essence or an active operation of it. The essence considered as passively related to itself is self-existent and simple; as passively related

* *Theology*, vol. i, p. 368.

to duration is eternal, to space is immense, to number is one. Self-existence, simplicity, eternity, immensity, and unity are not active operations of the divine essence, but inactive relationships of it. Eternity, immensity, unity, and simplicity, and the like, are not modes of energizing, but of existing." *

This we understand as precisely the equivalent of the view above expressed. They are not attributes, but predicates of modes of existence. When the essence is considered as active in any form of energizing it discovers inhering powers—not mere passive modes or qualities of existence. These are more properly attributes. Omnipotence, omniscience, love, goodness—comprehensively holiness, the all-inclusive moral power of God—and their active powers and implications are the only attributes of the divine personality. If, as we properly may, we separate the divine ubiquity or immensity from the divine omnipresence so as that the latter shall signify God's active presence in and with all being, omnipresence should be added to the list of attributes proper as showing an actual energizing in all being. Omnipotence is a direct exertion of the divine will, when related to things, a power of creating, sustaining, and efficiently ordering or carrying forward the material universe. The will is the seat of all efficiency and morality. Omniscience comprehends all intellectual activity in the divine nature, whether of wisdom or forms of knowledge, as perfect knowledge of himself and of all other being and all events, past, present, and future, and all possibilities. Love or goodness designates all forms of activity which emanate from the will and the moral affections, as desire for and choice of what ought to be—approval of right in creatures, disapproval of wrong; justice, mercy, sympathy, and whatever is involved in the perfect holiness of God.

* *Dogmatic Theology*, pp. 335, 336.

This will appear as we proceed with the more extended statement of these several attributes.

"The older theologians distinguished the attributes of God (*a*) from predicates which refer to God in the concrete and indicate his relations to his creatures as Creator, Preserver, Ruler, etc. (*b*) From properties which are technically the distinguishing characteristics of the several persons of the Trinity. There are certain acts or relations peculiar to the Father, others to the Son, others to the Spirit. And (*c*) from accidents or qualities which may or may not belong to a substance, which may be acquired or lost. Thus holiness was not an attribute of the nature of Adam, but an accident, something which he might lose and still remain a man; whereas intelligence was an attribute, because the loss of intelligence involves the loss of humanity." * The older theologians distinguished between the essence of God and the attributes, not as things different in reality, but as different modes of our thought of him—things different *non re, sed ratione*. This is explained by saying that things differ *ex natura rei*, when they are essentially different, as soul and body; while a difference *ex ratione* is merely a difference in us, that is, in our conceptions. Turretini says the attributes are to be distinguished not *realiter*, but *virtualiter;* that is, there is a real foundation in the divine nature for the several attributes ascribed to him. † The distinction between the divine essence and attributes is the same which is found in every other case. There is a difference, but it is impossible to define it, for the reason that when we come to describe the subject we must simply employ a name, or recite the attributes which inhere in the being—the essence of being refuses to be expressed in any other terms; yet we cannot doubt that there is a subject, or that which these attributes display.

* Hodge, vol. i, p. 368.
† *Examen Theologicum*, edit. Leipsic, 1763, p. 235.

In considering the moral nature of God there are several words used confusedly in common discourse and by authors as synonymous, which differ widely in meaning. It is important to clear thought that the student should discriminate carefully between them. The words are: quality, faculty, attribute, property, mode, predicate; not unfrequently subject is miscalled attribute, and accidents and acts are raised to the grade of attributes. Whatever in any form can be predicated of God, especially if it is peculiar to him and differentiates him from any other being, is often classed as an attribute. Nothing can properly be styled a divine attribute but a power which inheres in the very being of God, and which, if taken away, would abolish the being or so change it as to constitute it another being—which, in fact, it is impossible should be taken away, since it belongs to the eternal essence.

Nothing which implies an act of God in order to its existence can be classed as an attribute. He does not create his attributes any more than he creates his being. Attributes are not products, but inherences of the nature itself.

Spirituality is not an attribute of God, but is the substance or essence of his being; the attributes are inherences of it. Creatorship is not an attribute of God, but an accident or incident. He is God before and without it as much as after it; it does not in any sense pertain to his being, but is a result merely of a mode of his energizing in time.

Attributes are not elementary ingredients or component parts of the subject. Elementary ingredients exist apart from the substance which by uniting they constitute. The union forms a compound subject. Thus water is a compound material substance. Its essence is matter of which extension and figure are attributes. Its ingredients are oxygen and hydrogen gas; these are not attributes of it, but component parts of the substance. Fluidity, solidity, and vapor are possible accidents of it, not attributes. Whether in one form or another it is the same compound substance. The form is an accident occasioned by degrees of temperature. The properties did exist alone and may again be dissevered, and their disseverance would abolish the compound substance, but not the two substances which made it. The attributes of God are not of this nature. They are not elementary ingredients which uniting create him. He is not a compound.

The attributes are not identical. Power is not wisdom. The simplicity of the subject does not reduce the attributes to unity, but each diverse attribute inheres in the one indivisible and uncompounded subject.

God is the essential subject or being—not one, but all the attributes. He is not power, but he is not without power; he is not wisdom, but does not exist without wisdom; and so through all the circle of his attributes. He is not one or all of the attributes, but he is the being who possesses them all, and who has no existence apart from them entire.

We study the mind in its phenomena, and thus reach a knowledge of its endowments. This is the common method of science. We thus find the mind to be rationally constituted. This is one of the certainties of psychology. In like manner we determine the several forms of intellectual faculty. In the same manner we find the mind to be constituted with sensibility, and distinguish the different forms of feeling. Further, we find the choosing of ends and voluntary endeavors toward their attainment determine the mind to be endowed with a faculty of will. The several classes of mental phenomena are conclusive of these several forms of mental endowment. No phenomena of mind are more real or constant or common than the phenomena of conscience. But conscience means a moral nature, and can have no psychological explication without such a nature. Thus with the utmost certainty of scientific induction we reach the truth of a moral constitution of the mind. The phenomena of rational intelligence, of feeling, and of volition, which reveal themselves in the consciousness, no more certainly determine the mental endowments of intellect, sensibility, and will than the phenomena of conscience determine the moral constitution of the mind. Further statements may set this truth in a yet clearer light.

The history of the ages, the religions of the world, philosophy and poetry witness to the profound facts of conscience in human experience. The profoundest students of our mental nature unite in this testimony. Conscience is present in all minds, and asserts its right to rule all lives. This right is not disputed, however its authority may be resisted. In the sensibilities there are many incitements to action and in the absence of a supreme law the question as to which should prevail would be merely a question of secular prudence. "But there is a superior principle of reflection or conscience in every man, which distinguishes between the internal principles of his heart, as well as his external actions; pronounces determinately some actions to be in themselves just, right, good; others to be in themselves evil, wrong, unjust: which, without being advised with, magisterially exerts itself, and approves or condemns him, the doer of them, accordingly." "Thus that principle by which we survey, and either approve or disapprove, our own heart, temper, and actions is not only to be considered as what is in its turn to have some influence; which may be said of every passion, of the lowest appetites: but likewise as being superior; as from its very nature manifestly claiming superiority over all others: insomuch that you cannot form a notion of this faculty, conscience, without taking in judgment, direction, superintendency. This is a constituent part of the idea, that is, of the faculty itself, and, to preside and govern, from the very economy and constitution of man, belongs to it. Had it strength, as it has right; had it power, as it has manifested authority, it would absolutely govern the world." "Every man has conscience, and finds himself inspected by an inward censor, by whom he is threatened and kept in awe (reverence mingled with dread); and this power, watching over the law, is nothing arbitrarily (optionally) adopted by himself, but is interwoven with his substance."

While conscience is thus at once the central fact and the proof of a moral nature in man, it is the clear proof of a moral nature in God. "Hence, while the direct function of conscience is to discriminate the right and wrong in actions, while its immediate sphere is the human will, it goes far beyond this. In fact, it can perform those functions only in this way. It carries the soul outside of itself, and brings the will before a bar independent of its own impulses. It inevitably awakens in the soul the perception of a moral law, universal, unchangeable, binding under all circumstances; in short, of a moral order of the world analogous to the physical order which it is the province of science to trace and illustrate. The moral consciousness of man refuses to stop short of this conclusion. Man feels himself, not merely related to physical laws, but even more closely and more vitally related to moral laws, laws which not only enter into the structure of his own being, and go to form the framework of human life, but laws which extend beyond himself and his own hopes and struggles, and assert themselves as everywhere supreme. Such recognition of the moral order of the world is not only the highest, but the only conclusion that can satisfy the educated moral consciousness of mankind."

"Now it is in these phenomena of Conscience that Nature offers to us far her strongest argument for the moral character of God. Had he been an unrighteous being himself, would he have given to this, the obviously superior faculty in man, so distinct and authoritative a voice on the side of righteousness?

. . . . He would never have established a conscience in man, and invested it with the authority of a monitor, and given to it those legislative and judicial functions which it obviously possesses; and then so framed it that all its decisions should be on the side of that virtue which he himself disowned, and condemnatory of that vice which he himself exemplified. This is an evidence for the righteousness of God, which keeps its ground amid all the disorders and aberrations to which humanity is liable."

Thus in the moral consciousness of man there is the recognition of a moral law of universal obligation, and also of a supreme moral ruler to whom we are responsible. The moral nature of man is thus the manifestation of a moral nature in God. In the cosmological argument we found in the existence of the cosmos, as a world originating in time, conclusive proof of the existence of an eternal and infinitely potential being as its only sufficient cause. On the same grounds we found that this being must possess the power of self-energizing —must indeed possess an infinite potency of will. In the teleological argument we found in the adaptations of means to ends the proofs of a divine intelligence as their only sufficient cause. Then in grouping these truths thus attained we already have the proof of the divine personality. This same truth is confirmed by the nature and faculties of the mind as presented in the anthropological argument. The moral nature of man is his highest endowment and the crowning proof of his divine original. It is specially the manifestation of a moral nature in God ; and the truth of a moral nature in God is the truth of his holiness, justice, goodness.

DIVINE ATTRIBUTES.

By writers of eminence the divine attributes have been put in two classes: as, "active and passive; immanent and transitive; positive and negative; communicable and incommunicable; natural and moral." The elder Hodge very justly remarks: "That so many different principles of classification have been adopted, and that each of these principles is carried out in so many different ways, shows the uncertainty and difficulty attending the whole subject." * On the general subject of classification of the attributes he can be read with profit.† He adopts for his own: "(1) God is a spirit; (2) that as such he is infinite, eternal, and immutable; (3) that he is infinite (*a*) in his being; (*b*) in all that belongs to his intelligence, namely, in his knowledge and wisdom; (*c*) in all that belongs to his will, namely, his power, holiness, justice, goodness, and truth."‡ This is a good working scheme in treating of the divine Being, but it confounds subject and attributes, and so far lacks clearness.

Shedd, after some valuable statements on the subject of classification, adopts as his working scheme, deriving it from the same source which Dr. Hodge acknowledges, the Westminster Confession: "incommunicable and communicable." § It has, as we think, the same fault as that of Dr. Hodge, in confounding the nature with the attributes, and much greater fault, in fact, a serious blunder, in classing some of the attributes of God as communicable. In doing so he follows many distinguished writers, but none the less commits himself to a

---
* *Systematic Theology*, vol. i, p. 376. †Pp. 375, 376.
‡ P. 376. § *Dogmatic Theology*, p. 338.

great error. The attributes of God are infinite attributes of an infinite nature, and can be no more communicated to a creature than the nature itself. In treating the subject he abundantly recognizes this truth. Why, then, adopt a terminology which is misleading and calls for constant correction?

Dr. Pope seems to us to have propounded the most scientific classification yet reached; if not faultless, it is the nearest approach to perfection. He says: "Revelation in every possible form, directly and indirectly, explicitly and implicatively, affirms the being of God. It declares his essence and attributes; his works and his relations; his creatorship and sovereignty over the universe. It places him beyond all things and above all things, and makes all things subject to him and dependent on him for the beginning and continuance of their existence. It differentiates between him and all things. The universe is by him, but is in no sense a part of him. It is in him and of him as its causal ground, so that it could not exist without him, but it is not an evolution of his essence, but a product of his will. It is dependent on him, but he is independent of it. Once it was not. He forever has been. It might be abolished. He forever must continue to be. This is the teaching of the holy oracles concerning the being of God. It affirms not only that he is, but it imputes to him a unique quality and quantity of being. In quality his being is necessary, absolute, unconditioned. It is the only possibility of all contingent existence, the support of all actual being, so that nothing is or can be without him. His being is true and sole source of all being; but other being is not constituent of his being and does not spring out of it as an effluence of his essence. The majestic prologue with which revelation opens asserts the doctrine which is maintained throughout the great discourse: 'In the beginning God created the heaven and the earth.'"

There is another peculiarity of this classification. Under the common terms or general conceptions, as above stated, the things classed are essential, individual existences; whereas the attributes are neither essential nor individual existences, but are concrete realities of the divine personality.

With these profound differences we may still observe a scientific method in the treatment of the divine attributes. Such a method requires their classification on the ground of what is the deepest in God as their subject. This law must exclude all predicables which, however true of God, are not distinctively attributes. It follows that a catalogue of divine predicables, however complete and true, is not a classification of the divine attributes. Nor is any division on grounds which do not thoroughly differentiate the several groups a proper classification. A neglect of these principles results in artificial distinctions, of which there are many instances.

Dr. Miley says: "It will help us to a clearer view of the question if we notice a few instances of such artificial distinctions and groupings.

"Such is the division of the attributes into the natural and the moral. Instances of the kind are so common that it is needless to give any special reference. It might be proper to distinguish the spheres of the divine agency into the natural and the moral, but such a distinction of the attributes is groundless. God acts in the physical and moral spheres, but not by two distinct sets of powers. Such a distinction in the spheres of his operation cannot be carried back into the powers of his agency.

"A grouping of the attributes as positive and negative is equally artificial. It is artificial because this distinction in the terms marks no real distinction in the attributes. The negative terms have just as positive a sense as the class of positive terms. Infinity and immutability express the reality of the limitless and changeless in God, just as omniscience and omnipotence express the absolute plenitude of his knowledge and power. It thus appears that there is no ground for this classification of the attributes. It is a grouping without any real distinction. It will further appear that the divine predicables which we express negatively are not distinctively attributes.

"There is no scientific advance on the ground of a distinction between what God is in himself and in his manifestations: 'the *Majesty* which he has in himself, and the glory which he *outwardly* manifests; the inner brightness, consequently, and the outward radiance of the light; the attributes which relate to *his mode of existence*, and those which become known to us in *his mode of operation*.' There is no ground for such a distinction. In any proper sense in which some attributes are related to the mode of the divine existence all must be so related. Hence they cannot be thus divided into distinct classes. Further, all are eternally complete in God; hence no manifestation of a part in the mode of his operation can constitute a ground of classification.

"We may present together two instances of analysis and classification which, with verbal differences, are substantially the same. Dr. Pope gives, as the result of his analysis: 'First, the attributes pertaining to God as absolute or unrelated being; then, those arising out of the relation between the Supreme and the creature, which indeed require the creature for their manifestation; and, finally, those which belong to the relation between God and moral beings under his government, with special reference to man.' Dr. Cocker gives the result of his analysis and the grounds of his classification thus: '1. As related to our intuition of real being; by abstraction from all other being or personality—the *immanent* attributes of God. 2. As causally related to finite, dependent existence; by elimination of all necessary limitation—the *relative or transitive* attributes of God. 3. As ethically related to finite personality; by elimination of all imperfection—the *moral* attributes of God.' It will readily appear, on a comparison of the two instances, that the three divisions of the one are the same in principle and method as the three divisions of the other. They are both specially formal endeavors toward a scientific attainment. We must think the method a mistake and the aim a failure. In the grouping of the attributes according to the three divisions certain divine predicables are placed in the first which are not distinctively attributes. We may instance *spirituality*, which is of the very essence of God and not an attribute of his being; *eternity*, which is in no proper sense an attribute of the absolute being of God, and no truer of his absolute being than of his personal attributes which are grouped in the second and third divisions; *immutability*, which is not distinctively a truth of the essential being of God, as it is equally true of all his attributes; *self-sufficiency*, which, instead of being a distinct truth of the very essence of God, can be a reality only with his omniscience and omnipotence. In the second and third groupings, on a distinction of relations to the creature and to moral beings, with a resulting distinction of attributes as the transitive and the moral, it was impossible to complete the second division without placing in it some attributes which are necessary to the third—impossible, because that distinction is scientifically insufficient for the separate groupings. Omniscience, omnipotence, wisdom, goodness, which could not be omitted from the relation of God to the creature, are equally necessary in his relation to moral government. The insufficiency of these distinctions may be further noted, particularly in the analysis of Cocker. The transitive attributes of his second division are as immanent in God as the attributes of the first, and no more transitive than those of the third. In both instances the distinction between the second and the third divisions is really the same as that, previously noticed, between the natural and the moral attributes, and is open to the same insuperable objections.

"In the true method of science classification is open on the ground of what is most determinate in the subject. This is the natural method in distinction from the artificial. The same method should be observed in the classification of the divine attributes. Personality is the most determinate conception of God, and the truest, deepest sense in which he can be viewed as the subject of his own attributes. Personality is the only conception of God which immediately gives his attributes. Any other ground of classification must result either in a mere catalogue in which subject and attribute are confusedly jumbled, or in groupings without any sufficient ground of distinction. Personality gives all attributes which are properly such in distinction from what God is as their subject.

"Our method omits from this category certain divine predicables usually classed as attributes. Of these there are several classes. Some belong to God as subject, not as attributes. Some, however true of God, are in no proper sense his attributes. Others result from the perfection of attributes, but are not distinctively attributes themselves. We have previously noted spirituality as belonging to the first class. Eternity and unity belong to the second. Immutability and omnipresence belong to the third.

"As God in personality is the subject of his own attributes, so therein we must find their true category. This category must be determined by the constitutive and essential facts of the divine personality. These essential facts are the divine attributes.

"Intellect is in both common and philosophic use for the power or capacity of rational intelligence in the human mind. It includes all the cognitive faculties, but signifies simply the capacity for knowledge, while knowledge itself must be an acquisition through their proper use. There is the reality of intellect in God; and, so far, there is a likeness of powers in the human and the divine personalities. Knowledge in God, however, is not an acquisition, but an eternal possession. This profound distinction requires the use of another term for the expression of the whole truth in God. Intellect well expresses the power of knowledge in the human mind, but cannot express the plenitude of the reality in the divine mind. No term is more appropriate than omniscience—the one long in theological use. Omniscience implies the profoundest sense of intellect as a power of knowledge, but omits all implication of a process of acquisition, while it expresses the infinite plenitude of the divine knowledge.

"Sensibility is the term in philosophic use for all forms of mental feeling. It is also used without any qualification for all forms of divine feeling. It seems more appropriate for a philosophy grounded in sensationalism than for a philosophy which gives a proper place to the higher rational powers and to original truths. The profoundest motives of life arise with the activities of the philosophic and moral reason. Sensibility seems but a poor term for the expression of these higher motivities. Yet it is the term in philosophic use; nor have we another with which to replace it. It seems still more inappropriate and insufficient for the expression of the forms of feeling in the mind of God, and necessary to his personality. But the difficulty of replacing it with a better still remains. The term feeling is deficient in definiteness, and includes much of human sensibility which can have nothing analogous in the divine consciousness. Affection and emotion are in philosophic use for distinct forms of sensibility, and hence are too specific and narrow for the present requirement. Even love, while the deepest truth of the divine nature, does not include all the forms of divine feeling. It seems necessary still to use the term sensibility. But we here use it only in the sense of the higher forms of feeling, particularly the rational and moral, which render man the image of God. These feelings are the response of his motivities to the objects of his conception, and constitute the motives of his providence. Without such motives he could have no reason for any action. Neither teleology, nor justice, nor love could have any place in the operations of his providence. There could be no divine providence. Neither could there be a divine personality.

"Will is the third and completing attribute of personality. It is the necessary power of personal agency, of rational self-determination, of rational action with respect to motives and ends. The will is not sufficient for personality simply as a power of self-energizing for the attainment of the ends of one's impulses and appetences. Such a power is no higher than the self-energizing of an animal. It must be central to the personality, that it may be the working power of the rational personal agency. It is thus the power of election with respect to ends, and the executive power whereby one may give effect to his choices. The will is thus a necessary attribute of personality. It is such an attribute in God." *

There must be a best way of arranging the attributes, a most logical and philosophical order, one would think, but scarcely any two of the great writers agree as to the principles upon which the classification should proceed. This arises from the fact that the attributes of the divine nature, like its essence, are eternal, neither more essential than the others as to the divine nature. They equally partake of the dignity and worthiness of the nature itself. And yet there is a logical order in their manifestation. While it is true that the whole nature moves in every expression and manifestation, some one

---

* *Systematic Theology*, vol. i, pp. 175-179.

attribute takes the initiative in every act. There is thus a logical order in the exercise of the attributes. The nature and attributes which are of it are alike immanent and eternal, but all forms of causational activity and manifestation necessarily come under the conditions of time and succession.

If we can in thought place ourselves back of all created existences with God alone, and endeavor to find out the logical order in his modes of procedure in the great movement which he is about to inaugurate, we may possibly obtain some light on the problem of the logical relations of the attributes in carrying forward the movement. Most fundamental is the being, the essence. Can anyone doubt what the order would be? Would not the idea take logical precedence? But if so the omniscience, which in the form of wisdom gives the idea, would be the logical first subjectively. But could the idea of the proposed creation exist apart from the idea of the best possible? If not, then as a part of the idea would be an ethical affirmative; or the personal subjective action would involve the moral nature. Having now the idea of the best, can we doubt that the next subjective movement in logical order was the choice or determination of the whole nature acting in the form of will to it? Having so determined an act purely subjective, to realize the end does anyone fail to perceive that the logical next is an efficient or creative volition, by which the idea takes form in a real creation, or a forthputting of power objectively? Thus the first outward expression of God is in a creative act which is an act of omnipotence, manifesting wisdom; and as wisdom is the discernment of that which is best, the creative act also involves his moral nature in the choice of the best.

In studying the problem of the concurrent action of the divine attributes from our standpoint, as we are able to see their expression, the logical order is first his omnipotence.

Creation discloses to us the idea of an all-powerful Being. As we study its structure and constitution it discloses to us an all-wise Being. As we detect its tendency and the laws under which it exists and is governed, we detect an omnipresent agent, and as we follow it to its final outcome we detect a being acting from the inspiration of love, the basis of the moral nature, and ground of justice, mercy, and sympathy, and of absolute holiness.

To us any attempt to think logically of God, that is, to follow the order in which the mind proceeds, requires, first, that we should conceive of him as eternal Being, and, so conceiving, that we should next determine or find what kind of being he is, that is, whether he is a spirit or material. This, of course, requires us to bring into view his attributes, for these are determinative. They are only introduced as proofs of the nature or kind of his essence.

The subject being thus brought before the mind as a real existence or entity, the mind proceeds in logical order to find what predicates may and must be made of this Being to give his real and true differentiation. To do this it must consider his work. He is not an object of sense, and so it is impossible to describe him by sensible qualities; that is, we cannot describe him in thought, as a form, in terms of size, or figure, or color, or texture, or anything of this kind. These attributes or properties or qualities do not belong to him, or at least do not appear. Thus we eliminate all material predicates.

But as we do not cognize him as an object of sense the question arises, How do we cognize him at all? And we are compelled to answer, We cognize him only as he manifests himself, in things, to the reason as cause of things. When we find his being as cause—for to be a cause we intuitively know he must have being—the mind at once is logically thrown back on the question, What is involved in cause, that is, what predicates must be true of this Being in order that he may be cause—what attributes must he possess?

The logical order of the mind's movement is to ask, What must be the necessary predicates of such a Being, that is, what are the attributes with which we must of necessity invest him, and which of necessity he must possess? And following the line of rational thought we find as our first thought that he must be real, that is, have the quality of real being; as our second thought, he is cause of all, and therefore is not himself caused—he is not a creature; as our third thought, he is unconditioned and absolute. But then he must be eternal. Thus we reach what we may call the first predicate of this Being, namely, that of necessary existence—or eternity—self-being—underived independent existence. But now, returning to the ground of this affirmation, namely, that he is cause of all things, we are logically driven to ask next, What must we suppose of him in order that, being eternal, he may also be cause? And we are compelled to answer, He is an omnipotent being, for only a being of absolute and unlimited power can create all other being. Thus we reach what might be called the first in logical order, discovered essential attribute. But now, examining the effect caused or originated, we discover that it is a system of orderly arranged parts in order to infinitely ingenious ends; but these facts point to a mind of infinite wisdom. Thus we are driven to ascribe infinite intelligence or omniscience to the cause. He is eternal, omnipotent, omniscient.

If now we conceive the divine nature to be eternal and to include in it the attributes of absolute omniscience and omnipotence, not to name others, and the being possessing these attributes to be self-conscious and absolutely free, thus raising him into personality, we have the whole idea of what the Eternal is.

What does omniscience and self-consciousness give? They give the absolute and perfect knowledge of himself, of every attribute of his nature. Self-consciousness is knowledge of the self; perfect self-consciousness is perfect knowledge of the self. But perfect knowledge of the self includes a perfect knowledge of each attribute of the self, and of all the possibilities in these attributes; otherwise the knowledge and self-consciousness would be limited and imperfect. But perfect knowledge must also include the knowledge of all that will become actual, by the exercise of these attributes; otherwise we again reach limitation and the knowledge is imperfect.

But now this last form of knowledge, that is, of what will become actual, must include not simply a knowledge of what God himself will do and whatever will necessarily flow therefrom; but, if there be effects which will not necessarily flow from his acts, but other effects or results which will flow from the free acts of other free beings whom he will create, his knowledge must also include this or it will be an incomplete knowledge of the universe which he caused to exist; and so again we have not omniscience, but limited and imperfect knowledge, and a knowledge which cannot at any time be complete. But to know what he will do at any time, or what necessary effects will follow any of his acts, is not to know that he has already performed the acts and that the effects have already taken place, but is to know the very opposite; that is, that both his acts and necessary effects which will flow therefrom are yet in the future.

With these principles present in our thought we are prepared to examine the question, Is succession predicable of God? The principles are, succession is movement, and movement is temporal. Existence without movement is fixed, and stable or fixed being is eternal. Time as movement must be a product or creation, for without movement it could not exist. It is not predicative of stable, permanent existence. There must be stable being in order to movement, or there would be no cause of movement. Time implies and necessitates the eternal. The existence of movement involves the existence of the mover. The temporal demonstrates the nontemporal. To the question, then, Does the Eternal exist in the mode of succession? we have to answer, as to being and the essential perfections, No. In these respects he must simply exist in stable equilibrium. He is the I AM. If, now, he should translate his perfections into action or movement, this would be a mode of succession, and would be temporal, or under the conditions of time; but the succession or temporal thus reached, and predicable, would not be a predicate of his being or perfections, but of their mode of manifestation or exercise. Thus God would be seen to be eternal in his being and perfections, but temporal in the mode of their manifestation. As to mode, by action he would bring himself under conditions of time; in that respect he conditions himself and in turn is conditioned by the things made, but not in respect of being and perfections. Before acting he eternally possessed himself, and with himself the power to act; he forever knew all the contents of his power; he was forever conscious of all the moral principles implicated in his movement. These are eternal, and do not come and vanish, but are fixed and abiding. But the movement or manifestation must necessarily be temporal. The movement is creative and the product is successive events, and the succession is time. He therefore created time by movement, or the movement is time. Time denotes and measures the active mode of divine existence with relation to creative existence—it measures the act, not the actor. Dr. Shedd says: "God's acts of power are successionless. God creates all things from eternity by one act of power."* There could be no balder contradiction. If he creates from eternity, the thing created

* *Dogmatic Theology*, vol. i, p. 345.

is eternal; for when the creative act is performed the effect is. The entire section is remarkable for its fallacious reasoning. What is true of any act or manifestation is true of his acts or manifestations; they begin and are completed. They were not, they are, they will be. With respect to them there is a past, a present, a future. In the manifestation he acts under the mode of past, present, and future. There can be no properly eternal act, if by act we mean a movement, by which something is brought to pass that was not before existent. The divine creative and sequent providential movement must be regarded in thought, and must necessarily be in reality, a movement under the conditions of past, present, and future—current, successive, begun, progressing, completed, or advancing without completion. An eternal agent exists, that is, a being with power to act; but an eternal effect producing action is a contradiction in terms.

How then does the movement of God in manifesting or translating his perfections stand related to his being and eternity? The answer must be that though not present as acts before they took place, that is, though he is not eternally acting in each several act, each act is eternally with him, as known or purposed to be, or as having been, or as now being or possible to be. In this sense all his movement, though successive, is present with him from eternity. As to purpose, and knowledge, and all other implications of being, and agency, and potency, all events stand forever in his consciousness, as an eternal now, or present; as to the manifestation or expression, it is known as it will be in an orderly succession. There is a succession in the events themselves, and there is a succession in his acts, which is ground of the succession of the events, and he knows the succession in its exact order, and purposes to act in the exact order that will produce it. Thus he knows himself as acting progressively or successively. Thus we must conceive him as eternal in his being and perfections, and all his acts as forever present with his consciousness as known and purposed; but at the same time we must conceive the acts of the series as progressive movement or themselves progressive, and himself as forever acting in some mode of energy. The hypothesis of an eternal volition, which is eternally efficient or productive of effects, has in it this difficulty : It makes the system of effects eternal; for, if there be an eternal acting cause, there must be an eternal effect. We think this impossible, since beginningness seems to be the very essence of the term effect, and so of the mode of agency which produces them. Eternal being is necessary to agency and to effect, but it may be doubted whether eternal being and power must necessarily be eternally active as efficient cause.

Thus when we ascribe eternity to God we do not ascribe eternity to his acts necessarily or probably. Acts are not attributes, and attributes do not necessarily imply acts. The attribute of omniscience does imply the actual knowing of all things. It cannot be viewed as a mere power to know. This will appear in the statement of the doctrine on that subject. So likewise the predicate of immutability does not imply the power to be immutable, but actual immutability. So likewise the attribute infinity, if it be ranked as an attribute, does not imply the power to be infinite, but actual infinitude. But if now we consider the attribute of omnipotence, we discover at once that it implies the power to do all things doable, but it does not imply the actual doing of them. The attribute may exist and not be in exercise to its full expression, or to any extent at all. The omnipotence of God does not necessarily imply that he does all doable things, or that he will do them, but that he has the power to do them. It might exist in perfection though in fact he did nothing. It did so exist before it was exercised. That is before there was any creation. It has never been fully exercised. There is no evidence that he ever will do all that by possibility he might do. The power to do is the attribute. The doing is its exercise. It may never be exhaustively exercised. What power he will exert depends on other attributes. He will do what his wisdom and holiness prompt him to do at any given time in the future. To these promptings he is free. Thus an eternal being might possess the perfection of omnipotence without manifesting it. If for any reason he should determine to manifest it, the act of manifestation would not be eternal, but would be an event denoting a new mode of an eternal attribute. The attribute, as an essential inhering perfection of the being, would undergo no change, but its mode would undergo a change. This is precisely what would have to occur in order to the creation of other beings, and what necessarily must have occurred in the production of the universe. Thus all effect-making acts of the Eternal must come under the conditions of time, and whatever activity of this kind must be historic under the time order. In these respects there is a time order of succession in God, and the order of succession in events of his causation denotes an order of succession in his causal activity. This is clearly the doctrine of revelation. He created and rested—ceased from creation. He inspired the holy men of old; he wrought miracles; he providentially orders affairs; he hears prayers and answers them; he forgives sin; he sets up one and puts down another; he will raise the dead and judge the world. In all these and many other respects he acts under the conditions of time; but in all the process himself undergoes no change as to being or perfections. It is in vain to attempt to revoke this by assuming some one eternal act, not to speak of the absurdity of an eternal act. It is the eternal Being who acts, but his acts are not eternal.

If we are to think God as eternally having in his consciousness his own movement while yet it is progressive, the same is true of the effects which successively unfold as manifestations thereof. These are always present, but in their time order. Those past are present with him as past; those now existing are present to him as now existing; those to come, present with him as to come. The present are incessantly becoming past, and those future are constantly becoming present and past, and he notes the change in themselves or the movement; but they do not pass out of the present as permanent matters of knowledge with him, but only change their relation, and he knows the change. They are present in his knowledge all the time; they are present as actually existing only when they do actually exist. The whole order of succession lies under his gaze or in his consciousness perpetually, but just as it is in fact, as to itself, that is, as past, present, or future; and as to himself the past and future are always present as knowledge. There is, then, in the divine consciousness, that is, in his knowledge an eternal coexistence of all the events of time, while there is not a coexistence of the parts of the series, either as to themselves or the causal acts which produce them. It could not be predicated of the separate events that they coexist in a present moment, for they do not; some are past, some are present, some are future; but it could be predicated of them that they do coexist in his consciousness all the time as known. Thus in reality they are successive, but in his knowledge they coexist, but as they are in reality. The procession of events is relatively to themselves, and does not imply a procession in him, except as to his acts and relations. He changes not. But while there is no change in him his knowledge or consciousness forever conforms to the changing facts. The stream of events might be compared to a line stretched out on the bosom of immensity, of which the first event in the successive series is the beginning, and the event occurring the end. The first point is fixed, the second or the point at any time present or now existing movable and forever moving, and so the line is forever lengthening. Time is that lengthening line. But however projected, it is still a line with two ends, and can never, either in thought or reality, become anything else, or make the slightest approach to a line without ends—can never become infinite, but must forever be like a fragment on its measureless surface; and as the line had a beginning and end, so time had a beginning antecedent to which time was not; that is, time is not eternal. To-day marks a point on the line which is now its hither end; it may be millions of millions of ages from its thither end. To-morrow it will recede, and a period will come when to-day will bisect the line, divide it into two equal parts, our now being its middle point. That line will at date forever be the length of time, never will approach eternity. It will be the chronology of events, but not the chronology of divine existence. What means it, "One day is with the Lord as a thousand years, and a thousand years as one day?" Suppose now an omniscient eye of such power as to scan eternity at a glance, which, in fact, is the eye of divine consciousness, it would then forever behold that line at a single view from beginning to end. Suppose diamond-points thickly set along it, indeed touching each other, denoting successive events; then that eye looking upon it would behold all the events in a single moment, and looking before it forever would forever see them as coexisting in the vision, though not in themselves. The events as to themselves would forever be coming and vanishing, and the line as to itself would be forever lengthening. The events as to themselves would be characterized as past, present, and future. As to them the words would have meaning, as to the omniscient eye they would alike always be present, but present in the exact order of the events among themselves. He represents the eternity over whose measureless bosom the line of events stretches like a golden thread.

The treatment of this point by Mr. Watson, while in the main agreeing with the authors quoted, is in some respects at variance. Mr. Pope must have had the theologian of his own Church in mind, and very justly I must think dissents from a portion of his view. Mr. Watson says: "Duration, as applied to God, is no more than an extension of the idea as applied to ourselves." He says: "It follows, therefore, from this, that either we must apply the term duration to the divine Being, in the same sense in which we apply it to creatures, with the extension of the idea to a duration which has no bounds and limits, or blot it out of our creeds, as a word to which our minds, with all the aid they may derive from the labors of metaphysicians, can attach no meaning." "But it may be said that eternal duration, considered as succession, is only an artificial manner of measuring and conceiving of duration; and is no more eternal duration itself than minutes and moments, the artificial measures of time, are time itself. Were this granted, the question still would be whether there is anything in *duration*, considered generally, or in *time* considered specially, which corresponds to these artificial methods of measuring and conceiving of it. The ocean is measured by leagues; but the extension of the ocean and the measure of it are distinct. They nevertheless answer to each other. Leagues are the nominal divisions of an extended surface, but there is real extension, which answers to the artificial conceptions and admeasurements of it. In like manner days and hours and moments are the measures of time; but there is either something in time which answers to these measures, or not only the measures, but the thing itself is artificial—an imaginary creation. We apply the same argument to duration generally, whether finite or infinite. Minutes and moments, or smaller portions, for which we have no names, may be artificial, adapted to aid our conceptions; but conceptions of what? Not of anything standing still, but of something going on. Of duration we have no other conception; and if there be nothing in nature which answers to this conception, then is duration itself imaginary, and we discourse about nothing. If the duration of the divine Being admits not of past, present, and future, one of these two consequences must follow—that no such attribute as that of eternity belongs to him, or that there is no power in the human mind to conceive it." " But we are told that the eternity of God is a fixed eternal now, from which all ideas of succession, of past and future, are to be excluded; and we are called upon to conceive of eternal duration without reference to past or future, and to the extension of the idea of that *flow* under which we conceive of time. The proper abstract idea of duration is, however, *simple continuance of being*, without any reference to the exact degree of it, because in no other way can it be equally applicable to all the substances of which it is the attribute. It may be finite or infinite, momentary or eternal but that depends on the substance of which it is the quality, and not upon its own nature. Our own observation and experience teach us how to apply it to ourselves. As to us, duration is dependent and finite ; as to God, it is infinite ; but in both cases the originality or dependence, the finity or infinity of it, rises not out of the nature of duration itself, but out of other qualities of the subjects respectively." *

Watson's treatment fails utterly to distinguish between the radical implication of the two terms time and eternity. The terms duration, continuance, succession, flow, are all temporal terms of precisely the same import. They signify nothing in themselves. They describe nothing that is. They must be affixed to a subject, and then they imply simply a process of change in the subject. Until a changing subject is found the words are meaningless. If there were no such subject there would be nothing to be named by the terms. Duration seems to be the

* *Theological Institutes*, vol. i, pp. 57-59.

nearest approach to the name of something, but it simply means something which persists in being, or continues, or flows on into successive states. The very terms thus import change. Like time, of which they are equivalents, they describe a persisting but changing subject. And were the subject eradicated they would vanish. There would be no duration, no succession, no continuance, no flow—no time, if the changing subject were abolished. Eternity of being, on the contrary, describes a form of existence that does not flow—changeless existence. Continuance implies a kind of existence which can be atomized into moments, and which carries along from one moment to another. Composed of moments, it is resolvable into moments. Not such is the existence of the Eternal. The difference is not that there are more moments in one than in the other, but that the one is a flow or progress through moments and the other is not—moments exhaust the one but do not affect the other. If we recur to Watson's illustration the case will be plain: "The ocean is measured by leagues; but the extension of the ocean and the measure of it are distinct. They nevertheless answer to each other. Leagues are the nominal divisions of an extended surface, but there is real extension, which answers to the artificial conceptions and admeasurements of it." In this illustration he evidently intends to compare the ocean to a something which he calls duration or time, and by enlargement eternity. But here is where its weakness appears. The ocean has a limit, and hence, however extended, it can be expressed in leagues, and league therefore has meaning as a term of measurement. But take away the bounds, and the measure cannot measure it and ceases to be a measure. So moments are a true measure of time or changing existence, but they are not terms of measurement for limitless and changeless existence. The measure cannot measure the subject, and is meaningless. Eternity is not duration, as consisting of moments indefinitely extended. He is not made of moments, and moments represent nothing that is in his essence. But he creates moments by creating beings who exist in succession, or moment by moment. There is no other succession in him than the idea or knowledge of succession as it appears in things which exist under the form of succession, and these successive acts of his which give existence to things and are evoked in their governance and ordering. His own nature is such that there is in him a fixed and eternal comprehension of himself and of all beings and events of time, so that he is forever with them as knowing them, and they are forever coexistent in him as objects of knowledge in their exact order of past, present, and future alike. In them he beholds the relation of past, present, and future. He sees their continuance and flow, he knows the temporal order of their existence; he is conscious of his own successive acts, and he knows them as successive and puts himself so far under the time order; the entire moving procession is in him, and he exists in all and through all without partaking, as to his being and perfections, of the motion or flow. Our now is an instant vanishing; that is, our existence is always limited to a point. His now for himself is eternity, for he inhabits eternity. Our now could never, by multiplication, make his now. There may be a continuance or a flow of moments, but they must necessarily be limited between points, which mean only a series of successive events or becomings. The unlimited cannot flow. It is but another form of the absurdity of an infinite series, or an infinite composed of finite or measurable parts.

If we must predicate of the existence of God that it is in the form of duration or continuance similar to our own, in which there is a true past, present, and future, it will become us to consider what the words mean and whither the supposition will carry us. The words must be taken in their real import. The term "present" means this instant of time. The term "past" means all the instants of time that once were present but are now gone. The term "future" means all the instants of time that will become present and will vanish into the past. A being who exists according to this order never can have more than a moment's existence in his possession. The past he has no hold on. The future is not his. The mode of his existence is to flow from one instant to another, or to pass through successive stages; the continuity makes the unbroken whole of his existence. If we suppose him to transfer himself whole and entire from point to point it is easy to see how the being would be the same at each successive moment in the consecutive chain, however extended. It is thus that our personal identity is preserved, though our existence is always limited to the passing instant. If it is possible that our identity could be thus carried along without suffering impair it may be asked, Could not the integrity of the divine Being also be preserved under like conditions, and so may not the divine existence be limited likewise to the passing instant if he carry his unimpaired and immutable perfections along with him from eternity to eternity? Is there any need that we should suppose that his now should be larger than our now? Would not all the demands of the case be met by simply indefinitely extending the consecutive instants? We answer: (*a*) The fault of the conception is that it supposes that which is impossible, namely, that eternity is divisible into instants, or that by composition of measureable atoms of time he should be able to reach the timeless. This, we must think, is fatal to it. But (*b*) it labors under the further fatal difficulty that it supposes the actual existence of God to be constantly extending or enlarging. Moments add to the length of his life. In the amount of actual existence he employs he is variable, having more and more as time progresses. But we answer further, if the thing supposed could be allowed it would not alter the fact that eternity would be an eternal *now*—a *tota simul*—the *nunc stans*, or *punctum stans*, of the schoolmen. The assumption is that he exists only in the present moment—now—but that he transfers his unimpaired being and consciousness to the next and all succeeding moments, which become *now*, so that each moment is *now*. If we consider what is the unimpaired personality which is thus transferred, we shall find it to consist in changeless being and perfection. In this Being is a changeless consciousness of himself, and of all beings and events—the same millions of ages ago that it is to-day; the current moment, millions of ages ago as it is now; the events of millions of ages to come are as vivid in his consciousness now as they will be when they become now. Thus, all events coexist with the same vividness in his consciousness forever. In him they are eternally present—*tota simul*. Nothing is added, nothing is taken away. There is no successive flow. He is "the same yesterday, and to-day, and forever." There is no past, no future. This is his true eternity, not parceled out in moments.

But if now we pass to consider his efficiency or objective expression and manifestation, by which these forever present events are made real, we at once pass under the conditions of time; and He who is eternal in himself comes under the conditions of time in the manifestation of himself. Here, then, is true succession. The manifestation is in a measurable duration to which we give the name "time," and is under the form of a successive and continuous movement, moment by moment. There was a beginning; the line is ever lengthening, will never be endless, cannot become eternal. He is in the movement, forever unfolding what from eternity is in his consciousness as changeless purpose and knowledge. His eternal existence envelops it. It is in him, but it is not the measure of his existence, but it is the measure of a mode of his manifestation under the conditions of time or consecutive movement or working. His being is thus a *nunc stans* of changeless fullness of perfection. His manifestation is a continuous flow from a beginning point. The manifestation must have the being before or antecedent to it. What was he in that antecedent to all event? What was his consciousness? All future events were with him, or they were not. If they were with him, he did not reach them by continuance. They did not exist as events, but they were present as cognitions as really as when by his act they became real. The true Eternal antedates time, and cannot be reduced to the time order. *God is eternal. His acts are temporal.* All beings and events that have their origination from him are temporal. Their coming and flow create or are time. When they were not, time was not. Time is a creation. Eternity is unoriginated. To beings who exist under the time order—that is, the order of continuance and succession—the flow is discovered in the succession. But for this the time idea could not arise; there would be nothing to answer to it. There are two chronometric laws. The one is in the regular recurrence of phenomena external to the mind but observed by it—such as the uniform revolutions of the earth or the uniform recurrence of the seasons. This enables us to have common measures of the flow, denoted days and years. Take it away, and there would be no such periods and no such common measure. There could be no common means of determining the relations of events. The other is in the processes which go on in the mind itself—in the alternations of the mental life, in the processes of thought and feeling and other mental expressions. These are chronometric only to the extent of discovering to us successive states or continuance, not to the extent of a common standard. We could not tell whether a given state lasted for a minute or for years—whether it was long or short. This fact is often apparent now—a transient agony seems long. The mind absorbed in a thought reduces a day to a few minutes. The phenomena of dreams furnish illustration. The dream of minutes seems to extend over days, or even years. In essential Godhead there can be no such phenomena, and no corresponding consciousness. To him there is no such chronometer as regularly recurring phenomena to denote how his years are flying away—no such source of the consciousness of regular flow. The existence of the external phenomena and its regular recurrence make this flow; remove it, and there is none. To him, likewise, there can be no such chronometric order in his consciousness, without we suppose he is such a being as ourselves. But this would be manifestly to detract from his perfection. He can only be conscious of these things as they appear in the finite. They arise not from something in himself, but from things objective to himself. They represent nothing of his own essential life, but only those processes which he sets into motion in things. Thus, by setting up a finite universe, he puts himself under conditions of time as to it, not as to his own nature. He notes time as he creates it in others. He unites himself with it in the life of others, but himself lives in the changeless ineffableness of a being and perfections which do not vibrate, and only thus can he be eternal.

The doctrine on this point is thus expressed in the Scriptures: "In the beginning God created the heaven and the earth" (Gen. i, 1). Creation necessitates eternal being in the cause. "Before the mountains were brought forth, or ever thou hadst formed the earth and the world, even from everlasting to everlasting, thou art God" (Psalm xc, 2). "Of old hast thou laid the foundation of the earth: and the heavens are the work of thy hands. They shall perish, but thou shalt endure: yea, all of them shall wax old like a garment; as a vesture shalt thou change them, and they shall be changed: but thou art the same, and thy years shall have no end" (Psalm cii, 25-27).

"I am the first, and I am the last; and besides me there is no God" (Isa. xliv, 6). "The high and lofty One that inhabiteth eternity" (Isa. lvii, 15). "A thousand years in thy sight are but as yesterday when it is past" (Psalm xc, 4). "One day is with the Lord as a thousand years, and a thousand years as one day" (2 Peter iii, 8). "The same yesterday, and to-day, and forever" (Heb. xiii, 8). "Which is, and which was, and which is to come" (Rev. i, 4).

Taking these sacred utterances as the divine exposition of his own eternity, it would seem to embrace unoriginated being, changeless perfections, and actual possession of himself forever; and the permanent coexistence in him, that is, in his self-consciousness or knowing, of all events that ever have occurred or will occur, whether it be events of his own origination direct, or events arising from secondary causes, or events effectuated by other created wills. Their presence in him and his presence with them forever and ever denotes how it is that he is the Eternal—"the high and lofty One that inhabiteth eternity "—" with whom a thousand years are as one day "—" with whom is no variableness, neither shadow of turning "—" the same yesterday, and to-day, and forever."

With these sublime teachings of Holy Writ reason is obliged to agree. It is impossible to escape the thought and conviction that behind all phenomena there exists an eternal causal ground. The existence of these temporal manifestations necessitates the ante-temporal cause.

There are implications of this doctrine which should be noticed. Among these are: (*a*) the necessary existence of God; (*b*) his absolute independence; (*c*) his self-sufficiency; (*d*) the dependence of all being upon him, and universal creatorship and proprietorship; (*e*) absolute sovereignty; (*f*) immutability.

By *necessary* existence cannot be meant *necessitated* existence, but the very opposite. Necessitated existence implies a necessitating cause as the ground of it. Necessary existence implies the absence of any cause as ground of it. Necessitated existence is effect. Necessary existence is the true eternal Cause. He does not cause himself, for that would be a contradiction. He simply is, and cannot but be. It were a contradiction to suppose him not to be. "I AM" is his name. The acceptance of the fact is a necessity of thought, however its incomprehensibility amazes us. There must be such a Being —self-existing impossible not to exist. That which is unbegun must be unending. The idea transcends us, but we cannot escape from it. God is, and, being, he is necessarily.

By independence we must mean that the grounds of his existence are wholly in himself, not in his will, but in his essence. He is absolute, unconditioned being. There is nothing outside of himself to limit him, or condition him, or cause him to be, or to be what he is.

He is self-sufficient. As there is nothing outside of himself to determine anything that is of himself, so he is sufficient to himself. There is no necessity that there should be anything besides himself, as a complement of his existence. There need be no other Eternal. He is self-sufficing to exist alone. In his eternity and all other perfections he does exist alone. "The loneliness of God" is one of the amazing facts of his existence. He must forever be alone and self-sufficing. His resources are all within himself. He can borrow nothing. There is no one with whom he can share his thoughts or feelings. He must forever be his own counselor, his own lawgiver, his own companion. In the limitless expanses of his consciousness he must forever find himself alone. Of the majesty and eternal grandeur of his own thoughts and purposes and works he must forever be the solitary beholder. A lonely, self-sufficing, companionless God, "who only hath immortality, dwelling in the light which no man can approach unto; whom no man hath seen, nor can see" (1 Tim. vi, 16).

The dependence of all being upon him is a necessary implication of his eternal solitary existence. He alone is cause. All other being is effect. They are and must forever be what and as he makes them. Any agency they exert, either as secondary causes or free, spontaneous powers, is derivative. The universe has nothing apart from him.

The idea of self-sufficiency does not imply that there is not in the ineffable and independent nature of God a demand for the existence of other beings, or that he is such a being that he should forever find in his solitariness the perfect realization of his utmost idea or desire. The fact that he has become the Creator of a universe proves that this is not so. There was nothing outside of himself to move him to create. The reason, therefore, must be found within his nature. What is meant is that in himself are the adequate and sufficient grounds for the utmost realization of his ideals and desires. He has no unrealized or to him unrealizable desires. He needs no help, and can have no help outside of his own resources. He is adequate to his own plans.

Upon this point I quote from Mr. Pope: "Although this immanent and absolute attribute" (he names self-sufficiency an attribute) "by its very name shuts out the creature, and points to a Being who needs nothing to complement or complete his perfection, it nevertheless implies that in the infinity of his resources are all the possibilities and potentialities of the created universe. When we exchange the terms necessary, independent, self-sufficient for that of all-sufficient we begin to think of the eternal resources that are in the Deity—of *his eternal power and Godhead*. The word nothing vanishes both before his essence and his power. His sufficiency knows no limit but what he himself by word or act assigns to it. Of an eternal creation we dare not think; but we may speak of the eternal possibilities of creation. . . .

"By self-sufficiency we understand all that philosophy means by the notions of the absolute and the unconditioned. No relation in which the Supreme may place himself—he only becomes the Supreme by relation—throws any limitation around his being. No relation is a necessary relation. In saying this we say all that is needful. Some current definitions of the absolute have literally no meaning. The philosophy which admits that the finite cannot comprehend the infinite, yet asserts that the infinite cannot be a person, cannot be conscious of itself, because it can have no object over against itself as subject, is philosophy falsely so called. It must issue either in pantheism or in atheism. It has never been proved, it can never be proved, that self-consciousness necessarily implies consciousness of something not self. Even granted that it is so in the creature, the leap in the inference from the creature to the Creator is as unreasonable as it is certainly unscriptural." *

A further implication is his unlimited sovereignty. He who is sole cause of the universe must be sovereign in it and over it. There is nothing, there can be nothing, in it which he does not either create, or order, or permit and limit, or which could exist even without him. It cannot pass out of his hand or transcend his control. He must forever determine the metes and bounds of all its forces and agencies. Nothing that is made can successfully dispute or divide the throne with him. The powers which are derivative from him, and subsist only by his conservation, cannot take an independence and rivalship. The possession of himself involves the proprietorship of all things and the ultimate disposition of all things, according to his own immutable purpose. The bearings of this indisputable truth will be developed when we come to discuss the mode of divine

* *Theology*, vol. i, pp. 300, 301.

sovereignty over moral beings. To suppose that he is not sovereign is to suppose that he has originated a being greater than himself—that the effect rises above and dominates the cause—or that he voluntarily abdicates his own supremacy and of choice abandons the government of his own creatures. It is obvious that the first supposition is absurd and the second immoral. The doctrine is clearly taught, not only by rational inference, and the intuition of reason and the moral nature, all of which bow before the imperative of his law, but also, most fully, by revelation. Nature never mutinies. Moral rebels cannot evade the law or defy the sovereignty which enacts and executes its mandates or the alternative of its penalties.

A further implication of eternity is immutability. Whatever is eternal is necessarily immutable, and conversely. Whatever is mutable cannot be eternal. When we predicate eternity of God it is predicating immutability in the same respect, and *vice versâ*. The terms are equivalents. God is immutable in all respects in which he is eternal, and eternal in all respects in which he is immutable. In what respects is God immutable? (*a*) He must, as eternal, be immutable with respect to his essential being. He never began to be. He never had less being, and will never have more, than he now possesses. The inhering attributes are unmodifiable, and undergo no change. He is "the same yesterday, and to-day, and forever." His being is the ground of his infinite perfections, and his perfections are inherent in his being. Neither admits of change by diminution or increase. There is no change in his knowledge. "His understanding is infinite;" "Known unto God are all his works from the foundation of the world." His purposes are immutable. "I am the Lord, I change not." Mutation is change. If we could conceive of God as changing it must be in respect of being or perfection, that is, inhering attributes, or governing principles, or mere modes of manifestation. To suppose change of being is to suppose that he becomes some other kind of being—is to introduce into his nature a principle of disintegration—is to eliminate the idea of eternity entirely. This is not supposed by any. Here his eternity is admitted to be strict and his immutability absolute. It is an inherence of necessary existence. To suppose his attributes to change has the same consequence, for his attributes are requisites of his being, and make it what it is. To change they must become something other than they are—must augment or diminish; but this would be to make him other than he is. If perfect, there can be no augmentation by change. If they become less than perfect he ceases to be God. There can, therefore, be no change in these respects. The Eternal must forever remain the unchanging, infinitely perfect God. But if his attributes do not change the governing principles of his life cannot change. The same unchanging perfections cannot introduce new, better, or worse, or contradictory governing laws, or purposes, or expedients, or plans. He must forever remain the same "high and lofty One that inhabiteth eternity." Thus neither in being nor perfection nor plan can he ever change. "With whom is no variableness, neither shadow of turning," must forever be true of him. (*b*) In respect of his modes of activity or efficiency, and of his manifestations and relations, immutability cannot be predicated. Modifications here do not imply change or mutability of either being, or perfection, or plan. When he becomes a Creator, or puts forth his omnipotence, there is no change in his being, or attributes, or plan. When he administers over the beings he creates there is no change in these respects—no change in him, either as to power or purpose. In the entire expression, however varied, he but reveals what was eternally in him. The change is one in mode merely. His attributes eternally implicate the temporal expression they receive. There is every reason to suppose that the Infinite will forever continue to evolve in new and varied forms the mystery of his eternal purpose. We are certainly but in the dawn of the expression. As the illimitable ages roll away new and more marvelous revelations may be expected to burst upon the vision of adoring beholders. In the far-off places of creation there may be even now transpiring wonders of power and wonders of grace, displays of the divine glory, which we shall not reach until we have advanced through celestial cycles. In the far-off times still greater discoveries of an eternal plan may ravish angelic hosts, which will require the developed faculty of countless cycles for us to reach. We have only to remember that we are in the ongoings of an infinite and endless movement— that it is God who is unfolding the mystery of his own thought and love on a scale commensurate with his own perfections.

Martensen well says : " As the Being who has life in himself (John v, 25), in whom is contained all fullness, God is the Eternal. In the eternal God are all the possibilities of ex istence—all the sources of entire creation. The Eternal is the one who is the I AM, who is the Unalterable and Unchangeable. But his unchangeableness is not a dead unchangeableness, for it is to produce himself with infinite fruitfulness out of himself. His eternity is, therefore, not an eternity like that of the 'eternal hills;' it is not a crystal eternity, like that of the eternal stars, but a living eternity, blossoming with never-varying youth. But his self-production, his becoming (Werden), is not the fragmentary growth or production we witness in time. Created life has time outside of itself, because it has its fullness outside of itself. The Eternal lives in the inner, truer time, in a present of undivided power and fullness, in the rhythmic circle of perfection. The life he lives is unchangeably the same, and yet he never ceases to live his life in something new, because he has in himself an inexhaustible fountain of renovation and of youth."

This quotation shows how difficult it is for our finite faculties to reach the height of this great mystery, or to intelligibly formulate a statement of it. We are simply driven back to the conception of a timeless Being who manifests himself under conditions of time.

"While it has ever been seen that the apparently most simple questions are at the same time the most profound, this is certainly the case with that which now arises: when did the universe come into existence? Assuredly, that which God willed from eternity he has called into being in a certain moment of time; but nothing, perhaps, is more difficult than to conceive of a period in which the All arose out of the Nothing. The doctrine of a so-called eternal creation has therefore been defended in different ways during all ages. Not to speak of the Manichæans, we see this idea rigorously defended in the Alexandrine school, and above all by Origen. Without regarding matter— which he considered to be the seat of the evil one—as an independent power, he assumed an eternal creation of countless ideal worlds, partly as having taken place before this of ours, partly as to be looked for after this, since he could not conceive of an inactive God (*De Princ.*, iv, 16). Although rejected by the orthodox Church, this idea continued to live on in various forms, especially where the influence of the Platonic philosophy made itself felt. Erigena (Duns Scotus) defended it, and the pantheistic mysticism of the Middle Ages regarded the whole of creaturedom as a sort of decadence from God. While the Reformation confessed with fresh alacrity the creating of the universe in time, and a later scholasticism sought even to determine the day and the hour of creation, the newer theology and philosophy, on the other hand, under the influence of Spinoza, has declared itself ever more distinctly in favor of an eternal creation. Kant regarded the whole alternative as a cosmological antinomy, the solution of which surpassed the power of theoretical reason. And even among believing theologians of our own day we observe here and there a hesitation on this point, which certainly pleads for their modesty, but no less really shows the difficulty of this question.

"Yet, as far as we can see, the idea of an eternal creation is not less self-contradictory than that of a square circle; for to create, in the proper sense of the word, is nothing else than to bring into existence that which hitherto had no existence. 'No creature can exist,' as has been well said by Quenstadt, 'unless after previously not existing'—*Nulla creatura esse potest, nisi post non esse*. By the theory of an eternal creation— Strauss, also, has acknowledged this—the idea of creation is thus, in fact, destroyed; and he who favors this view would do better, for the avoiding of misunderstanding, no longer to speak of a creation at all. Moreover, the above-mentioned theory is in irreconcilable conflict as well with the Christian idea of God as with the nature of the cosmos. It may be defended, indeed, from the dualistic or pantheistic standpoint, but never from the supranaturalistic theistic one. The universe presents itself to our vision as something which is not absolute, but relative, contingent, exposed to all kinds of variation; in a word, not as existing from eternity, but as having at one time begun to be. That with the opposite mode of view the doctrine of a creation out of nothing also disappears has scarcely need of proof; the *nihilum* in this case exists nowhere else than in the imagination alone. No wonder, accordingly, that profound thinkers—a Nitzsch, for example—maintain the idea of a beginning, however difficult to comprehend, as absolutely necessary. The pure idea of history is sacrificed so soon as its starting point must be relegated to the list of fictions. Every teleological view of the world at once loses its support, since the final aim (τέλος, *terminus ad quem*) presupposes a beginning (ἀρχή, *terminus a quo*). If the world is without a beginning it will also continue to exist without end; and what is thus in itself eternal and independent needs for its infinite revolutions no longer a center in the personal and living God.

"On the ground of all this it must be maintained that God was, indeed, from eternity God, but not from eternity the Creator of the world. If it is said that in this case a change must have taken place in the Infinite, the fact is overlooked that a change in the working of God by no means compels us to speak of a variation in his nature. Or must God, then—to speak after a human manner—never be able to create anything new, lest thereby the unchangeableness of his being should be brought to an end? Assuredly we cannot possibly conceive of an inactive God; but we need not do this, if we again revert to the doctrine of the divine plan of the world as seen in Section lv. [The part referred to we introduce here: "If God is eternal and omniscient he must also have foreseen what happens in time, have foreseen, yea, even have determined and ordained, or the whole world would not be unconditionally dependent upon him. If he is wise and holy he must have had, also, a perfect aim before his spirit, and must will the attaining of this end by means worthy of himself. If he is supreme and sovereign he must be absolute disposer of all that exists; and if nothing of an arbitrary kind is to be ascribed to this Sovereign he must have a plan in regard to the world. The existence of such a world plan is a postulate of the thinking mind, but, at the same time, of the religious feeling, which cannot possibly rest satisfied with the conception of an inactive God. Certainly the question what God was doing before the creation of the world has often been put in an unbecoming manner, and in that case has deservedly been discountenanced. But this question cannot always be answered by authoritative utterances, and the dogmatics of the Church has acknowledged its relative right in treating the doctrine of God's decrees before that of his works.

It felt the necessity to make for itself a representation of God as from all eternity thinking, willing, determining, preparing that which should take place in the course of time. As well earlier as later philosophers, in so far as they have approached to the recognition of the personality of God, have admitted this element in their notion of God, and the earlier ecclesiastical conception of a 'counsel of peace' also originated in this necessity. Nothing is easier than contemptuously to mock at all teleology; but if this be wholly denied there results a naturalistic view, which only too easily slides into practical atheism. If we are not to assume that the universe has no higher ground and aim than that which is to be found in itself, then the purely æsthetical view of the world must alternate with an ethical-teleological one; that is, we must seek to comprehend creation as the work of a Being who from all eternity had conceived it in his mind. Naturally this will and counsel of God is not to be separated from his essential being, which, on the contrary, is therein shadowed forth and expressed. But although (in point of fact) one therewith, this counsel and will must be able to a certain extent to disclose itself to the eye of thoughtful believers. It is, as it were, the *inner* work of God which precedes his activity *without*" (p. 296).]

"Or does anyone stumble at the difficulty of not being able to conceive of a point in eternity at which time has begun? Augustine has already expressed this difficulty in the well-known words, 'Nor could the ages revolve before thou hadst made the ages'—*Nec præterire potuerunt tempora, antequam faceres tempora*—but he afforded at the same time the only tolerable solution, when he reminds us that the world was called into being not *in*, but *with*, time—*non in sed cum tempora*—or, to speak more exactly, time *with* the world. Time, indeed, is the succession of moments for finite things; so long, thus, as these latter did not exist there could be no room to speak of the former. A time before creation did not exist; then it was only eternity. Or yet better, with Augustine: 'If before heaven and earth there was no time, why is it asked, What wast thou then doing? For there was no *then* when there was no time. And thou dost not in time precede the ages; but thou art raised above all the past by the height of thine ever-present majesty.'

"To bring the matter into greater clearness we must carefully distinguish between the two senses of the word "creation." It signifies, namely, as well the proper creative *act* of God as the whole of *created objects* themselves which are called forth by this act. In the former case we can say that the creation is an eternal act, because the Creator himself is, in his living and working, exalted above all time (?). In the latter case we must assume that that which is created at *some time*—when, is for us now a matter of indifference—received a beginning, since it could not otherwise be spoken of as created. The world *began to be* so soon as this was willed by God, who placed it in time, and for it—at its birth (*wording*)—gave to time a beginning. On this account time has existed precisely as long as the world, and the world precisely as long as time. And time? This is God's secret; but enough—natural science proclaims it as well as Holy Scripture—the realm of creation at some time received a beginning, precisely because it is essentially distinguished from the eternal Creator." *

It is evident from this quotation that the learned author employs the term duration as the equivalent of existence. When he affirms that "there is no eternal now," that "the terms are contradictory," he says what seems to be true; but if from eternity God knew all things, all moments were always present with him—which is the exact meaning of an eternal now, or an all-embracing now, in his consciousness; there is no

* Van Oosterzee, *Christian Dogmatics*, vol. i, pp. 303-305.

contradiction in the thought. That is precisely the truth; all transient passing nows are encompassed by his permanent now. When he says, "being must exist in duration," he cannot mean that it is forever a flowing existence. He cannot mean that the Eternal exists in moments, or by enduring from moment to moment. The Eternal cannot so exist, or it could be reduced to moments. God *is*—not has been—not will be.

OMNIPRESENCE OF GOD.

IMMENSITY, ubiquity, omnipresence, are terms applicable to God. They practically represent one and the same attribute. We, in our thought, associate these with the idea of something which we call space, and which we conceive as limitless. It is clear enough that it is not an entity of some kind. If we should conceive that God were annihilated, and with him, as a necessity, that created beings were annihilated, and should then raise the question, What would be left? we should be compelled to say, *Nothing*. The sum of all being is God and the forms of being which he originates. If some one would say, Yes, eternity and infinite space would remain, we answer, These are not beings, but only predicates of a kind of being.

When we predicate of him, or when he predicates of himself, that he is omnipresent, we are not to attempt to conceive of an immense place, and to suppose that he is diffused through it—infinitely extended. Such an attempt would be both misleading and abortive. All terms of place relate to finite things, or to God's relation to finite things, not to God himself. When we predicate immensity of God we mean this, that he is such a Being that he has power to make a universe of extended things, and also unextended beings, and that his presence is commensurate with them; that he could repeat the creation, *ad infinitum*, and would be still present with each atomic part and with the whole, however extended. They are practically terms of relation to created being. All being is within him, and there never can be any being without or beyond him. If we were to conceive a myriad of angels to start from the rim of the universe and fly for myriads of centuries with the rapidity of thought in every direction, they would still be within him, not because he is extended, but because his power would still uphold them, without which they could not exist; and at the points which they should reach by their immeasurable flight he could build new universes vaster than now exist. *Where* does he live? With himself, and wherever other beings are posited by him. This is practically the doctrine of omnipresence, and any other conception serves no purpose of thought or end of doctrine. Where being is God is, and he is such that he might indefinitely extend being where now nothing is, and were he to do so he would be there also—is there in the possibilities of his power. This idea of omnipresence is free from the idea of extension of substance, which is materialistic, and to be rejected. This is the doctrine of revelation : " Whither shall I go from thy Spirit? or whither shall I flee from thy presence? If I ascend up into heaven, thou art there : if I make my bed in hell, behold, thou art there. If I take the wings of the morning, and dwell in the uttermost parts of the sea; even there shall thy hand lead me, and thy right hand shall hold me." " Do not I fill heaven and earth? saith the Lord." " Am I a God near at hand, saith the Lord, and not a God afar off?" " Thus saith the Lord, The heaven is my throne, and the earth is my footstool." " Behold, the heaven and heaven of heavens cannot contain thee." " Though they dig into hell, thence shall mine hand take them ; though they climb up to heaven, thence will I bring them down." " In him we live, and move, and have our being." "He filleth all things." It is obvious enough what all these passages mean, namely, that there is no possibility of escaping by distance from the presence of God; that wherever being is, or should go, it would still find him present. It is no limitation of unextended being, that is, being that has not the property of form or extension, to declare that there is nothing in it which answers to that idea. That which thought demands is that the eternal cause shall be present wherever effects are, and that as infinite it should be able to manifest itself everywhere, and that wheresoever it does manifest itself the eternal Agent is, in all forms of presence of which unextended being is capable, or which may be predicated of it.

It has been the fashion to distinguish between the immensity of God and his omnipresence. Dr. Hodge says: "These are not different attributes, but one and the same attribute, viewed under different aspects. His immensity is the infinitude of his being, viewed as belonging to his nature from eternity. He fills immensity with his presence. ["He fills immensity with his presence" is a phrase without meaning, or a contradiction.] His omnipresence is the infinitude of his being, viewed in relation to his creations. He is equally present with all his creatures at all times and in all places. He is not far from any one of us. 'The Lord is in this place,' may be said with equal truth and confidence everywhere. Theologians are accustomed to distinguish three modes of presence in space. Bodies are in space circumscriptively. They are bounded by it. Spirits are in space definitely. They have an *ubi*. They are not everywhere, but only somewhere. God is in space repletively. He fills all space. [This phrase is absurd and self-subversive.] In other words, the limitations of space have no reference to him. He is not absent from any portion of space, nor more present in one portion than in another. This, of course, is not to be understood of extension or diffusion. Extension is a property of matter, and cannot be predicated of God. If extended he would be capable of division and separation; and part of God would be here and part elsewhere. Nor is this omnipresence to be understood as a mere presence in knowledge and power. It is an omnipresence of the divine essence; otherwise the essence of God would be limited. [How can that which has no extension be limited by extension; or how can that which is not extended be conceived under terms of extension? To fill space makes space a receptacle and puts God in it.] The doctrine, therefore, taught by the older Socinians, that the essence of God is confined to heaven (wherever that may be), and that he is elsewhere only as to his knowledge and efficiency, is inconsistent with the divine perfections and with the representations of Scripture. As God acts everywhere he is present everywhere; for, as the theologians say, a being can no more act where he is not than when he is not." *

Mr. Pope says: "The omnipresence of God is no other than his immensity referred to the creature and restricted, so to speak, within the universe. There are three ways in which we may regard this attribute, as we find it everywhere present in Scripture. (*a*) It is the actual presence of the Deity in every part of created nature. 'Do not I fill heaven and earth? saith the Lord.' This is one aspect, and it asserts that the divine essence, though not extended nor diffused, is to be regarded as present to every portion of the universe, whether more material or more spiritual. God is not present by circumscription of space, nor by the occupation of any one locality rather than another. He is present in every force or energy of created things; nor can he be absent from any region of the universe or any act of the beings he has created. This, with all its inevitable consequences, may be called his absolute or, so to speak, natural omnipresence. (*b*) But there is another view of the matter which we may profitably take: 'In him we live and move and have our being;' which makes God's omnipresence the presence of every creature to him.

* *Systematic Theology*, vol. i, pp. 383, 384.

The relation is rather of the creature to him than his relation to the creature. (c) There is yet another, which connects it specially with the divine omnipresence : 'Whither shall I go from thy Spirit? or whither shall I flee from thy presence? If I ascend up into heaven, thou art there : if I make my bed in hell, behold, thou art there. If I take the wings of the morning, and dwell in the uttermost parts of the sea; even there shall thy hand lead me, and thy right hand shall hold me' (Psalm cxxxix, 7–10). This makes the God of the universe present wherever the special operation of his power is. Thus we may speak of him as present in the mightiest and gentlest forces of nature, which no physical science can account for or explain without this fundamental supposition. . . . All these must be combined in our reverent study of this attribute. God is in all things; all things are present to him; and his energy is everywhere felt, though not everywhere alike felt. Thus the attribute is protected from pantheism on the one hand and from every limitation of the divine essence on the other."*

Knapp says : "The *omnipresence* of God is that power by which he is *able to act everywhere*. This attribute, when correctly viewed, cannot be distinguished from the divine omnipotence and omniscience taken in connection; and so it is exhibited by Morus. We justly conclude that He who knows all things, and whose power is so unlimited that he does whatever he will, must be present in all things and cannot be separated from them by time or space. In thinking on this subject we have need to guard against gross conceptions, and especially against the danger of predicating of God what can only be said of presence of *body*. This caution is especially necessary here, since we are apt to transfer the forms of time and space, which are applicable to the sphere of sense, into the world of spirits, and, in so doing, to come to conclusions

* *Theology*, vol. i, pp. 314, 315.

which are false and contradictory and dishonorable to the purely spiritual nature of God.

"*Extension* is not predicable of God, who is spirit; to say, therefore, that he is in infinite space, or, with Philo, the Cabalists, and many modern writers, that he is himself infinite space, is altogether erroneous. Such expressions necessarily involve a material and limited nature. Space is a mode of thought, in which, as in a frame, we must range everything which belongs to the sphere of sense, but within which nothing relating to the spiritual or moral world can be brought. The omnipresence of God was often mentioned by the ancient philosophers, who ascribed to him a corporeal nature, or who regarded him and the world as composing one whole.

" By the presence of a spiritual being with us we mean that he thinks of us, and in this way *acts* upon us. But in order to this we need not suppose his local presence or the approximation of the spiritual substance. . . . If we attempt to go beyond this we fall at once into fruitless subtleties. We would be content to say with Moses, *Deus rebus præsens, est Deus in res agens.*"*

"In order to set forth clearly the whole truth of the doctrine a threefold distinction has been made. Thus God is everywhere, *per scientiam, per potentiam, per essentiam*—by his knowledge, by his power, and by his essence. Turretini presents this distinction with his usual clearness and ability. In accordance with it Calovius defines the omnipresence of God as the attribute by which he is present with his creatures, not only by the *propinquitate*—nearness of his essence—but also by his knowledge and power.

" It would seem to the common mind that the rational and scriptural view of this subject is that which has gained the general assent of the Church, which predicates the omnipres-

* *Christian Theology*, pp. 105, 106.

ence of God, not only of his knowledge and power, but also of his being. God himself, in a way congruous to his spiritual nature, fills the universe. One source of error in the matter probably exists, as Hahn has remarked, in confounding the idea of body and substance. By denying to God a body, and thus avoiding the error of pantheism, they have at the same time denied to him being or substance. They have thus changed God into an unessential thought, and placed him at some point beyond the universe, whence he surveys it and acts upon it, being present in it only by his knowledge and by such influence as he can exert through second causes." *

I have quoted these several authors for the purpose of pointing out the intrinsic obscurity of the subject, and to show how learned mind has attempted to grapple with it along the ages of thought. Finite mind will probably never reach a clear and perfectly satisfactory conception, so long as it must think under conditions of space and time. These are probably predicates exclusively of being which exists only under forms of succession and extension, and which can never be employed of the essential Infinite, but only of him as by creation he brings himself under their conditions. As he exists in time, he exists in space.

All agree that, whatever we mean by his immensity, he is not to be thought under terms of extension. All agree that he is truly present with all being, and that he has power to multiply being. This is as far as our faculties will carry us. All words and sentences which attempt to go beyond this are probably mere sounds, which have nothing for thought. The sum of all our knowledge is: He has created a universe; he has power to create others; he is, and must forever be, present with all created existence; there is nothing to limit him; and there is no spatial limit to his existence. Spatial limits, or

* *Christian Theology*, p. 135.

any space relations whatever, to a subject which has not the property of figure or extension, that is, to a being whose essence is spirit without admixture of matter, is not only an impossible conception, but also an absolute impossibility. God has no other relations to space than that of having created the idea of it by creating material substance. His presence is not simply a presence of knowledge and power, but is a personal and essential presence. When he energizes or exerts power he is, but he is an unspatial, unextended, spiritual, absolute, infinite Being, energizing under conditions of time and space. For all practical ends, and for thought and in accordance with the word of revelation, this is the import of the predicate omnipresence. The other terms in frequent use, immensity, ubiquity, if they have other, wider, and truer meanings, have nothing for our finite thinking.

When we think of the vastness of the universe, spread forth in the infinite abysm of what we call space, itself immeasurable, and of the illimitudes of time through which its history extends, and attempt to conceive of a Being whose mysterious presence fills all, so that no atomic part or increment is without him; whose presence and power touch all, and always; who lives and moves through all, holding the stars in his right hand, moving the most delicate tissues of the minute life cell; painting the tint of each perishing flower; supporting the infant's breath, and guiding the archangel on his adventurous flight; bearing the whole magnificence on the shoulders of his unwearying power forever and forever, we may well be filled with awe and wonder. It is not more a doctrine of revelation than a necessity of thought that there is such a Being. We fail to comprehend him, but we are certain that he is, and that every atomic part of the vastness is full of him. He hides himself, but our eyes behold the tokens of his presence. We do not touch him, but we touch nothing which does not report of him as pervasive ground and cause. "For all things were made by him and for him, and by him all things consist." The doctrine rests upon revelation and upon reason also, as do all truths. The reasons of the doctrine aside from the teachings of the word are these: (*a*) Where there is action we are compelled to posit a being that acts. This we do not simply spontaneously, or from the force of habit, but we do it necessarily. The laws of thought are such that we cannot do otherwise. (*b*) We cannot think that this is a mere law of thought, but by the same necessity we are compelled to think that the reality is as the thought affirms. The necessity is not simply that we should so think, but that it should so be. All attempts to conceive that there is no such reality are abortive. (*c*) The same necessity compels us to connect the act with the being who acts, that is, he must be present to it, must be in it and with it. There can be neither temporal nor spatial disconnection. He can no more act where he is not than he could act if he were not. The power which acts must be at the point where the effect is produced, and must be resident in the agent who exerts it at the same moment. If disconnected from the agent it is nothing, and if disconnected from the effect there is nothing effected. The cause must be conterminous with the effect, that is, must pervade it. There can be no part of the effect without the cause. These necessary principles of reason determine the conclusion that the unitary ground of the cosmos must be omnipresent with the entire cosmic order in every atom and part thereof, forever and forever. The tendencies and outcome of all scientific investigations are in accord with the biblical teaching, that a unitary world ground is forever acting and permanently present throughout the entire system, continuously realizing his idea, thus proving that God is an omnipotent person.

But, it is answered, whatever the necessities of the case are in point of fact, we cannot think a being of this kind, that is, pure, changeless, unextended being—a bodiless, omnipresent agent. There is thus an alleged contradiction. We are brought face to face with the inadmissible implication of a necessity to think what it is impossible we should think. Is there ground for this allegation? We answer, If by thinking such a being be meant either conceiving a mental image of him, or understanding how he exists, it must be admitted that we cannot think him. But these are not the things we are required to think. No necessity of thought requires us to conceive the *image* of an agent, or *how* he exists or acts, before we can admit *that* he exists and acts. The proof to us of his being is that he acts, and it is completed, whether we can form a thought-image of him, or understand the how of his act or not. That which we are required in this case to do is to think an agent who possesses adequate power to build the universe and perpetuate and govern it. This we can do, and cannot as rational beings escape doing. If we go beyond this and undertake to figure him, or form an image of him, or to explain how he exists, or how he handles himself, our minds immediately refuse to think at all, for we have broached the unthinkable.

Here, there, and yonder are terms of limitation. They can be predicated only of limited existences; of the unlimited they are meaningless, except as they are applied to his agency. They apply to things which exist here, there, and yonder, and to the exertion of power here, there, and yonder, but they do not apply to an essence which is not spatial. To God there is only here, for all things with him are here, and nothing there or yonder; that is, all things are present with him, and nothing is apart from him. Though unextended himself, and without spatial existence as to his essence, he has spatial relations in energizing spatial things—his power is manifested with and in things of space, and where his power is he is present exerting it. The same is true of the term everywhere. It simply includes all limited points—limited by the presence of finite things. As predicates of God they mean simply in every place where things are. He is present with them. If nothing exists which occupies space and is limited or circumscribed by space, they mean nothing. God's relations to such points arise from the fact that he creates substances which with relation to each other give meaning to the terms here, there, yonder, everywhere. The terms are relative as applied to him, as well as applied to the finites of which they are proper predicates. Does God exist, then, nowhere? That which exists nowhere is nothing. To this we answer, If these terms imply presence by extension, God is nowhere. There is no north side, or east side, or south side, or west side to a pure spirit—no up or down, or right or left to it any more than there is to thought or power. He creates all terms of place when he creates things which have a place. To say that God fills immensity of space is simply to say that he fills nothing, for space is nothing but an idea, which idea could not exist were it not for finite things; it is purely relative, and its conditions are created. The immensity of God means simply that his power is not limited within the boundaries of the finite creation. He is such a Being that out beyond creation in any direction he could energize new creations, and would be present with them where he so energized. If more than this be supposed there is no escape from the idea of extended substance, and no extended substance can be infinite. The terms are strict contradictions. A pure spirit is unextended, and fills no place, but creates places by creating extended objects, and is in place relations only by making things which are limited and figured. "The omnipresence of God is that power by which he is able to act everywhere. . . . To say that he is in infinite space, or, with Philo, the Cabalists, and many modern writers, that he is himself infinite space, is altogether erroneous. Such expressions necessarily involve a material and limited nature. Space is a mode of thought, in which, as in a frame, we must arrange everything which belongs to the sphere of sense, but within which nothing relating to the spiritual or moral world can be brought." *

Perhaps the best idea we can get of what is called the immensity of God as a form of his infinitude or plenitude of being is that he is such a Being as is without shape or figure, body or parts; this he discloses of himself; and such that his entire perfections are concentrated in his entire essence, and not divisible in parts; and such that he pervades the entire universe and is wholly present at every point in it; and such that the universe does not circumscribe or include him, but is circumscribed by him; and such that out beyond the limits of the limitable he so is as that in any point in any direction and at all points in all directions he could without spatial modification of his essence exercise and manifest all of his infinite perfections in creative and providential and administrative acts, both moral and natural, as they are now exercised within the limits of the created universe. *Vide* Hodge, Shedd, Knapp, and Smith on the Immensity of God.

* Knapp, *Christian Theology*, pp. 105, 106.

THE OMNIPOTENCE OF GOD.

OMNIPOTENCE is the term employed to designate the power of God. It is of primary importance that we have a clear idea of the import of the term power. In strict signification it is simple adequacy to effects; that is, it is that attribute of an agent to or by which effects are possible. It has close affinity to the terms cause, causality, causation, and agency. A cause is a being to whom effects are possible; causality is an exercise of power; power is an attribute of the being by which he is able to produce effects; causation is the exertion of the power by which effects are produced. Thus power is seen to be an attribute which, considered simply in itself, may be a latent inherence of a being, but which, considered in relation to effects, is active. "The general idea of *cause* is that without which another thing, called the *effect*, cannot be."* "Causality, *in actu primo*, is the exerted energy in the *cause* by which it produces the effect. Causality, *in actu secundo*, is *causation*, or the operation of the power by which the cause is actually producing the effect."† Thus it appears that a cause is something which not only *precedes*, but has power to produce, the effect. And when it has been produced we say it is in consequence of the power in the cause having been operated. The idea of power is not given in sense perception. It is primarily given in consciousness. We are conscious of power in ourselves to produce effects. We are conscious of having exerted power when we produce effects. We intuitively cognize the connection and relation between our exercise of power and the

* *Metaphys.*, lib. i, chap. iii.
† Fleming, *Vocabulary of Phil.*, pp. 75–77.

effect. The intuition broadens into the maxim, "There can be no effect without a cause."

"The sensuous school of philosophers deny that there is any efficiency or power in existence. Their principle is that knowledge is derived from the senses, and consequently that, as we cannot know anything of which the senses do not take cognizance, it is unphilosophical and unreasonable to admit the existence of anything else. Our senses, however, do not take cognizance of efficiency. It cannot be seen, or heard, or tasted. Therefore it does not exist. A cause is not that to which an effect is due, but simply that which uniformly precedes it. All we can know, and all we can rationally believe, is the facts which affect our senses, and the order of their sequence, which order, being uniform and necessary, has the character of law. This is the doctrine of causation preferred by Hume, Kant, Brown, Mill, and virtually by Sir W. Hamilton, and it is this principle which lies at the foundation of the positive philosophy of Comte."*

"Now, that our idea of *power* cannot be explained by the philosophy which derives all our ideas from sensation and reflection is true. *Power* is not an object of sense. All that we observe is succession. But when we see one thing invariably succeeded by another we not only connect the one as effect and the other as cause, and view them under the relation, but we frame the idea of *power*, and conclude that there is a virtue, an efficacy, a force, in the one thing to originate or produce the other, and that the connection between them is not only uniform and unvaried, but universal and necessary. This is the common idea of *power*, and that there is such an idea framed and entertained by the human mind cannot be denied. The legitimacy and validity of the idea can be fully indicated."†

---
* Hodge, *Systematic Theology*, vol. i, p. 408.
† Fleming, *Vocabulary of Phil.*, pp. 394, 395.

"In the strict sense *power* and agency are attributes of mind only; and I think that mind only can be a *cause* in the strict sense. This *power*, indeed, may be where it is not exerted, and so may be without agency or causation; but there can be no agency or causation without *power* to act and produce the effect. In intelligent causes the *power* may be without being exerted; so I have power to run when I sit still or walk. But in inanimate causes we conceive no *power* but what is exerted, and, therefore, measure the power of the cause by the effect which it actually produces. The *power* of an acid to dissolve iron is measured by what it actually dissolves. We get the notion of *active power*, as well as of cause and effect, as I think, from what we feel in ourselves. We feel in ourselves a *power* to move our limbs and to produce certain effects when we choose. Hence we get the notion of *power*, *agency*, and *causation*, in the strict and philosophical sense; and this I take to be our first notion of these three things."

That we do have the idea of *power* and causality cannot be disputed, except on the most arbitrary grounds. The philosophy which denies it can allege nothing in support of its position but the inadmissible postulate that we can form no idea of anything not given in sense. (*a*) It contradicts our consciousness —we know that it is not true by directly cognizing in ourselves that which it denies. (*b*) It contradicts the most certain and positive intuition of the mind, namely, that an effect is impossible without the action of a cause. (*c*) It takes all meaning out of the connection of events which we behold transpiring around us every moment of our conscious existence. Succession explains nothing. (*d*) The connection of effects with our acts, consciously exerted to that end, is such that it is impossible we should believe that there is nothing in the one causal of the other. Antecedently, we believe, *we know*, that we can do certain things. We consciously put forth the power and do them.

We do this in order to a given effect which we believe will follow; we see that the expected and purposed effect does follow. To say that all we discover in the case is one thing following another is what the human mind can never believe, while the laws of thought remain and reason and consciousness are permitted to be heard.

There is such a thing, then, as power, and we consciously possess and exert it. But we no less consciously know that our power is narrow and limited and its exercise restricted and conditioned in many ways. We express all this by giving to it the general name finite. Inanimate things *seem*, likewise, to possess power. To this we give the name *secondary cause*, by which we mean that the power is not original to them, but to the agent constitutive of them. To them is appointed the function of making visible the real ordering cause, who himself does not directly appear. These, like ourselves, are circumscribed.

To the *power* of God is given the name Omnipotence—which strictly means all power. But this is not to be so construed as to imply that there is no other power than the power of God, any more than the infinitude of God is to be so construed as to imply that there is no being but the being of God. Such a construction would resolve all things into God and mere modes of his acting, and thus reduce to sheer pantheism. Things are real and have real power. But they have neither being nor power in themselves. They are products of the Infinite, and their powers are derivative and conferred. They are created with limited powers which they cannot transcend, and which it is their nature to exert, and which they cannot refrain from exerting. The constraint is in them as an inherence of their existence and dower of their being. When we rise out of things which thus have limited powers under the law of necessity to the contemplation of mind we detect a higher range of powers, which are exerted in freedom, but these, while real, we are compelled to trace to God as original source; so that there are no powers which do not ultimately emanate from him. He sets them up and determines their limits, whether they act under the law of freedom or necessity. If they exist under the law of necessity he creates them to that end, and they can but fulfill the function of their existence. It is the sun that shines and warms and vivifies; the atom that attracts; and they can do nothing other than that which they are created to do. If, on the other hand, they exist under the law of freedom, they can do with freedom certain things, but they are limited and restricted within certain bounds, in which they were created to move. He not only creates all finite powers, but he determines their kind and fixes their limits.

There are such concreated powers—powers given and imparted to created things. We cannot get on with thought without admitting and recognizing this. Every atom is a throne of power which, in a sense, is its own to exert. It does instrumentally exert it. The whole universe quivers with interaction—is alive with contending and yet coworking forces. They work to an end, but to an end which they do not propose or understand. Science discerns that they work according to laws fixed and universal; laws of whose existence they know nothing, yet which they obey with infallible and undeviating fidelity. The reason is obvious. They were created to work for those unknown ends, and for nothing else. The ends are apprehended by their Creator, and their existence is given simply to accomplish them. The story which they relate to discerning science is not simply of their existence and working, but beyond that of the Infinite whose will and purpose they were made to serve—of the Infinite from whom come both their power and its working. All other powers are thus witnesses of the omnipotence of their source and unitary ground.

Omnipotence is viewed under two aspects by philosophers

and theologians, and with some advantage to the clearer comprehension of the subject. A distinction is made between the power which is exercised in creating and that which is exercised in the ongoing of things—not that there are two kinds of power, but two modes of exercising the same power, or two forms of manifestation. To the former they give the name *absoluta*, or *potentia absoluta*, or *potestas absoluta*; to the latter *ordinata*, or *potentia ordinata*, or *potestas ordinata*. This distinction is found to be serviceable in many ways. Of this Dr. Hodge says: "By the latter is meant the efficiency of God, as exercised uniformly in the order of creation of second causes; by the former, his efficiency, as exercised without intervention of second causes. Creation, miracles, immediate revelation, inspiration, and regeneration are to be referred to the *potentia absoluta* of God; all his works of providence to his *potentia ordinata*. This distinction is important, as it draws the line between the natural and supernatural, between what is due to the operation of natural causes, sustained and guided by the providential efficiency of God, and what is due to the immediate exercise of his power." *

Knapp, on the same point, says: "The absolute omnipotence of God is that immediate miraculous exertion of his power which is seen in the creation of the world. His *omnipotentia ordinata* is that common, regular exercise of his power by which he makes use of the course of nature, which he himself has established for the promotion of his own designs. Thus he produces the warmth of the atmosphere, not *per potentiam absolutum*, but *ordinatum*, in causing the sun to shine. The same thing is expressed by saying he acts *per causas secundas*."†

Dr. Pope holds similar language. "Once more," he says, "the wisdom and goodness of the Supreme conditionates his omnipotence. Here there is a twofold range of suggestion, one more

* *Systematic Theology*, vol. i, p. 410.   † *Christian Theology*, p. 102.

simple and comprehensible ; the other bringing us to the threshold of unfathomable mystery. It is not difficult to understand that in the providential arrangements of the universe omnipotent agency is limited by wisdom. There is a definite and clear distinction between what is sometimes called the *potestas absoluta*, or the absolute power that creates all at first and places it under the government of secondary laws which represent the *potestas ordinata*. This distinction between the supreme and the economical omnipotence of the Creator is important in many applications. It does justice to the regular, orderly, uninterrupted process of created things, in which occasional interventions are rare, and, indeed, no more than exceptions to general rule. But it gives room for these interventions in creation itself, and in the miracles which sometimes introduce a new creation into the world. The one idea of the divine omnipotence reconciles the two and harmonizes with both. But there is another aspect of the subject, before which the human mind must bow down in amazement. In the infinite wisdom of God things contrary to his will in one sense are permitted by his will in another. This leads us up to the original mystery, that Omnipotence created beings capable of falling from him ; and down again to the present mystery, that Omnipotence sustains in being creatures opposing his authority ; and then forward to the same mystery in its consummate form, that Omnipotence will preserve in being, not, indeed, active rebels against his authority, but spirits separated from himself. It is the awful peculiarity of this attribute, in common with wisdom and goodness, as we shall see, that is traversed and thwarted, so to speak, by the creatures which owe to it their origin." *

We cannot doubt either the justice of this distinction in the mode of divine efficiency or its importance in interpreting the relations of the Infinite to the world order. Nothing is more

* *Theology*, vol. i, p. 313.

certain than the affirmation that the absolute power of the Eternal unitary cause must have been exerted, with immediateness of efficiency, in creating and establishing the world order. It is not an inference, but a necessity. The effect is a direct product of the cause. There can be no intermediates. In order to the effect all requisite power must be found in the cause absolutely. We thus by necessity of thought trace causation to its ineffable source, and find in the Infinite the home of omnipotence, and from the Infinite its direct expression. The existence of the universe cannot otherwise be accounted for. Reason joins with revelation in the postulate that the universe is product of absolute power directly exerted. All capable scientists admit it in effect.

So nothing is more certain than that in conserving the world order, in its ongoing, the same omnipotence or infinite power employs second causes, or makes the creature itself the medium of efficiency—makes it serve ends by forms of power which it was created to exert. It is his power which makes the sun to shine, but the sun shines, and by its warmth and light vivifies things which grow out of the earth. The secondary form of power is as dependent on him as the primary, but differs in mode. He is as really in the ongoing of things as in their origination, but in a different manner. The universe could no more continue without him than it could begin without him, but the modes or forms of power employed in its continuance are not identical with the mode employed in its production. It is the same omnipotence which works in all and through all, now originating, thenceforth conserving.

The rational, as well as scriptural, idea of omnipotence is that it is that power of God whereby he is able to do whatsoever he wills to do—a power which nothing external to himself can hinder or limit. Restraints to the exercise of his unlimited power do not arise from external impedimenta, but are restraints employed by coordinate perfections of his own nature. It is by removing all the limitations of power, as it exists in us, that we rise to the idea of omnipotence of God.* It is no limitation to power to say that it cannot do the impossible, that it acts only by choice, that its exercise is determined by coordinating perfections. We reach the highest idea of infinite power when we ascribe to God power to do whatsoever his infinitely perfect nature determines, or whatsoever he pleases to do.

In defining the omnipotence of God to be the power whereby he is able to do what he wills to do there are several things to be observed, as, (*a*) the distinction which is made between his causality and his will ; (*b*) the seeming limitation that he can only do what he wills ; (*c*) whether he must will to do all that he has power to do ; (*d*) whether the willing and the doing are not identical. On these points we have to remark : (*a*) That the will of God is that perfection of his nature by which he determines himself to certain ends, that is, by which he purposes certain ends ; as such it is always coördained by wisdom and goodness. (*b*) It is also the perfection of God by which he effectuates his chosen ends by a forthgoing of efficiency or power; power is thus in the will and of the will. (*c*) The form of the will, which is determined to ends, is purpose in harmony with the coordinate perfections of wisdom and goodness ; he wills to do all that he ever will do in the sense of a choice or purpose to do it, and he never will do anything else, or other, than he purposes to do. (*d*) The form of will, which consists in the forthgoing of causality, is under conditions of time, and is his infinite will exerted constantly to the realization of its purposes in time. (*e*) The will as efficient or causational can never transcend the will as purposing; whensoever he puts forth causational energy or power it will be in accord with his purpose, and it will be by an act of will under

---

* Hodge, *Systematic Theology*, vol. i, p. 407.

the conditions of time. (*f*) The forthgoing of causational energy is not exhaustive of causality or of the infinite power as power, but will be exhaustive of infinite power coordinated by wisdom and goodness. To infinite power, as infinite power, many things are possible which will never take place, simply because the infinite will, coordinated by love and wisdom, does not choose them as ends, and not from lack of power in him to cause them.

And now, having sufficiently cleared the term of false and crude meanings and determined its true significance, that is, that power whereby the Infinite can do whatsoever he chooses to do—a power inherent and eternal—we are prepared to attend to the proofs that he does possess such power, that he truly is omnipotent.

In the foregoing statement the divine omnipotence has been postulated. It remains that we more distinctly point out the grounds which have been intimated in the course of the statement, but the proofs of which are yet to be developed. The proofs are in two parts and from diverse sources, as, (*a*) those reached by the reason and arrived at from the study of nature; (*b*) those derived from revelation, each supporting the other.

If the so-called positive philosophy, which limits our knowledge to sense perceptions, were true, we could know nothing of God nor have any proof of his existence or of any of his attributes. Neither he nor they come into the range of sense cognition. God is strictly invisible. His works and word furnish the only sources of knowledge of him. In his works we comprise all created mind and all forms of material existence. We have shown in former discussions that these are his product—that he is the eternal unitary ground of the world order, or all cosmic phenomena.

From this established fact we deduce his omnipotence in

two ways: (*a*) As the universe is wholly his creation, all the power that is in it or implicated by it, of every degree and kind, is derivative from his power, and as such can in no sense transcend its source, but of necessity must come within it. His power thus embraces, and is the equivalent of, all the power that is. In this sense he is omnipotent. (*b*) As he is the only absolute Being there is nothing to impose limits upon him or restrict any of his perfections. His necessary existence involves the infinitude of his attributes. He who limits all cannot himself be limited. When once the mind rises to the apprehension of eternal cause it intuitively excludes all limitations and ascribes infinity. It is seen not only to account for everything, but in order thereto is conceived as perfect. Over against the finite, the imperfect, the dependent, the conditioned, there arise in thought the Infinite, the Perfect, the Independent, the Unconditioned, the Absolute. To his power reason refuses to set bounds, and assumes and irrevocably insists that there can be no bounds. The feeling that he can do whatsoever he will, that his power is absolute, is a mental instinct which has all the force of an intuition. It cannot be reasoned down. It is ineradicable. The limited forces of nature often make us tremble, but that which pervades the thoughtful mind with profoundest awe is the consciousness of a power which transcends all local and visible forces—a power out of whose grasp it is impossible we should escape, which may either preserve or destroy us—on the sole decision of whose will our destiny, the destiny of all things, depends. There is a mysterious sense of the Infinite in the soul of man, which is forever finding us in unexpected forms and overwhelming us in unexpected moments. We feel the swell and hear the sounds of the infinite sea. Of nothing are we more conscious than the idea and dread of eternal power or hope in it. Our own insufficiency and sense of dependence—absolute helplessness—begets in us, over against itself, the idea of absolute, self-sufficient, infinite power, and without an effort we believe there is an answering reality. When, if ever, we would disenchant ourselves of the thought, we become conscious that it holds us with the unrelaxing grip of necessity.

Creatorship implies unlimited power. The proof rises to its highest point when we contemplate the extent of the creative act measured by the extent of the created product. Power to create an atom implicates power to create a world. In its nature it is limitless. "The power displayed in the act of creating not only exceeds all finite comprehension, but is plainly so great as to exclude every rational limitation. It is impossible to believe that the power which originally gives existence cannot do anything and everything, the doing of which involves not a contradiction."* But if our minds, in their feebleness, fail to grasp the abstract principle, we have but to turn to the concrete fact of the universe to feel the force of the argument. Think for a moment of its vastness, only a part of which, and with its high probability only an infinitesimal part, as compared with the reality, is yet known to man. It is intimated that, within the sweep of the largest telescopic instrument, there are thousands of millions of solar systems the solar centers of which are visible, and which indicate planetary arrangements like those of our own. Think of the immeasurable spaces where those solar centers burn and shine—an abyss so deep and broad that it requires millions of years for a ray of light to traverse it, flying at the velocity of twelve millions of miles in a minute of time. Think of the velocities of those ponderous bodies themselves, moving in vast orbits, at a rate of speed equal to thousands of miles in a second, or almost unappreciable moment. Think of the unfailing energy which supports them and guides them in their courses from age to

* Dwight, *Theology*, vol. i, p. 152.

age, so that no one fails. The illustration is scarcely impressive if we turn from these stupendous exhibitions to the minutest parts. Think of the interplay of the atoms, the constructive force pervasive of each organism, the abiding energy which holds each particle in its place—which elaborates the completed and perfect whole from the rudimental germ. Surely the power which originated the vast system and carries it forward over such limitless spaces in exact and complete harmony through infinite ages is omnipotence—is inclusive of all the forces which play in the wondrous system.

OMNISCIENCE OF GOD.

IN discussing the subject of divine omniscience it is important that we preliminarily have definite understanding of what we mean by knowledge and the conditions of knowing. For a full discussion of this subject the reader is referred to Treatise I of this series, *Prolegomena*, pp. 74–184; but for convenience we present the following points here:

(a) Knowledge or knowing is an act or state of mind in which it is intuitively possessed of truth, that is, a concept of reality as it is. (b) In order to knowledge there must exist a knower and a thing known—subject and object. (c) The subject and object may be identical or different. (d) When identical the knowing is simply self-consciousness of the subject as to his own state or act; the knower knows himself, that is, he knows that he is, and in a degree what he is—what is in him as essence and attribute, and what he can do and will do—everything that can be predicated of his being and of his doing. When the object is different from the subject the knower knows the object and himself in the same act—self-consciousness is integral to all knowledge. In the first case, in order to knowledge there is no need that there should exist any other being than the subject—any objective of any kind external to the subject. In the second case, there must exist an object of knowledge external to the subject, or other than the subject.

Omniscience is the eternal and exhaustive knowledge the subject has of himself; and the complete and the perfect knowledge he has of everything other than himself.

The Omniscient is himself the only eternal object—subject-object. In the knowledge of himself is the perfect knowledge of his own nature and attributes, and what is contained in himself; and in knowing these he must know all his concepts and purposes with respect of as yet nonexistent objects. Thus nonexistent things may be eternally known, as they will be.

Thus God himself as subject-object furnishes the conditions of eternal knowledge. There is besides himself a universe which did not eternally exist. Omniscience requires that this also should be eternally known. But if there cannot be knowledge without an object, how could that which at a time had no existence be matter of knowledge? If we attempt to answer this by affirming that they really do exist in him we can only mean that they exist in him from eternity as concepts, or as concepts which he purposes shall become real. We thereby affirm that they are yet not real, and have for the matter of knowledge, not the objects, but simply the concepts and purposes of God. We may say that the one statement is the equivalent of the other; but we can never convince ourselves of the truth of the affirmation that a universe existing merely as a concept in the mind of God, and which he purposes shall become real, has the quality of existence before it in fact exists—is identical with the actually existing universe. The one part of the statement, that is, that the concept is eternal, may be true, but its truth proves the nontruth of the other, that is, that there is a corresponding reality. That which he knows is simply himself, his concepts and his purposes; and of all possible concepts he will give real existence to some and not to others. Nothing is eternally known to be real, that is, to have real existence, but himself and what is purely subjective to himself. That the universe may be known to be real, it must be real; but its reality is not eternal. Knowledge of a universe which once was not must be conditioned on its having become real or the certainty that it will become real.

Two things enter into the conditioning ground of knowledge,

namely: (*a*) his purpose to make the universe and knowledge that his purpose will be effectual to the end; (*b*) the actual existence of the reality. The first part (*a*) may be eternal, but the second part (*b*) must be in time. The first part (*a*) furnishes ground for the knowledge of what will be; the second part (*b*) furnishes the knowledge of what is.

According to the Calvinistic philosophy, God's knowledge of what will be has its ground in his knowledge of his purpose. He eternally knows all that ever will be because he purposes it shall be, and he knows that his purpose cannot fail.

To this philosophy there are these objections: it grounds all futuritions in the purposes of God, and thus at the same time denies freedom to man, and makes God the efficient cause and author of sin.

The position we hold and maintain is that God's eternal knowledge of himself in self-consciousness is, among other things, the knowledge of his purposes with respect to nonexistent events, and that so far as his purposes are efficient thereto he knows future events in this way. But further we hold that there are innumerable future events which he never did purpose, and especially that any purpose with respect to them was not efficient to them, and that these are also matters of his eternal knowledge; but if so his purpose is not the only ground of his prescience. His eternal purpose is one ground of knowledge of some things, but it is not the only ground, even with respect to those same things. His purpose to create a universe was a ground of knowing precisely what kind of a universe he would create; but it was not the only ground. He lives with the universe, and it is eternally open to him as a thing to be, and he thus knows it, not simply by knowing his own purpose, but by actual cognition of the universe itself; and this before it existed.

This last sentence needs special attention. A postulate laid down a few pages back was this: In order to knowledge there must be a knower and a thing known. The above sentence seems to contradict this postulate. If it does it is false. Does it contradict it? The seeming contradiction is that when the universe did not exist it was open to his observation as an existing reality; he knew it not as something purposed merely, but as something actually under his observation. We are free to admit that the supposition has all the appearance of a direct and bald contradiction. How can it be reconciled? We answer: That there was an indefinite period during which the universe itself did not in fact exist is certain. This is admitted by all the parties in this contention. The position taken here is that during this period when it did not exist in fact it was even then open to God as if actually existing; and we affirm that the position is not contradictory; and the explanation is this: We have found in the discussion on the eternity of God that his mode of existence is such that he exists in all time, nay, that he inhabits eternity; not that existing in one time he looks forward through all time, but that he exists in all time. There is no time when he is not. Now, if this be true, then he was actually existing from eternity, at the point of time when creation arose, and in all the time which creation occupies; but if he was and is present himself or existing in all that time, then the events of that time were always matters of real and direct cognition. As to themselves, there was a time when they did not exist, and in that time he knew them as nonexistent, but as to be; but as he was at that very time also existing in all coming time, he knew them in that coming time as existing. If the mode of eternal existence is permanent existence in eternity, and not a passing from one time into another, which we have seen it must be, the position here taken is irresistible. Things not existing at one time, and existing at another, are always under his gaze as reality. If we could suppose ourselves to be existing to-day, in a day a million years hence as well as to-day, we should then see what now is, for it would be under our present gaze; but we would also to-day see what will be nonexistent for a million years, for by supposition we are also to-day existing in that day a million years hence, and are seeing as real and present to us the events of that day. This represents what we are compelled to believe is the actual mode of divine existence. Things that will be are to him who now lives in the time when they will be. Thus, because of the mode of divine existence, things that are not in themselves existing are under his gaze; and however in themselves they are transient, in his knowledge, that is, direct vision, they are forever with him. Past and future now are with all their contents in his cognition. This point will be fully developed as this argument progresses. Thus God's purposes are not the only ground of knowledge. He knows by direct cognition of what is.

The importance of this point is found in its bearing on the question of how God could know from eternity the acts of free beings. The Calvinistic answer which ascribes his knowledge to his purposes, as we shall see, absolutely excludes all such acts from existence. To its theory, however it may affirm freedom of creatures, the fact must remain that freedom does not exist. Some of those who deny the theory as subversive of the idea of freedom, not seeing how prescience can be in any other way, find refuge in the denial of prescience.

We contend both for prescience, or absolute knowledge of all events of time from the eternity which precedes time, and also that among the eternally known events many are brought about in absolute freedom. The position we hold requires us to deny that God can only know future events by having fixed the occurrence in inevitability by his efficient purpose that they shall be. If among the all things known from eternity as certain to occur are some things which are not efficiently caused by his purpose, the grounds of the knowing must be different from the knowledge of his efficient purpose that they shall be. But if he does not know them by knowing himself as cause of them, there can be no other ground of knowing but the actual existence of the things known. To have this knowledge he must be present with them at the time of their actual existence, and they must be under his observation. His eternity explains his prescience; or prescience is simple knowledge of what is in fact matter of observation. The knowledge of God as to things created and caused by him is the knowledge of himself as cause and the perfect knowledge of the thing caused. It is not exhausted by the knowledge of his act, but also includes the effect in all its contents. He knows, not simply that the effect exists, but what it is—its innermost essence, all its properties and potencies and relations and collocations forever and ever; nothing in it or in its history is hid from him for a moment. Thus every atom in existence is forever open and naked to his ever-present gaze. As it derives its existence from him, it can have no existence without him. He is as much present with it each moment as he was present with it the moment he called it into being, and as directly observant of it. He lives in it and with it in all its history, as really as he lives in himself and with himself. It is not himself, but it has nothing apart from him.

Was there no knowledge of the real universe in the eternal omniscience? If we must so conclude, then there was no knowledge of all those events of the real universe which were not actually product of the divine purpose and causation, that is, all the free acts of free beings. His only ground of knowledge was the existence in him of concepts and purposes. There could be no other ground of knowledge of nonexistent things if they were not purposed. It would so seem, but can we be certain that it is really so? By concession the objective universe did not exist; but he who did exist existed in a mode of eternity, that is, not in a mode of succession.

The omniscience of God is thus as to events absolute prescience. He knows them from eternity or before time; not simply because he knows his purposes with respect to them, but because the time when they will be is, as included in his eternity, present with him.

With respect to events which are not immediately caused by God's agency, and so cannot be foreknown because foreordained, the question how he can be prescient of them is answered in the fact that, as above stated, he is present with them, and knows them, as we know events by beholding them. The eternity of God is the solution of prescience. He is with all events coexistent. Events are not coexistent with his eternity, but his eternity is coexistent with all events. The man of sixty years is coexistent with every day of his sixty years; but no day of the sixty years is coexistent with the sixty years.

If God's omniscience includes the knowledge of all events, it includes the knowledge of the thoughts, feelings, motives, and purposes of all minds. Prescience of them is in no respect more difficult to explain than the knowledge of them at the time when they exist. The whole difficulty is in explaining how they can be known at all; and arises from the fact that *we* have no such power by which to interpret them. We see or know through observable phenomena. Spirit itself to us is only seen by some external act. He discerns the thoughts of the heart. How prescience stands related to freedom will appear as we progress.

Omniscience is the term employed to designate the knowledge of God. The term defines itself in its simple etymological import. It signifies all knowledge, or the knowledge of all things; that is, first the perfect knowledge of himself, absolute and perfect self-consciousness of all that is in him, and the perfect knowledge of all that exists or shall exist apart from him, whether by creation or otherwise. The term knowledge is well understood. Those who find the worldground in matter, or impersonal force, logically deny any knowledge back of the universe, or in the eternal impersonal cause, and consistently hold that the evolution implies no mind.

This is what the human mind will never admit. It is impossible to conceive of such an unfolding without preexisting and pervading intelligence in the causation. We are compelled to construe the system under laws derived from our own consciousness. These necessitate the belief that mind is in, or rather is, the primitive world ground. Mind, as we find it in ourselves, *attains* to knowledge in a limited degree and under fixed laws. Its primary condition is that of a being who has faculties of knowledge. It will acquire knowledge under given conditions; and, under favorable environments, it will forever enlarge the scope of its knowledge. It is impossible that we should conceive of God as a being of this kind. With all his essential attributes his knowledge must be eternal and perfect, for from whom, or what, can he, who alone is eternal, derive anything? Knowledge may be viewed as wisdom and cognition. The distinction should be made. Omniscience includes perfect wisdom, that is, the knowledge of best ends and the best means thereto, and the knowledge of all existences and of all events.

Infinite wisdom cannot be viewed as an acquisition, but must be viewed as an attribute of the infinitely perfect. What is that attribute? Can it be anything else than the inherent knowledge of the best possible creation? As he, alone, is source of all things, all the implicates of wisdom in things must come from himself. Can the things which he has made teach him anything? Do they contain anything which he did not knowingly bestow? How can they have any secrets which he did not confide? Do they not, so far as they are intelligible, that is, construable in thought, represent antecedent concepts according to which they are formed? The entire mentality expressed by them of necessity preceded them in the cause. The attempt to confound the power which builds with the idea according to which it builds, or to suppose that the cause unfolds itself simply as force according to perfectly intelligible forms, without admitting a knowing along with the process, and, so, in the cause, which exerts the power different from the power exerted, and giving direction to it, is not only contrary to all experience and consciousness, but is absurd. Nothing can be more certain than that the cause was a knowing cause before it became a producing cause. The knowing was original, inherent, and eternal. The power which gave expression to the knowing must have also been inherent and eternal, but its *exercise*, of necessity, could not be eternal, but under conditions of time.

If we consider the world process we are forced to the following conclusions: (*a*) The process itself is in time; (*b*) as such it is an effect; (*c*) in order to it there must have been a preexisting cause; (*d*) the process evinces intelligence; (*e*) the intelligence must reside in the preexisting cause; (*f*) the process evinces power or causation; (*g*) the power must reside in the cause; (*h*) the action of the power is according to thought, and is not the thought itself; (*i*) the thought must be presupposed, in order to the exertion of the power, in the form and manner in which it was exerted; (*j*) the thought must be original to the cause, and eternal, since there was no source from which it could be derived but the Eternal himself; (*k*) the exercise of the power must be subsequent to the idea which it expresses, and necessarily under the conditions of time, since the effect is in time and must be contemporaneous with the exercise of the power which produces it. The result of which is that an eternal personal being who possessed the knowledge of it, in the form in which it should be, and who possessed the power to realize it or create it, but which power was not eternally in exercise but was exercised at the moment when the evolution of the world process began, must have existed before the universe. Thus, while intelligence and power are both attributes of the cause, they are distinct and differentiable. Knowledge selects the ends and the times, and determines the order—fashions the archetypes or ideals; power produces according to the pattern. Which is only saying that the universe was primitively a thought, afterward it became reality. In the eternal, mind was eternal as a thought; in the power of God, eternal as a possibility; in itself, as a realized idea or product of power, an effect—and in time. If we should undertake to suppose that power built without a mind directing we must encounter the difficulty of accounting for the most perfect result of wisdom by mere chance. If we deny the eternity of the ideals we must encounter the difficulty of accounting for the origin of the most perfect wisdom without a cause. Either dilemma must be fatal to the supposition. The only alternative is the admission of the ideals in the builder himself—not made or derived, but unoriginated and eternal. Thus it appears that the eternal Cause must have a perfect knowledge of all his works, so far forth as they emanate from him, and fill out the measures of his thought and changeless purpose.

Implicit in a universe which once did not exist, but which afterward does or did exist, is its cause, or a being who created it. Implicit in the cause is the idea of that which passed from nonexistence into existence. If the cause be conceived as a being of infinite perfections of power, wisdom, and goodness, it is implicit that there should be coexistent with these perfections an idea of something to which these attributes stand related. There is no meaning to the term power, and no function for the attribute apart from an object, for the realization of which it is power; there is no wisdom apart from an end; there is no goodness that is not for a good. The perfections are subjective, but they demand a conceptive object. The object is implicit in the attributes, first as idea of nonexisting reality, then as reality wrought by, and exponential of, the attributes exerted in its existence, and in the procurement of its good when it became actual. The idea is as eternal and necessary as the perfections themselves—implicit in their existence. It is the idea of a possible other than the sole existing Infinite; possible not without, but to, the Infinite. The idea is complete and perfectly definite in all its inclusions. It is not the idea of one thing, but of a far-reaching plan—a plan covering infinite areas and infinite time, that is, endless successions and limitless extension. Thus the one only universe that ought to be is in idea coexistent with its eternal Cause—the only one possible, because the best possible, and because infinite wisdom, power, and goodness will permit only the best possible, even in idea. The possible best may not be the ideal best, for it may not be possible to realize the ideal best. There are things conceivable which are impossible even to infinite power, because not objects of power. The idea of the possible best, and also the idea of the ideally perfect, have actual existence in the infinite mind; but neither the possible best nor the ideally perfect have the reality of being. The universe that is was potentially the best possible, but the possible is marred so as not to be equal to the ideal best. Free beings have caused it to fail to realize the ideal.

The possible is contingent—may become actual. Will it become actual? That depends on the will of God. It can only acquire the reality of being by a creative act; but if it shall become real it will conform to the eternal idea, and as the contents of that are perfectly known to the Infinite the corresponding reality is forever perfectly known in all its contents; thus eternal prescience covers the whole domain of possible existence.

The idea of the possible best exists simply in the divine consciousness and is the basis of eternal self-consciousness, that is, the consciousness of the self over against the not self. In the idea the *future* reality is present as a thought, but not as a reality. The divine knowledge corresponds precisely with that fact; it includes an ideal that is present, and a reality that is not at present existing. The knowledge of reality is prescience of something that is not, but that will be, and exactly as it will be. There are two modes of eternal knowing. The eternal knowledge with respect to an as yet nonexisting reality does not make it real. It makes the idea real. Its existence remains contingent upon the exercise of the creative will. That is something which has not taken place. The power is eternal, but its exercise comes under conditions of time, that is, of a beginning and eternally future progressive movement. Henceforth the eternal Absolute wills with and in the contingent finite, and brings himself under conditions of succession and extension, called time and space. The knowledge of the idea remains an ever-present knowledge, but the creation and ordering of real existence is the occasion, not of the changes of the substance of knowledge, but of the mode of it. From eternity he knew that he would act creatively. He now knows that he does act as before he knew he would. The act was before present in the divine mind as something to be; it is now present as an accomplished and accomplishing fact, and the knowledge conforms to the fact. There is thus a permanent now in the prescience, but a transient now in the realization.

The idea or plan of the finite is an eternal fact and changeless, but the act which realizes it has a beginning, and is unintermittently continued forever. Thus God has in the finite a life of ever-varying activity—a life in which there is a true past and present and future, a continuous becoming; and this is matter of self-consciousness. He knows himself as having done certain things. Concerning these he knows himself as not now active. He knows himself as doing in the present moment what occupies him at the time, and, knowing the changeless plan which he has, he knows just what he will do when the time comes for doing it.

A contractor engages to build a road across a continent. He has carefully charted the route he is to pursue. He knows every tunnel, every bridge, every winding of the way. Make his knowledge perfect. He would then know precisely what is to be done each day—would then know exactly how it will come out. All is present with him in his perfect plan. The reality will correspond precisely with the plan. But he also knows that the plan is not the road, and he knows that in order to the road work is to be done, and he knows that the work must be begun and continued, and he knows that work will fill out the plan. If his knowledge were absolutely perfect he would know from the start, yea, before he commenced, just what work he would be doing each moment to its completion. The work would keep him busy from its inception to its end.

The case is in no respect different when we think of God as founding and ordering the universe, except as he is infinitely perfect. Here we have first an eternal plan of a work to be accomplished in time. The work has not been done, though in him the knowledge of it is complete. It is a vast plan, extending over infinite ages, and of infinite extent. He who possesses it engages his infinite wisdom, power, and goodness to carry it out. His prescience sees it from beginning to end, or forever, for it has no end. The plan is thus forever present with him in all its minutiæ as an idea. He knows all the tunnels and bridges and incidents. He knows that the plan will not execute itself. He knows that work is required—that each moment in the future will call for its specific work. He knows what the specific work for the moment will be, and that he will be or is to do it. So much is included in his eternal prescience. But he also knows that the work that the plan calls for must be begun, and until it is begun he knows that it has not begun. When begun he knows that it is just begun and not completed. The mode of his knowledge, but not its contents, changes as the work progresses; he knows yesterday's work has been done and is past; he knows to-day's work is being done; he knows to-morrow's work remains. There are sunrisings and sunsettings in his work, and in the mode of his knowledge, but not in its substance. The ages come and go and find him busy; busier to-day than yesterday; busier to-morrow than to-day—busy forever, and finding his joy in seeing the walls go up; doing to-day what he did not do yesterday, because the time had not come, and doing to-morrow what he does not do to-day, because the conditions do not exist. His infinite happiness is thus found in thus realizing his eternal idea. It is an eternal plan, but the joy and fact of its realization are in the processes of time. The corner stone has been laid. It exists as a pleasing mode of changeless knowledge. The walls are partly up and are progressing. The under courses have been laid in beauty and are viewed with delight; some great arches are now being lifted and keyed, and each added stone brings new pleasure. The dome is in the perspective of far-off ages, but in due time will be set, with shoutings of "Grace, grace unto it," and in all the process the works of his hands will glorify him; the finished universe will be his everlasting crown. In the ongoing the finite changes, parts become obsolete and fall away, like useless scaffolding, needful once, but no more required; new parts appear, for which the old was preparation; but he changes not, but tirelessly works and will forever work to realize his idea and immutable purposes.

We have said that in creating the universe he brought himself under conditions of extension and succession called time and space. Prior to the creative act nothing existed of which extension or succession could be predicated. The idea of a universe included the idea of extension and succession, but it did not include the fact of either extension or succession, for these are not predicable of an idea. There was no extension or succession in the idea, and nothing in the essence or attributes of the Infinite of which these modes of being could be predicated. But the creative act began a series of divine activities and effects which were successional. Things created existed moment by moment, and new phases constantly emerged; this was succession as a law of things. The divine acts which produced the changes in things were also a series of activities, and as to acts the divine Being came under the law of succession. There was no succession in him, but there was succession by him. He was, in essence and attribute, "the same yesterday, and to-day, and forever;" but he acted yesterday as he does not to-day, and to-day as he does not forever. This does not imply any change in him, but only in the mode of handling of himself. He is "the same yesterday, and to-day, and forever"—the same when he acts and when he does not act, as the man is the same whether he is passive or active, when he walks as when he rests. So, also, there was nothing in the idea of creation of which extension could be predicated. But the creation of material substances, of which extension is an essential attribute, not only created extension in the thing, but brought the Creator under conditions of extension. He exists with and in extended things, and acts in them as he does not act where they are not. As extended things have an area or scope, God's presence pervades that scope, and *as working* in certain ways is bounded by it. He is thus omnipresent with being. We know of no other form in which extension can be predicated of him. The universe does not contain or limit him, but it proclaims his presence in it and in a mode in which he does not exist outside of or beyond it. His acting is bounded, but not his power to act.

There is a difference between a purpose and an idea, and also a difference between a purpose and an effect-producing act. The idea exists in the intelligence, and is an inherence of the eternal and unoriginated wisdom of the cause. We cannot conceive of it as an evolution or product of volition. It is of the essence of the infinitely perfect in the same sense as power is. He does not exist without it—he does not originate it. Purpose is an act of the will, and if there be freedom in God it is a free act, and if free it cannot be among the necessary inherences of his being. Even Dr. Hodge says that "God was free to create or not create." But how could he be free not to create if creation was eternal? There is a difference between the being and essential attributes of God and the acts of God. The former are eternal and necessary; the latter are sequent and self-determined. Certainly there is a logical necessity that the idea of a thing and consciousness of power to realize it should exist antecedently to the determination to realize it. Is the necessity simply logical, or also real? There is a difference between the eternal idea of the good and the choice of it or the purpose to realize it; and such may be the perfect nature of God, that along with the idea the purpose may exist as a free choice. The purpose may have the quality of eternity in it without the quality of necessity.

Purpose is used in the sense of choice of, or self-determination to, an end. The end must first be apprehended. After the end is apprehended is there a necessity that the purpose to realize it should exist, and, if it exist, must it not be originated, and, if originated, was there not a time when it did not exist? Is there any reason why the purpose should not exist in immediate connection with the existence of the idea and the discernment of its wisdom and goodness?

The universe we absolutely know is not eternal. What is gained by assuming that the purpose of it existed eternally before it was created? The eternal purpose accomplished nothing. In order to the realization there must be an executive volition. Why separate the purpose and the executive volition by the breadth of an intervening eternity? Does it not answer all the demands of the problem to say that the divine Being antecedently to all existence purposed—determined to create a universe after the pattern of infinite wisdom which existed in him? It is true that purpose as choice of an end logically precedes volition to attain to it or to realize it, and also that there may be any amount of intervening time; it may be a purpose not to do a thing now, but at some future time, near or remote. In this case, if we suppose the purpose to be eternal, the intervening time is a past eternity during which the purpose remained fallow. But the phrase, "*Eternitas a parte ante,*" and its counter, "*a eternitas a partis post,*" is itself misleading and meaningless, or false. Eternity is not a line which can be bisected so as to make two eternities. At the imaginary point of bisection we have an end beyond which the past does not extend; but a line which has one end must have two. Eternity has no end —is beginningless and endless, and must include past and future, or is rather that which properly has no past nor future. Past and future are temporal terms, and can only relate to things which have beginning and end. However inexplicable the idea, we have seen that God is a being whose existence and perfections are beginningless and endless—who does not pass out of a past into a future, but whose existence is in the forever of all past and all future, or is beginningless and endless.

Such may be the nature of God that with the presence of all possible things in his consciousness there is also in his consciousness an eternal choice of that which is best, and an eternal purpose to realize it, and that choice may be an immediate and immutable self-determination. We do not doubt that such is the fact. It is the free, spontaneous, preferential state of the divine nature.

Dr. Shedd says : "The instantaneous vision and successionless unchanging consciousness of the divine Omniscience, in comparison of the gradual view and successive increasing knowledge of the creature, have been thus illustrated. A person stands at a street corner and sees a procession passing whose component parts he does not know beforehand. He first sees white men, then black men, and lastly red men. When the last man has passed he knows that the procession was composed of Europeans, Africans, and Indians. Now, suppose that from a church tower he could see at one glance of the eye the whole procession. Suppose that he saw no one part of it before the other, but that the total view was instantaneous. His knowledge of the procession would be all-comprehending and without succession. He would not come into the knowledge of the components of the procession, as he did in the former case, gradually, part by part. And yet the procession would have its own movement still, and could be made up of parts that follow each other. Though the vision and knowledge of that procession, in this instance, are instantaneous, the procession itself is gradual. In like manner the vast sequences of human history, and the still vaster sequences of physical history, appear all at once, and without any consciousness of succession, to the divine Observer." *

This is an admirable illustration, but we should have to make one criticism upon it. The last line, we think, is not exactly true, " without any consciousness of succession to the divine Observer." The exact truth is the divine Observer would be conscious of the succession in the component parts thereof, for that conforms to the fact, but he would not be conscious of any succession in his knowledge of the component parts. There is

* *Dogmatic Theology*, vol. i, pp. 344, 345.

no succession in his knowledge, but there is a succession in parts of the moving line. The knowledge is simultaneous, but parts of the procession pass a given point at different times.

But the next position taken by the learned author we think entirely erroneous, namely: "Not only is God's act of knowledge eternal and successionless, but his act of power is so likewise. God creates all things from eternity by one act of power, as he knows all things by one act of knowledge, and as he decrees all things by one act of will." *

This statement is a strict contradiction. No creative act can be eternal. The power to create must be eternal; it is a divine attribute, but the creative act cannot be eternal, for the reason that the effect cannot be eternal. The effect is simultaneous with the creative act. There can be no creative act without a creative product, but we know that the universe is not, and cannot be, eternal, as its Maker is. All effect-producing acts must be in time. Acts are not attributes. His reasoning on the subject is by no means satisfactory. On this subject Dr. Hodge says: "We know that God is constantly producing new effects, effects which succeed each other in time; but we do not know that these effects are due to successive exercises of divine efficiency." [*They can be due to nothing else.*] It is indeed incomprehensible that it should be otherwise. The miracles of Christ were due to the exercise of divine efficiency. We utter words to which we can attach no meaning when we say that these effects were due, not to contemporaneous acts of volition of the divine mind, but to an eternal act, if such a phrase be not solecism." †

Nothing can be more certain than that both reason and revelation imply the idea that God does work successively and continuously in the creation and ongoing of the universe. If Dr.

* *Dogmatic Theology*, vol. i, p. 347.
† Hodge, *Systematic Theology*, vol. i, p. 388.

Shedd's meaning in the above statement is that "God creates all things from eternity by one act of power" continuously carried forward without cessation in successive forthputting, it would be nearer the truth; but this is manifestly not his thought, if so be he has a thought; but even then it would be a solecism, as intimated by Dr. Hodge. There can be no eternal creative act as above stated, simply because no effect can be beginningless, or eternal, and the creative act must be contemporaneous with the effect. Of nothing can eternity be predicated but God's existence and essential attributes; and his creative acts are not an attribute, but exercise.

God possesses his purposes and executes them, and priority of existence and power to do so is a necessary implicate. We must constantly remember that the purposes of God are not an attribute of God, but an act of will or self-determination. This is a most important fact in this discussion. Attributes are eternal, as coexisting with the essence; acts are not. They emanate from the being, but are not of the being, but by him. Prior, logically, if not really, to the possession of his purpose, not only must he exist, but his purposes must be the outcome of principle of goodness in him and of wisdom. His purposes are acts which precede executive volitions and condition them. Neither the choice nor the executive volition, which means exercise of causational agency, are of the essence. All his purposes which relate to the existence of the universe antedate its existence, and are purposes of an eternal being which are determined by himself, and which therefore are independent of all other beings; and they are purposes which will not change, but will stand fast forever, not of necessity, but of free choice, being in harmony with infallible wisdom and irreversible goodness and perfect knowledge. In respect of unchangeableness they are eternal, but in respect of existence they are originated. They are not an attribute, but a free exercise of an attribute, in harmony with other attributes. We do not see how it is possible to make the purposes of God eternal in the same sense that his being is without annihilating his personality, and at the same time imparting necessary existence to things eternally purposed. There is, by supposition, an absolute necessity that things should be as purposed, and the purpose partakes of the eternal and necessary existence of the being who purposes, and so created existence partakes of the necessity of the eternal Being. Where, then, is the freedom of God, and where is his absoluteness? There is no escape from the dilemma but by allowing that God has absolute power over his purposes which involves alternatively to create or not to create—to create now or farther on. The alternative power belongs to the nature, and the free choice or purpose is in accord therewith. As being he is eternal, absolute, out of all necessary relations to any possibilities. He is spirit, which is intelligent self-consciousness. As self-conscious he knows himself, his power, his freedom; that he has power to do as he may will. Things cognized by self-consciousness as possible to his power, if freedom belong to him, that is, if he have the attribute of personality as a positum of his necessary existence—a quality of his essence, that personality which consists of intelligent freedom must now assert itself in answer to the question which now confronts him, Shall the possibilities be made actual? It is entirely certain, however it may be with respect of purpose, that executive volition which is necessary to effectuate purpose must fall within time and have a beginning. This absolute necessity is discernible in the fact that executive volition, wherever it exists, connects with the effects which it produces, and does not exist antecedently to the effect, but contemporaneously; but every effect must have a beginning, a time when it becomes, and behind which it did not exist. The executive volition of God cannot be eternal.

The answer to the question, What will he choose to do,

that is, what will he purpose? must be freely self-determined, and it will determine whether the unconditioned will condition himself by bringing himself into relations to a universe which he will create.

The logical requirement with respect to God's relation to the contingent is first to posit the eternal as absolute and out of all relations; to posit him as a being of infinite power, intelligence, and freedom—as a person unrelated and unconditioned and self-conscious, having the sense of power to do as he will, that is, to determine himself. Thus existing he has ideas of nonexisting things possible to be, that is, possible to be made by his power. Will any of them ever become actual? That is contingent upon his free self-determination. If he shall so choose, they will; otherwise, not. Let us keep in mind that the problem is concerning the free act of a perfectly free being with respect to nonexisting things. There is nothing outside of himself to condition his act; nothing to necessitate him; he alone exists. The ideals have no power to necessitate him, for they are merely subjective states of his eternal wisdom. Will his own nature necessitate him? If so, the necessitation is eternal, for his nature is eternal; then freedom vanishes from the universe. There is no contingent existence, for the necessity which determines his choice and purpose binds all up in absolute necessity. If this be true, then there was a mistake when we started with the supposition that there were some things known as possible merely; when necessity binds all it matters nothing what kind of necessity, there is nothing contingent or merely possible. The universe so originating, and every incident in it, is as necessary as God. True, it did not in fact exist, but the necessity of its existence is absolute, and is as eternal as the nature of God which compels its existence.

There is no escape from this reflection on the nature and character of the eternal Being, but in the admission that his plan of the universe, and his purpose to create it, emanate not from a necessitated nature, but from self-active intelligence and from a free choice and act of self-determination.

To be free himself God must have power over his own self-determinations. But if his self-determinations are eternal, it is impossible he should have power over them any more than he could have power over his own existence, for no power can reach behind eternity or be operative as condition of that which is eternal, or be determinative of that which is eternal. Thus, under the supposition, freedom in any respect is eliminated from God. He never possessed the power to do anything which he does not do, or to avoid doing anything which he does do, or to vary the shadow of a shade in any respect with regard to any of his acts or purposes. It is said, in answer, that that is precisely what is implied in his infinite perfection and immutability. We answer that such an implication destroys his infinite perfection, since it absolutely deprives him of an ethical nature and character, and reduces him to the grade of unfree being, and imparts to him impossible immutability. He can only be immutable in respect to what is eternal inheritance of his being; but his acts, which proceed from him and produce effects, cannot be eternal without eternalizing effects, which is a contradiction. He is not immutable, therefore, with respect to acts; for there is a time when he acts and when he does not act with regard to such effects. His immutability is of nature and attribute, not of acts, and is not contrary to his freedom. His ethical principles are immutable.

But if the supposition with which we started destroys his own freedom, much more does it do away with the freedom of any created being. Given the postulates, God's purposes are eternal, and his purposes effectuate or cause all futuritions; and his purposes are that every act of every being shall accord therewith; absolute and strict necessity and divine necessitation binds all events. Freedom exists only in name.

There may be eternal possibilities to eternal powers, but the things that are possible cannot themselves be eternal. The fact that they are possible only proves that there may not be. A will-act that is only possible does not exist; if it did exist eternally it never could not be, or be different, and freedom is shown not to exist. God's own character depends upon the power he has over his purposes. There is no such thing as an ethical character or ethical being without power of self-determination, or in the absence of the exercise of that power. There is nothing ethical in spirit simply as such, or in absolutism, or in eternity, or in intelligence, or in self-consciousness, or in the power of self-determination. These are the inclusions of an ethical nature, but they only furnish the possibilities of an ethical character; that depends upon the free act of determining himself to an end, and not upon anything included in his necessary existence. A perfect ethical nature, such as the infinitely perfect being possesses, requires that there should be in him the idea of right and the feeling of good will, which, whenever contingent existence should be created by him, would find in him a disposition to beneficence—pure and perfect love, or delight in its welfare, and a disposition in every way possible to provide for its greatest good. That perfect notion was eternal in him; it was of his nature, as much as power, wisdom, intelligence was of his essence. It belongs to a perfect nature. But he was a person as well as a nature, that is, he had power of self-determination. His ethical character as the actually good and holy did not consist simply in his nature, but for its completion required action. His primal unchangeable act of free self-determination was to the good of being and his own as well. He chose the good and thus passed from a perfect nature to the character of a holy person. His choice is final, so that his holiness is eternal as to the future, and before temporary things as to the past. Self-consciousness of a being who possesses all power gives him the necessary knowledge of all possibilities. The ethical intelligence indicates what among the possibles is best; it is called wisdom or the discernment of best ends and best methods or means to realize the best ends; so far the essential nature carries, but now the being confronts a question which he, as free, must as a person determine, whether he will choose the best—the good which wisdom points out. His character depends upon that choice and the efficient volitions which freely follow it. As every other being to acquire ethical character must be under this law, so must the highest. His purpose to create a universe and the kind of universe chosen, if governed by the highest wisdom and the purest beneficence, and if unchangeable, all of which we know to be, constitute him the perfectly and unchangeably holy God. Purposes condition and make ethical quality.

The free act of determining to regulate his handling of himself according to the dictates of wisdom and goodness gives eternal worthiness in an infinite degree to the divine character. It was the initial, primary act of the eternal will—but it was a free act and was not an inherence of necessary being, as no determining act of a free and therefore moral being can be. A perfect nature necessarily existing can have no personal merit in it; it has a kind of worthiness, but not moral quality. Moral quality depends upon freedom, but is not inherent in freedom. It must be personal, and is created by a personal act; it cannot exist in a thing; it cannot exist of necessity. A driven machine cannot be ethically good or evil. God is perfect goodness and absolutely holy, because he freely determines himself to the perfectly good. The infinite glory of his character does not arise from the fact of eternal existence and the inhering attributes of his unchosen nature.

It is impossible that these should constitute him personally worthy of homage or love. That must depend, as in the case of every other being, upon how he freely uses his power. "He is glorious in holiness," because of his determination of himself to goodness, righteousness, and truth. To assume that his necessary perfections are such that he could not determine himself otherwise is not to show that he has a perfect moral character, or even moral nature, since moral nature implies freedom, but that he has no moral nature at all. He is good because he wills to be good. He is infinitely good, that is, there is absolutely no defect in his moral character; not because it is impossible he should will otherwise, but because he freely and unchangeably determines himself to be absolutely good. Being infinitely wise he can make no mistake; his knowledge is perfect; he has absolute power over his acts, and power to accomplish the choices he makes—to do whatsoever he wills; he is immutable in his nature and unchangeable in his self-determination to the good. This is the ground of confidence that all his creative and administrative acts are, and will forever be, perfect in goodness and righteousness. It is his glory that he is the unchangeably good. It could be no glory if it were not a free choice—if it were like gravitation, a necessity. The universe might be safe if it were possible that impersonal force working infallibly to ends of safety and welfare reigned over it, but the supposition is inconceivable; but were it possible, it would forever be impossible to feel toward the impersonal sovereignty the sentiments of reverence, worship, love. Such a sovereignty could be a fate, but could not be viewed as ethical. It could beget confidence of safety, but it could not beget in the soul the feeling that the administration springs from a holy personality. The moral nature—the conscience and heart of man—and reason itself demand that a person shall be on the throne of the universe; a person that can be loved, adored, and worshiped; a friend, a sympathizer; one who feels, and who understands the feelings of his creatures; not an irresistible fate, but a loving Father. Banish personality and leave mere force, no matter how beneficently it works, the heart becomes an arid waste, and the affections shrivel and perish; hope dies; prayer, the last refuge of the soul, becomes impossible; there is no more place for gratitude; praise ceases; not a single flower of the affection blooms in the desert waste of life.

It answers all the demands of theology, natural and revealed, and accords with the dictates of the highest reason, and the teaching of revelation, to say that all finite existence is by the will, and under the domain of an absolutely holy Being—holy before all creative acts and unchangeably holy forever and ever, but self-determined in his holiness.

Dr. Pope is responsible for the paradox that "absolute necessity is perfect freedom."* We assert that a balder paradox was never penned. If we suppose his meaning to be that the absolutely perfect *must* act in accordance with absolute perfection or he could not be the absolutely perfect, we answer that by bringing him thus under the law of necessity we not only contradict the position that he is the most free, but we contradict the position that he is the most perfect, for we deprive him of that which is the highest perfection, namely, a moral nature and personality. That which ought to be affirmed is that the most perfect *will, not must*, infallibly, but not of necessity, act according to his perfect wisdom and goodness. This is the only position which will admit of freedom and moral perfection in the divine nature, and the only one that is consistent with personality and a holy character in God.

But it is affirmed by some of the ablest thinkers that after all it is possible that a free purpose can be as eternal as the attribute of freedom itself; that there is no impossibility in the posi-

* *Compendium Christian Theology*, vol. i, p. 309.

tion that any act, even a creative act, may be eternal or coexistent with an eternal being. That an eternal being may have a form of activity which is of his essence is not disputed. Being implies it. If intelligence be an inherent attribute of his essence, self-consciousness is an implicate of his existence. These are eternal forms of activity. If power, wisdom, love, and freedom are of his essential being, self-consciousness is active with respect to them, and the feeling that he can do whatever he wills to do is a form of eternal activity which belongs to being itself. The range of pure subjective activity to the most perfect nature may be as infinite as the nature itself. Solitariness does not produce sterility; for in the infinitely perfect there is infinite potential variety and infinite enjoyment of existence. The actual infinite is excluded as unnecessary to him and as forever other from him: it is nonexistent and he is existent; it can never be without him, but he is without it. Without that mode of activity which would issue in finite existence there might be a true thought life, and a true moral life, simply in subjective exercises; all possibles, conceptions, and ideals would be open to him, and the moral approval of the good and disapproval of the evil which the ideals suggest, which approval and disapproval would be moral affections and of the nature of moral action—self-determinations. Thus there is a necessary distinction between God and his free purposes. He is not his purposes, but cause of them. They are contingent upon his free act; he is not contingent upon his act. They are purely subjective and unconditioned, except as he conditions them; he as to being and attributes is necessary and unconditioned even by himself, as he cannot condition his own existence any more than he could create himself. And no more can he condition his own eternal perfections. He does condition his own acts. They are not of his necessary nature, and are not necessitated by it, but are his creation and are free.

But if now we pass beyond these purely subjective exercises, and conceive an act by which nonexisting things are created, we come to an act which is conditioned by the thing to be made, and pass beyond the merely subjective to the objective. It is impossible that this act of efficient causation of the new existence should be eternal. Any objective movement toward the nonexistent involves contingency and excludes necessity and eternity. Whatever is eternal includes the quality of the necessary, and excludes the quality of the contingent or merely possible and free, since whatever is eternal cannot not be.

The purposes of God are grounded in his wisdom, power, and goodness. He has no purposes which are not in accord with and which do not arise from these eternal attributes, by a free act of self-determination. That he has perfect knowledge of these only implies that he is self-conscious—is a person.

The knowledge of himself is as eternal as his self-consciousness is, and as perfect and exhaustive. It leaves nothing, so far as his infinite being and attributes are concerned, to be known. And his omniscience includes the knowledge of all events which will flow from his purposes. Thus there is nothing that can ever come to pass in the remotest future, which is in fulfillment of his purposes, which is not from the time of his purposing fully and perfectly known to him as certain to occur and be as purposed. He needs only to know himself to know all things which he purposes to effect, in the exact order in which they will arise. Present knowledge of his purposes before creation began was absolute prescience of all events connected therewith and predetermined thereby.

But it must be observed that this form of omniscience relates simply to self-knowledge and effects produced by predetermined personal agency; that is, it is knowledge of his attributes and of what he himself will do directly or by necessitated second causes. It is a complete knowledge of the universe in all its history, so far as it is a created and necessitated product.

What appears with perfect clearness is that for rational thought the world ground is a being of infinite wisdom. The proof of this is found in the continuance and ongoing of the system. But a popular theological idea of omniscience includes more than this. All but the most obtuse mind must advance so far. But the common theological idea goes further. It holds to absolute omniscience. It adds to the idea of a wisdom which is capable of devising the world order, and providing for its harmonious and faultless ongoing, absolute knowledge of all the events of its history. It goes yet further, and believes that this knowledge is not simply a knowledge of events coetaneously with the occurrences, but a perfect prescience of them, in their exact relations of space and time, from eternity. It ventures even beyond this, and does not doubt that all possibilities are likewise known unto God, and that all this infinite knowledge is immutably in his consciousness.

The attribute of omniscience is not, in theological thought, the power to know all things, but the conscious knowing of all things. There is this difference between the attribute of omniscience and the other ineffable attributes of the Infinite nature. Omnipotence does not imply its exercise in order to its existence. The eternal consciousness with respect of it is the consciousness of ability to do all things that can be done. It might be complete, and was complete, before he put forth a single act or exertion of it. Not so with the attribute of omniscience. The consciousness in this case, it is assumed, is not a consciousness of ability to know, but of *de facto* knowledge of all things. There is doubtless a difference between the power to know, and knowing, and a difference between a consciousness of a power to know, and the consciousness of actual knowledge. This is a difference which appeals to our consciousness. We are conscious of a power to acquire knowledge, even as we are conscious of knowing some things. But this is the consciousness of a limited and improvable intelligence. If such were the consciousness of God, it is assumed that it would degrade him at once from the All-perfect to the grade of a finite and imperfect being. It is not necessary that he should do all things in order that he should be infinite in power; but it is necessary that he should actually know all things in order that he should be perfect in knowledge.

There is a phrase in extensive use among theologians, even those who are most careful of statement, in treating of omniscience to this effect, and often in these exact words: "Omniscience is that attribute of God by which he eternally knows all things and all possibilities." The phrase "all possibilities" is so employed as to imply that God is eternally conscious of everything that is possible to his power, and all things that might by possibility arise from any other source. Rightly guarded it might represent a truth, but it is frequently so put as to convey the idea that there is forever present in conceptional form an infinite number of things that never did have, and never will have, existence. It is sufficient to say that omniscience is the perfect knowledge of what has been, is, or ever will be.

But does the answer to the question which has now been reached satisfy the demands of the question, What is meant by the divine omniscience? It has been simply affirmed that God perfectly knows himself and of all forms of existence and of all events which he efficiently purposes shall be. Is this all? So a popular form of theology has long taught. It declares that there is nothing of being or event that God has not determined shall be, and therefore to know himself and his purposes is omniscience. It is an easy explanation of infinite knowledge, but for many reasons we find ourselves unable to receive it.

There is a universe of free beings. These, like the universe of things, he created, and to know of them, therefore, as to their existence he needs only to know his purpose that they should be—the time and place when and where they should have their existence and the kind of beings they will be, the external environments in which they should pass their time and their providential allotments. But he endowed them with freedom—power of self-determination, and other high emoluments of responsibility. Was he prescient, also, of how these beings would use their freedom? This is an entirely different question. To know necessitated things he needs only to know of his own acts, but to know of the determination of free wills is to know of the non-necessitated acts of other beings. It is obvious that this latter case is a much more difficult conception than the former. Are we to suppose it impossible? So many have thought, and for the thought they have alleged many plausible reasons. But the reasons alleged we are compelled to think collide with indisputable facts.

The difficulties embarrassing the idea of prescience, it thus appears, all relate to contingent, that is, non-necessitated, events. With respect to things which are comprised in a plan which is predetermined, and which God himself is to work out by his own direct agency, the doctrine presents no difficulty whatever, since it requires only that he should know his own purposes, which he will certainly carry out. Any idea of prescience which leaves God nothing to do in the ongoing of the universe but to stare at it as a fixed and finished piece of mechanism is no more to be tolerated than the idea that he acquires new ideas and forms new plans; both are equally false. What is perfectly clear is that his knowledge of his own work, and all that emanates from him, is so complete and perfect that it permits of no mistake or fault of any kind, and will admit of no improvement; is such that he will encounter no surprises and need to make no corrections; what he at first purposed he will carry out.

But when, now, we pass from the realm of things in which his efficiency is alone cause, and in which his wisdom is the sole determiner, to the realm of personalities, prescience becomes a much more perplexing problem. The Calvino-Augustinian theory that here, as in the realm of things, he fixes every act of every free agent by an unchangeable decree in such manner that the event must fulfill the decree simplifies the problem of prescience, but it does so at the sacrifice of the character of God and the utter overthrow of moral government. If the theory of divine prescience can be sustained on no other ground it must be at once abandoned as simply blasphemous.

There is certainly great difficulty in any view we may take of the question, but it is the common difficulty which we encounter whenever we attempt to deal with matters which lie in the obscurities of the infinite. Some things we can see must be; some we clearly know cannot be; others we imperfectly understand. Reason halts and hesitates for the want of clear light. The ablest minds do not reach absolute certitude. It is not modest to pretend that this is not a question of this kind. I quote from a few of the leading minds who call the doctrine in question; who either absolutely deny prescience of free acts, or who affirm doubt.

On the relations of the divine omniscience to the events of time Dorner says: "We have been obliged to affirm, if there is a world, no mere negative relation of God to it, to space and time, and their contents, but a positive relation, and thus the necessity has been proved to us that in the mode in which God knows everything not merely an eternal uniformity may be thought, but that there must be a movement in the divine knowledge in order that it may be a true knowledge, because a movement is seen in things, a decay and a birth, and thus God cannot always know the same things as present. But we were not able to discover as yet, in the ethical essence of God, how to combine this with his eternal self-identity. Growth and change cannot certainly be supposed in the divine knowledge in the sense that an absolutely new and unforeseen thing may present itself to him even by the agency of human freedom. For nothing can become real which was not possible; and the possibilities of all things are known in God from eternity. But still it is insufficient to think of God as not merely knowing everything at all times from eternity to eternity, but in spite of growth and decay simply knowing in the same way, as existing or present in eternal uniformity. For the divine knowledge is not in reality eternally similar, otherwise decay would be a semblance as growth would be. . . .

"Consequently in the interests of the truth of the divine knowledge, as well as in the interests of a living idea of God, there must belong to that divine knowledge, which alike eternally comprises everything necessary and possible, and which will be at any time existent, a knowledge also relative to time, and the present constitution of the world, individually and collectively, and concomitant with that constitution. The divine knowledge accompanies, step by step, so to speak, advancing time and the development taking place therein, which in the ultimate resort is certainly conditioned by Him who alone has deity. We must, therefore, say that God even knows what is past as past, and not as present, and knows the future as not yet being, and that only by that means does he know of the world of history; and can he have a relation there towhich is not eternally identical and rigid?"*

On the relation of the divine prescience to the free acts of the creature he says: "It is allowable to think the divine knowl-

* Dorner, *System of Christian Doctrine*, vol. i, pp. 329-331.

edge in the sense of a knowledge which is historical, and which advances with history, so that God does not know at all beforehand the free acts which will actually take place in the future, as such acts as will come to be realized before they have been freely done in time; or it is that which is eternally possible, but which has not yet become realized, immediately separated in God, who knows eternally everything possible, from those possibilities which attain realization by the agency of free causalities. . . . But if God's knowledge embraces different things to his will or himself, the question comes: Is God, in such knowledge, so dependent upon the thing known that only by the realization of free acts does he at all perceive that they will take place, or does he know the certainty of their realization previously?"*

His summing up to these questions is as follows: "At this stage we are only able to lay down the following points as suggestive positions relative to this question:

"1. Predestinationism is to be excluded, as well as the denial of all creaturely causalities, if freedom is to remain; but no less, if the absoluteness of God is to be preserved, must a falsely ethical and deistic mode of thought be excluded.

"2. Since God eternally knows all that is possible, future free acts are not to be excluded in every case from the divine prescience; God at any rate comprehends them as what is possible, since only the possible can become real; by virtue of his *scientia media* he knows in allcircumstances his own actions proportionally to the acts of the creature, however it may fall out.

"3. All that is real is at all times illuminated by the divine knowledge.

"4. But whether there is to be supposed in God a prescience of what free acts will really come to pass, or only a privity to

* *System of Christian Doctrine*, vol. i, p. 333.

those acts when realized, at any rate God does not become conscious of their actual *being* before they have become present. He does not know them as present before they have become present; just as, on the other hand, he is previously prepared by his *scientia media* for every possibility of realization." *

It is clear from the whole tenor of Dorner's treatment of the subject that his mind was in doubt as to God's prescience of unrealized free acts, with a preponderating tendency against the idea. The same is probably true of Rothe, while it is certain that Martensen entirely discarded the idea. He says: "The contradiction which has been supposed to exist between the idea of the free progress of the world and the omniscience of God rests upon a one-sided conception of omniscience as a mere knowing *beforehand*, and an ignoring of the *conditional* in the divine decrees. An unconditioned foreknowledge undeniably militates against the freedom of the creature, so far as freedom of choice is concerned, and against the undecided, the contingent, which is an idea inseparable from the development of freedom in time. The actual alone, which is in and for itself rationally necessary, can be the subject of unconditional foreknowledge; the actual, which is not this, cannot be so; it can only be foreknown as possible, as eventual. But such an unconditional foreknowledge not only militates against the freedom of the creature; it is equally opposed to the idea of a freely working God in history. A God literally foreknowing all things would be merely the spectator of events decided and predestined from eternity, not the all-directing Governor in a drama of freedom which he carries on in reciprocal conflict and work with the freedom of the creature. If we would preserve this reciprocal relation between God and his creatures we must not make the whole actual course of the world the subject of his foreknowledge, but only its eternal import, the essential truth it

* Dorner, *System of Christian Doctrine*, vol. i, pp. 336, 337.

involves. The final goal of this world's development, together with the entire series of its essentially necessary stages, must be regarded as fixed in the eternal counsel of God; but the practical carrying out of this eternal counsel, the entire fullness of actual limitations on the part of this world's progress, in so far as they are conditioned by the freedom of the creature, can only be subject of a conditional foreknowledge; that is, they can only be foreknown as possibilities, as *futurabilia*, but not as realities, because other possibilities may actually take place. In thus asserting that God does not actually foreknow all that actually occurs, we by no means imply that every event is not the subject of his penetrating cognizance. God is not only *before* his creatures, he is also with and in his creatures in every moment of their development. While God neither foreknows, nor will foreknow, what he leaves undecided, in order to be decided in time, he is not less *cognizant* and privy to all that occurs. Every moment of his creatures, even their most secret thoughts, is within the range of his all-embracing knowledge. His knowledge penetrates the entanglements of this world's progress at every point; the unerring eye of his wisdom discerns in every moment the relation subsisting between free beings and his eternal plan; and his almighty hand, his power, pregnant of great designs, guides and influences the movements of the world as his counsels require."*

Dr. McCabe, Professor of Philosophy in one of the leading universities, and an orthodox of the orthodox of Arminian faith, has written two very learned and able works in which the doctrine is called in question, and indeed as to the contingent acts of wills prescience is declared to be impossible. See his treatises on *Divine Foreknowledge* and on *Divine Nescience*. They are worthy of a careful reading, and present all the difficulties of the doctrine in their full strength. But it is not a question to be settled by

* Martensen, *Christian Dogmatics*, pp. 218, 219.

authorities. The position of Dr. Adam Clarke is well known as among the rejecters of the doctrine. The denial of the doctrine of decrees as held by the Calvinistic Churches has been so closely associated with the doctrine of prescience that all who deny the former are classed by some writers who ought to know better as denying the latter. In fact, Wesleyan Arminianism has held as firmly to the doctrine of prescience as Calvinists, but upon entirely different grounds. No abler defense has ever been made of the doctrine than that of Richard Watson, long regarded as the highest authority by Arminian divines. There can be no doubt that the imagined impossibility of prescience without some mode of fixing future events in inevitability in some such way as the doctrine of decrees does, has been the chief occasion for the revolt against the doctrine of prescience of the acts of free beings; but it is not the only ground. Many minds, and among them some of the most philosophical, reject it on other grounds. It must be regarded as an open question, though so almost universally supposed to be closed. There are difficulties which no theory successfully relieves; but there are also, it must be said, real difficulties, and, we must think, greater, which beset the rejection of the doctrine.

The position we hold, and shall attempt to defend, is this: God is an absolutely and eternally perfect Being, to whom nothing can be added, and from whom nothing can be taken away; who, therefore, is immutable and unchangeable in essence and attribute. Among his ineffable perfections is that of knowledge, which is so perfect that from eternity he has a perfect knowledge of all possibles and he has known all that he ever will or can know—all, whatsoever, that ever can be matter of knowledge; that, antecedently to creation, he not only knew himself as to all his powers and attributes, with all the primary and secondary effects that would be caused by him to exist; but, further, that such, from his eternity of being, including in himself all time, is his relation to all free beings that he knows not only what they do and all that they do at the time of its occurrence, but has, before they had existence, and, indeed, before there was any being but himself, known all their free acts, as well as all their feelings, thoughts, notions, and purposes—that so his knowledge of events was originally all prescience as to events themselves. All events were as to themselves once nonexistent; as to Him who is eternal they are forever existent in knowledge as they will be when they become real in fact. Thus, if our position is sound, omniscience covers all beings and all events, whether free or necessitated. The events are known in themselves, and not simply in their causes. They are forever present as cognitions in the consciousness of God as they are, that is, as having been, being, or to be, the mode of the knowledge being determined by the actual case. The mode of the knowledge differs, as the objects differ, but its substance does not improve or increase.

The ground of omniscience here affirmed is found in the eternity and infinite intelligence of God. His eternity is such as to include all time history as forever *present* with him, but also as progressing in themselves in a time order.* It is a difficult, but absolutely necessary, conception. His omnipresence connects him in real presence with every event. Nothing occurs from which he is absent. It occurs not in every case by his agency, but it is in every case in his actual presence and under his observation. Nothing is, ever was, or ever can be hid from him, or wholly apart from him. Thus filling all time, and having all parts of time in his undivided and indivisible eternity, and filling all the boundaries of finite existence with his absolute presence, his infinite intelligence is cognizant forever of all events which transpire. The knowledge of all is simultaneous and permanent—it is simply beholding

* See discussion of the Eternity of God.

what is present and what can never escape from him. If he is everywhere, and if he is eternal, thus filling all time and all space, and if he is infinitely intelligent, it is obvious that he must know all things and know them eternally—know them as really and truly before they have existed as afterward. Their futurition is clasped in his abiding now. It is not necessary that they should actually exist in order to be known. If at some future time they will exist, and if the infinite Knower has a mode of existence which makes that future time present with him, then the event now nonexistent will be known to him as then actually existent. Nonexistent itself, it is not nonexistent to a knowledge which covers the time when it will be existent. The knowledge in the case is prescient as to the object; that is, it is a knowledge of it *before it exists*, and a knowledge of what it *will be*, but to God it is a knowledge of what is, because his present now or mode of being includes that future; but while known as existing in a time now present to God, it is also known as yet to be in itself nonexistent until it comes to be. In attempting to interpret omniscience—the all-embracing knowledge of the Infinite—we must remember that we cannot interpret his knowledge, or the mode of it, by our knowledge. All of his knowledge is direct, perfect, intuitive, independent; ours is indirect, superficial, dependent. We know things externally by observation, and only so much as they give us by perception, that is, phenomena; we know minds by witnessing the effects they produce, or by manifestations external. He knows things and minds internally in their constitution and essence. He is in all and pervades all, and directly cognizes all. He discerns thoughts, motives, unexpressed feelings, purposes, will-acts, as we discern things. To him as objects of knowledge, because of his eternity, they are real and actual before they exist. His insight is exhaustive and complete, leaving nothing for future discovery. Prescience is only another form of his knowledge, which transcends ours, and is in no respect more inscrutable. The moralities all ultimately lie in the interior action of free wills, and the power to cognize such actions is no more explicable to us than is prescience of them, when we remember that He who cognizes them by his absolute eternity is as really present with them, though in the far-away future, as he is when they are actually transpiring. But he must have this power, or it is impossible that he should know the real moral character of his creatures, and therefore impossible that he should administer in righteousness.

The difficulty of the problem of prescience as a mode of divine omniscience is not to understand how it is possible for him to be prescient of all events which are predetermined and fixed in necessity by his immutable purpose that they should be. Of all such events it is only necessary that he should know his own purposes and efficiency to be certain of their futurition.

But the difficulty here is to know the future acts of beings who do not yet themselves exist; who, when they are brought into existence, are perfectly free as to their acts, being determined thereto by no constitutional necessity, and by no external agency, either divine or creaturely.

The question assumes that there are such beings—beings who are constituted so that they act in absolute freedom; who in any case have the power when they choose one course of action to have chosen another, and whose choice is one of pure self-determination. Whether there are such beings or not is a mooted question, and whether there is any such freedom is matter of dispute; but allowing that there are such, the question is, Could their free choices be matter of prescience?

The position we maintain is that such free acts are prescient to God's omniscience.

The question is, Is it impossible to God to be prescient of the free acts of free beings, or must he wait upon the action of free beings to know what they will be? If we answer in the affirmative, then we have this as the result: God can only be prescient of such acts and events as are necessitated. Then, if there are free beings, he can know nothing of their future conduct and destiny. He cannot know that a single angel in heaven will not turn rebel against his throne and heaven itself become depopulated. He cannot know that any soul of man will ever be saved. He cannot know that the atonement will not prove utterly in vain. He cannot know that all intelligences will not ultimately sink into endless perdition. To secure certainty of knowledge of any event it must be brought about by necessitation. We think that it must appear that the principle is not a rational working principle. There must, to justify the existence of free beings, that is, the existence of a moral universe, be a possibility of prescience of the outcome, and a knowledge that it would not prove utterly disastrous. But to know this requires that it should be known that some free beings would so conduct themselves as to make being a blessing to them; that is, it must be possible to be prescient of the fact that they would act in such a way as to secure blessedness. But if prescience of some free acts is possible the prescience of all free acts is possible.

If there were no difficulties of sequence, it must still be admitted that the concept itself at first view seems incredible. In this respect it may not differ from other infinite attributes, but it lacks that overpowering obvious proof which make seeming impossibilities less. The idea of a mind that can grasp all present and past facts and hold them forever is amazing to us—a mind that penetrates the universe at a glance, so as to know it all perfectly: all atoms of matter—all their past mutations and present condition; and all minds—all their past thoughts, imaginations, feelings, purposes—their entire history to the minutest circumstance, so that nothing will ever be forgotten. The idea of such a mind, when we reflect on the extent of the universe in both time and space—the myriads of myriads of intelligent beings, each having a complex experience each moment of time—the millions of millions of changes occurring at the same instant—to think of a mind that can note all these and preserve the record complete so that all will stand in exact order in a permanent consciousness, is so amazing that nothing of difficulty is added when we project the thought further and assume that he also knows the future free acts of free beings as well as the past. If the first supposition can be true, the second may. It has no force to say that the knowledge of things that have not yet transpired seems impossible, since the other admitted fact seems equally impossible. Both facts awaken in us the consciousness that the Being of whom they are predicated is infinite, incomprehensible—out of comparison with finites such as we are—exists in a mode and is invested with powers that can never have adequate representation in our thought—is the topmost end of an ascending series, between which and the next is the impassable abyss of infinitude. His methods of knowledge differ from ours, as he differs from us. We cannot reason from one to the other. We can understand as well how he can know future events as how he can know thoughts. In fact, we know that in some way he does possess both kinds of knowledge. The knowledge of things contingent adds nothing of difficulty that is not already implied in the former facts. The whole subject of the manner of his presence with us and his power of cognition is involved in mystery, and the fact only is known.

I think it just to say that prescience of contingent events does not seem to my own mind absolutely necessary to a just and perfect administration of the universe. I can conceive how the Infinite might perfectly conduct the affairs of the universe by having an immediate and perfect knowledge of all events as they arise, by adjusting the administration to the exigency as it occurred. But evidently such is not his method, and were it practicable it would not seem so fitting or creditable as that he should have foresight of the results of his own plan, and not be under the necessity of adopting expedients necessitated by comparative defects of knowledge. It is not an answer to say that there would be no defect of knowledge, when there was nothing in fact existing to be known, which is the case with regard to events prior to the time of their occurrence. In one sense it is true; in another, it is not. But the supposition must be rejected on the grounds that it ultimately reduces God, as to his highest perfections, to the law of succession, and leaves him at the starting point of his moral administration in absolute ignorance of the tendency and outcome of his own work; and for the reason that his knowledge is infinite—that known unto him are all his works from the foundation of the world—and from the fact that he has shown perfect prescience of the thoughts, free volitions, and deeds of man, in innumerable instances, ages before the men themselves lived, as appears from the prophecies contained in the holy record; and in the fact that the scheme of redemption antedates creation, showing perfect foresight of the events that would arise. Along with the doctrine of omniscience, which is necessary to the current administration of the affairs of the universe, and to the final just awards for moral deeds, we accept the doctrine of prescience, even though it is incomprehensible to us.

The attempt to explain it by the Calvinistic scheme we must reject as impossible on moral grounds. That explanation is in substance this: God from eternity determined upon a plan of the universe so minute as to comprehend with perfect exactness all things and events that were to be—the detail of the plan was so minute as to include the slightest changes in the worlds both of matter and mind. This plan he determined should become real, and in order thereto he decreed the occurrence of whatsoever comes to pass, so that nothing comes to pass, or can, but according to his decree. What he decrees he efficiently causes, so that it cannot fail. In the world of matter he operates all the decreed effects by power and according to natural laws, which are only his fixed methods of action. In the world of mind he operates by motives and according to the laws of mind or freedom, but with the same inevitability of the event. Prescience, therefore, is simply the knowledge of his own changeless decrees, which must make certain the event—to know all is simply to know himself. It is a simple explanation, and makes it easy to understand how all events could be foreknown—in fact, it strips the difficult subject of prescience of its mystery. It differs, advantageously in some respects, from the theory of materialistic fatalism. That theory necessitates all events by reducing them all to the categories of cause and effect, so that each event is chained to its antecedent by inevitable causational force, and reduces mind and matter to unity, so that to know all future events would be simply to know the first cause, in its endless necessary evolutions—implying nothing more than power to look along a line of mechanical effects. In the end the theories are the same as to the certainty and inevitability of events. The one may or may not admit a God. If it allow of his existence, it reduces his method of creation and government to mechanical fate, and confessedly denies all freedom. The other makes God the only efficiency, and distinguishes between his method of securing the certainty of events in the two realms of mind and matter, reducing the latter to mechanical fixity, but asserting the law of freedom for the other, in an impossible and contradictory form. We reject both as immoral, and in the end, as we shall see, substantially one. But it is just that we should admit that we have no theory for explaining the how of prescience at all comparable to either of them, as to ease of understanding.

Foreknowledge is an accommodated use of language. In the real fact there is no foreknowing, but simply knowing. The state of the Infinite mind is an abiding state of simple knowing. The event which is known is future, and hence the knowing is called foreknowing, or foreseeing. Suppose an eye could be so adjusted as to see all the time the events of a thousand years. The result would be simple seeing; in it there could be no difference, such as past seeing, or future seeing, but simple seeing of the entire series all the time. The series would have before and after, but the seeing would not. So of knowing; if it is perfect and includes all events forever, in it there is no difference. But in the events there is a difference. At any time some part of the series has elapsed, some part is elapsing, some part has yet to come. The knowing is not affected by this circumstance. Even if we add the idea that the knowing is a knowing that some part of the events, as to themselves, are past, and some present, and some in future, this does not change the quality of the knowing. It is still simple knowing, and results not from some peculiar exercise of the power to know, denoted by a looking into the future. There is with the Infinite and Eternal no looking back and forward, but a simple seeing—no past, no future. That is, with him there is a coexistence of all time—no past, no future, but the fullness of all things and events forever in his knowledge. The coexistence in him of all things always makes the mystery of his omniscience. The seeing the whole universe at a glance would be to see it at a given moment as it then is. To see it from beginning to end as it will be forever in all its flow of changes, and hold the vision from eternity to eternity, is omniscience. The former implies an inconceivable power. The latter is *only* inconceivable. We can comprehend the one just as well as the other.

To some minds it is extremely difficult to conceive that an event may be foreknown as certain and yet not be inevitable. To them the doctrine that God foresaw all events from eternity is equivalent to the statement that he fixed them in absolute inevitability. But the one fact does not at all involve the other. If certainty did involve inevitability, it would then be true that no event has ever occurred, or ever will occur, that might not have been, for whatever will be was certain from eternity to be, whether foreseen or not. But it is impossible for the human mind to believe that all events, great and small, are *inevitable*—might not be otherwise; that no word has been spoken, no act performed, that might not have been omitted. The certainty of events conforms to events, and not events to certainty. Free beings have alternative powers, may do this or that; they are not shut up to inevitability. If what they will do is foreknown, they do not do it that it may conform to a foreknowledge which necessitates it, but the foreknowledge grows out of the fact that they will freely do it when they have power to the alternative.

Still, we cannot but feel that the choice of a universe with the absolute knowledge of all events, whether they be evitable or inevitable, does involve the Divine Being in responsibility, and place him in the light of seeming cause, as having chosen that whatever will be should be, that whatever is is because he willed to have it, and would not have been had he not willed it.

Let us try to see the exact truth. May we not conceive that many things are caused by God directly; that many others are caused by other beings, but according to his will; and that still many others are caused by other beings, but not according to his will? May not all sins be of this last class; nay, is it not certain that they are? Could they otherwise be sins? We cannot doubt that he has both relation and responsibility. They are in and of his universe, and could not be here without him. In a certain sense they owe their existence to him. Let us endeavor to see in what sense. To ascribe them to him as absolute Author and Cause would be blasphemous; but we cannot wholly disconnect him from them. Had he not created moral beings sin never could have entered his universe. He might, then, have prevented it. He did that which made it *possible*, and without which it would have been forever impossible. This cannot be disputed. It must be added that he did that which made it *possible*, with full knowledge that it would become actual. He knew that the creature he made would make it to be actual. So far we go. Others go still further. We dare not. It is difficult, even with these facts, to see the righteousness, much more to see the goodness, of his part in the dreadful history. The only possible ground of defense is that, though he knew it would come, he did not desire or cause it; did what he could to prevent it, without, in preventing it, he would cause greater harm than to permit it; so ordered that it could only come by abuse and misuse of his beneficent laws; and further, to hinder it would involve plans and processes that would make any creation abortive. He provided amply for its possible nonexistence. It serves no purpose of his. It is an intruder. True, it emanates from powers which he created, but he did not create them to produce it. He did create them to do the very opposite, and in the opposite to find their highest, and the highest possible, good; and that they might do this the *possibility* of the evil was permitted. But, it is said, after all he knew the evil would come, and his good would be destroyed; he ought not, therefore, to have created, since that which he meant for good he knew would result in evil. To this there is but one possible answer: He must have known that, despite the evil that would come, and much as it would mar his work, and much as he wished it might not be, it was for the greatest good that he should so create; better to have the system with sin, if he might not have it without, than not to have it at all. As Cause he has no connection with it, but only as noncause as not preventing it. As Cause he created the being who could as cause create sin, but who as cause also might refrain from it. The sin itself was not his product, but that of a free being, whom he restrained in every possible way, without destroying his freedom, from the act. It is here by his non-preventing, not because he preferred it, but in violation of his express command.

Still, it is said, what he knows will be will be, and we have no power to prevent it, and there is no use of concerning ourselves about it. The first part of the statement is true; the remaining parts are not true. What he knows will be will be. That is indisputable. That we have no power to prevent it is not true. It will be because we will have it, not because we have no power to have it otherwise. Therefore, there is reason why we should concern ourselves about it. If we cause the "will be" to be evil, when we have the power to make it good; if we make it evil, when we are able to make it good, and when we know that we ought to make it good, we shall find, when too late to remedy the mistake, that there was great reason that we should concern ourselves about it. We shall find that it is not God, or certainty, or prescience, or fate that causes what will be to be, but we ourselves. For no one but ourselves can be responsible. The only relation that God has to it is that he so made us as to make it possible, and that he did not interfere to prevent it. That is his responsibility. What is the effect of it? We are no more conscious of anything than we are that we are cause now, sole, absolute cause of our free deeds; we but delude ourselves when we attempt to persuade ourselves of some mysterious metaphysical necessity which subtly determines them. What consciousness attests now it will continue forever to attest, that our deeds in the sphere of morality are our *own*. The moral reason will continue to assert forever, as it does now, that our sins are in no sense caused by the plan or prescience of God, but that they are offensive to him; that he desired and provided for their nonexistence; that he did everything consistent with having a moral universe possible to prevent them, nothing to originate them; that whatever of shame and odium attaches to them attaches to us. On no other principle can an ethical universe exist. Obliterate it, and the idea of morality expires. God becomes sole agent in the universe, and his administration simply an administration of force, for its evil he is alone responsible, and the self-accusations existing in us are but refined methods of torture.

If the doctrine that personal acts are governed by motives without alternative power in the actor be true, then this is true, that no event has ever occurred, or ever can occur, that might not have occurred. If we are to understand that he arranges the motives, or in any way causes them, it is not possible that anything should be different from what it has been, is, or will be—there is absolute necessity pervasive of all being and events; for there can be no event of will without motive, and each event is produced by the adequate motive, and the motive is eternally fixed by determination of God. Motive is to the act, cause; it is followed by effect, as in any and every other case. Where is the possibility that any volitional act should have been different, if each one was necessitated by its adequate motive? There is absolutely no such thing as freedom, except the freedom of effects to be as caused—such freedom as matter has when it yields to gravitation. As gravitation is always present with matter, and always adequately attracts it to the mass to make impossible that it should release itself, so motive always precedes volition, and controls its action, so that no volition can be freed from its determinating power. All beings and events are thus locked up in the absolute fixity of necessary sequence. The idea obliterates the whole nomenclature of ethics as absolutely meaningless. And if yet further the motive be under the control of and created by God, either directly or by the constitution of the mind and its environments, so that it emerges by a fixed law, then he is the alone cause and the only responsible agent in the universe. If the admission of this theory were necessary to the truth of divine prescience, we could not hesitate a moment in renouncing the latter doctrine. There can be no evidence adduced in support of the doctrine of prescience of the acts and choices of free beings of comparable strength with the proof that such an explanation of the doctrine is false and impossible. The doctrine must stand on other grounds, or it cannot stand at all. The knowing a fact concurrently with its occurrence does not necessitate its occurrence; no more would the knowing of it before its occurrence. To assume that to know it before fixes it in necessity is to attribute causation to knowledge, which we know is not true. It is the causation of the event which necessitates its occurrence, and not the observation of it. If it should be said that in order to the knowledge of it it must necessarily exist, again we assert the knowledge of it does not make it *necessary* that it should, but simply implies that it will certainly exist, without determining anything as to whether it will exist by necessary cause, that is, a cause which must act, or simply an adequate cause that will freely act. A cause that freely acts produces effects as certainly as a cause that necessarily acts, and the events produced by one are just as certain of occurrence as the events produced by the other. The only difference in the cases is that the event in the one case could not be otherwise; in the other it might have been otherwise, but certainly will not be otherwise. In one case the knowledge that the event would occur might arise from the knowledge of the necessary cause from which it would take its rise, and the prevision would be simply the result of a knowledge of an existing causation which would necessitate it. This would be an easy way to account for prescience, but it would reduce the whole ongoing of mind to the pure mechanism of materialistic necessity. In the other case, it supposes a mind which sees events themselves and the operations of free wills which give them existence. It is more difficult to conceive of such a mode of knowing, but it is not impossible, and if it implies increased difficulty in this respect it escapes what is impossible on ethical grounds in other respects.

The fundamental fact that we must keep in mind is this: Knowledge is not causational of that which is known, and it in no way affects the fact of the existence of what is known; it is simple cognition of what is. This is so whether the fact be a present fact or a future fact—just the same in one case as the other. Present knowledge does not cause the existence of the thing known—has nothing whatever to do with it. Knowledge of future events in no sense differs; it is simple cognition of what will be; it in no sense causes it. The knower may be cause, or he may know that he is not the cause, and that some other agent is the cause. The cause, whether the knower or some other agent, is not in the knowing, but in the energy which produces the effect, and in the being who exerts the energy. We sit quietly in our home and see through the window what is going on in the outside street. Our seeing is knowing, but it is in no sense cause of what is transpiring in the street. Now, if we had the power to see it a thousand years in advance the case would not at all be changed; as our seeing when it occurred did not cause it, so our seeing a thousand years in advance would not cause it. We know things of which we are not the cause. So God knows things of which he is not the cause. If he is cause of all that he knows, and if he knows all things, he is the cause of all things—or whatever he knows he causes. If his knowing is not cause of what he knows at present, his knowing is no more cause of what he knows will be at some future time. Knowledge is not agency, but is simple cognition.

But, it is said, the knowledge of an event, whether present or future, is the certainty of its existence. Of this there can be no question. That which is known to be is; and that which is known will be in the future it is certain will be. But then, it is said, its inevitability is fixed before its occurrence—*it must be*. To this we answer, that does not follow. That certainly will be which certainly will be, whether known or unknown; but the certainty is not the equation of necessity—events will be that might not be. They may be certain, but not necessary. But then, it is said, when they are known as certain to be it is impossible they should not be—the knowledge makes the occurrence necessary. This brings us back to the point that knowing causes nothing, and that which does not cause an event cannot be its necessity. But then, it is said, it would be impossible to know it as certain if it were not fixed in necessity—if it were contingent; to know it, therefore, involves the necessity that it should occur even if the knowledge does not cause it. To this we answer that what is certain does not involve necessitation. What is certain may be inevitable because necessitated; but if there be free beings who do not act from necessity, they may act as causes, and events will follow just as certainly as if they acted from necessity; but their acts being free are not necessary, and so the effects which follow are not necessary, but if they follow they are certain, and if they could be foreknown they would be foreknown as certain, but not necessary.

The only point of difficulty is in the question, How can the free acts of free beings be known before they occur? When they have perfect power to act either of two or several ways, how is it possible to foreknow which way they will act? To this we answer: Of the how of such knowledge we have no theory; of the fact we cannot doubt. We have no such power of knowing. We cannot interpret the Infinite by ourselves. We see things that are. He sees things that will be before they exist. We see thoughts when we see them expressed. He sees thoughts directly and forever, and so of all free acts of free beings. He sees them not by seeing himself as determining that they shall be, but because he is forever present with all being, as well that which is not but will be, as that which is and has been, and because he knows what is in mind intuitively and not simply by manifestation. The how we do not attempt to explain.

We have no theory as to how God exists. There is positive proof that he does exist. We attempt no explanation. We have no theory as to how he is eternal. It is a necessity of thought that he is eternal. We have no theory as to how he is infinitely perfect. We cannot think him otherwise. We have no theory as to how he created the universe. The proof is that he did create it. We have no theory as to how he can be cognizant of thoughts. We are compelled to think that he is. We have no theory as to how he knows futuritions of free acts. To us the proof is conclusive that he has such prescience. We have seen that the difficulty in this case is no greater than in other cases with respect to which we can have no doubt. We have seen that the idea interferes with no other idea which we are compelled to accept; that it does not involve contradiction; that it does not collide with the principles of moral government; that it leaves man free and responsible for his acts; that it does not cast a shade over Infinite benevolence; that there is not an atom of proof against it; that any theory which seeks to escape it falls into no less difficulties than those which beset it, but really into greater; that the Calvinistic mode of explaining it is inadmissible on ethical grounds. So far we have progressed in the discussion.

We now allege briefly the reasons for accepting the doctrine. These are, first, in general, that it seems to be necessary to the absolute perfection of God; that the opposite view reduces him from the Infinite to the finite. Explain it as we may, it leaves the fact that there is a large department of the universe which he has projected, and by far the most important part, of the outcome of which he is absolutely ignorant; he has made creatures whose destiny he does not, and by assumption cannot, know. To us this seems to be a frightful conclusion—a conclusion which seems inconsistent with both his wisdom and goodness. If there be possible evils—and all admit there are —and if they are such as cannot be averted in a system including free beings, it would seem that at least prudence and beneficence would require that he should know the measure of the possible evil that would become actual, before he ventured upon the creation of such a system; but this would demand that he should know beforehand what these free beings would do, that is, that he should be prescient of their acts, and know that any disaster that would arise would still leave the result such as Infinite wisdom would discern to be better than that to be reached by any other system or by abstaining from any. It is not enough that he should know what he would do in any emergency that might arise. He must, to justify his creative act, know precisely the measure of the emergency, and know that it would involve only an evil which, despite it, would leave the good which could not otherwise be attained so immeasurably greater than the evil that it would justify his work as both wise and good. To be prescient of such an outcome he must be prescient of all free acts that would in any way affect it.

If we answer that God is ignorant of the acts of free beings before they have committed them—that is, that he does not know what they will be—it must be either because he does not choose to know them or because he cannot. To say that he does not know them because he chooses to be ignorant of them can scarcely be a creditable supposition to the Infinite, especially since it is a choice to be ignorant when it is most important for the vindication of his character that he should choose to be informed; and further, to say that he chooses not to know free acts, and therefore cannot know them, involves that he has the power to know them if he chose to do so. To say that he could not know them is a high judgment for the finite speck that we are to pronounce upon the Infinite. We do not say that the judgment is certainly erroneous, but that, for reasons which will be assigned, we are constrained to an opposite conclusion. The ablest defense of the position we have seen is that made by Dr. McCabe in his two learned and masterly treatises, *The Foreknowledge of God* and *Divine Nescience*. Much as we admire their ability, and feel the force of his reasoning, we have to confess ourselves not convinced, and still of an opposite opinion.

But, second, passing from these general grounds for rejecting the doctrine, we come to name some facts which cannot be reconciled to the theory—facts which show that he is prescient of free acts. The principle would be perfectly established by a single case, but we think revelation, which is God's personal testimony on the point, is full of them, in both implicit and explicit form.

The first case we allege in point is this : The atonement is declared to be an arrangement in the divine plan concomitant with the plan to create—from the foundation of the world (Matt. xiii, 35 ; Rev. xvii, 8 ; 1 Peter i, 19, 20). There is every reason to believe that the human creation would not have taken place but for a prearranged redemption. But this proves that God was prescient of human sin before it was committed; but it was impossible that he should know it without prescience of the free act of transgression. Prescience of sin was not merely prescience of the external act of transgression, but it was prescience of the interior revolt of the will against the divine command. For it was the interior act of the will which constituted the essence of sin for which atonement was needed and provided. If the atonement was prearranged from the foundation of the world, then was prescience of sin from the foundation of the world, that is, from the time when the world itself was purposed to be.

Sin is a free act, that is, a purely contingent act, or it is a necessitated act, that is, an act which was made inevitable, either by direct necessitation of the will, or by some constitutional and inevitable tendency thereto in the will. If of this latter origin, it locates the cause of the sin in God, and removes its guilt from the transgressor. In this case, to be prescient of the sin it was only necessary that God should be prescient of his own act in the same way in which he is prescient of his own act in the realm of natural events, the necessitation of which is in him. This is practically the view of Calvinism. But is this credible?

But if sin was not necessitated, but was an act of pure freedom, then the knowledge that it would occur, which is implied in a prearranged atonement, was prescience of a purely contingent, that is, free, act of the will itself. It was insight into the act of a mind which as yet had no existence. What was true in the case of the first sin may be true in the case of every sin. We confess ourselves to believe that it is a universal fact.

The second proof we name as compelling our assent to the doctrine is found in the numerous prophecies contained in revelation and establishing the impregnable bulwark of its defense.

These are numerous and convincing. We will not burden this discussion by the enumeration of them.*

The proof of prescience of contingent events derived from prophecy is found in the fact that the prophecy in every case preannounces events the occurrence of which shows absolute prescience of acts contingent on the decisions of wills which at the time of the announcement were not in existence, and whose existence at any future time was itself dependent on contingencies of freedom.

There is no possibility of accounting for these marvelous predictions, and their subsequent fulfillment, except by admitting what they constantly assume; that is, that they are forthgivings of a mind to whom the future is as open as the past or present, and who is able to see the decisions of wills, in anticipation, as clearly as he sees events in the chain of necessitation.

The attempt of Dr. McCabe to break the force of this argument we must think is a failure, and puts him in line with the system of Calvinian necessitationism, a system which he detests with unmitigated abhorrence. A libertarian of libertarians, for the sake of his argument he becomes a necessitarian, in part at least, and lends a kind of support to the system, to avoid which is the inspiration of both his treatises.

His argument first expends a good deal of ingenious force to prove that the acts of the will are not always free, but are in some respects, on occasions, under the law of necessitation; that it is possible for the will in some cases to be overpowered in such measure as to be bereft of its freedom. We do not question the correctness of the position. In every such case there is volitional action, and in no such case can there be either freedom or responsibility—the act, though the act of a characteristically free being, is in no proper sense a free act. The loss of power of freedom may be by abuse; in that case responsibility

* See *The Supernatural Book*, by the author; argument on Prophecy.

would remain not for the nonuse of power which had ceased to exist, but for the free course of abuse which had destroyed the power. Where there is no such loss of power, it is conceivable that a combination of influences may in some cases be such as to overpower a finite will. So much is freely granted.

Proceeding upon this principle, the argument explains the whole scheme of prophecy by denying that it implies any prescience of contingent events. The prophecy is not foresight of what will be by cognition of the free acts of those who are its subjects, but it is simply knowledge of a system of influences which God, together with environment, will bring to bear, which will constrain actions, and thus secure their fulfillment. I quote, that the author may represent his own somewhat peculiar theory. He says, in *The Foreknowledge of God*, pages 37-40 :

" The moment divine or diabolical influences are brought to bear on an individual will which are out of exact proportion to its strength of resistance, the will loses its freedom and comes under the power of the same law that rules material forces. True, the will requires occasions for its action. These occasions are reasons presented to the intellect, or motives presented to the sensibilities. These occasions of human volition, these influences, without which the will does not act, are, in the normal state of the soul, merely influential, but not causal; they are testing, but not controlling. But there are limits to our mental and moral forces, to our powers of endurance and of resistance, just as there are limits to our physical strength. Now, when these testing influences are out of proportion to the strength of the will, the will is simply overpowered, and its freedom of action, in that instance, is prevented ; it acts under constraint, and its accountability therefore is annihilated. These influences, in such cases, then cease to be merely testing or occasioning, and become causal. In these instances the reason of the will's action is not in the will itself, but outside of itself in causal antecedents.

"Hosts of perplexities have arisen from a failure to make this manifest and pregnant distinction. 'Because the will does sometimes act under constraint, under the law of cause and effect, therefore it always acts under that law;' and 'because the will does sometimes act under the law of liberty, therefore it always acts under that law,' are the hasty conclusions which have sadly bewildered theologians, especially in their interpretations of Holy Scripture. Doubtless both these kinds of causation are found in the action of the human will. Sometimes it acts freely from its own voluntary choice, sometimes consentingly, because objective influences overmaster its capacities of resistance or endurance. When the will acts *freely*, the incipiency of the volition is in the will itself; that is, the incipiency of the volition is *subjective*, and the will is active. When the will acts only *consentingly*, the incipiency of the volition is in the *objective*, and the will is not positively active, but passive, rather. In the *free* action of the will, the occasions of its volitions are merely influential, merely afford the necessary test. In the *consenting* action of the will, the occasions of its volitions are causal, controlling, and necessary.

"Strikingly in harmony with this rigid teaching of philosophy, the inspired apostle declares, 'God is faithful, who will not suffer you to be tempted above that ye are able, but will with the temptation also make a way to escape, that ye may be able to bear it.' In this passage, God assumes that reasons, motives, influences, and occasions for disobedience do exert a testing influence upon a free agent in his choices. He assumes that without these influences there could be neither loyalty nor manifestation of character worthy of reward; that they are indispensable to test adherence to the right; that it is possible to make a choice worthy of reward, or of punishment, when these influences are in due proportion to the moral strength of the free agent; and that the moment these influences are in excess of the strength of any person's will his free agency disappears, and his accountability for his choices ceases. He therefore pledges, in this passage, that on the arena of probation for eternity, in the actions involving responsibility, these influences shall never be disproportionate to the strength of the free agent. The moment the choices of a being are not the choices of a free agent, they become strictly the effects of causes *ab extra*, and can involve no moral character.

"Man is so constituted that his will can be brought under the law of cause and effect by bringing overpowering influences to act upon his reason and his sensibilities. God, therefore, can use him as an instrument in his hands. He can make use of him as easily as he can make use of fire, water, light, air, sun, moon, or stars. To deny that God can place man in such circumstances that his choices would not have or involve any moral character, or to deny that God can use man merely as an instrument, would be to limit Omnipotence, and prevent the possibility of a superintending providence. God uses the material universe, the animal and vegetable kingdoms, in carrying out his own various plans and purposes. He spake to Balaam through the mouth of a dumb beast, and he commanded the stars in their courses to fight for his chosen ones. So in like manner he uses intelligent beings with the same wise and benign designs. When he wishes to accomplish any end through intelligent beings he may bring such influences to bear upon them, or offer to them such suggestions, or mysteriously so lead them by some of the resources and instrumentalities within his almighty embrace, that the action of their wills shall be under the law of cause and effect. Such influences may be brought to bear upon them as to interfere with their free agency.

"In those acts of the will which involve moral character there must be occasions for the action of the will in choosing. If upon such occasions there be nothing to exert an *influence* over the choice, there could be neither test, character, nor reward. But if there be in them anything to *coerce* the choice, then there could be neither freedom nor accountability. The moment that degree of intensity is reached in the force of these occasions which determines the choice, free agency and moral character disappear from the arena of human action.

"Hence, if God desired a certain providential work to be accomplished five hundred years hence, he could predict it with absolute certainty. All that would be necessary would be to influence the will of some one then living with the requisite intensity to secure a consenting volition, or, as in many cases, an unconscious instrument. The volitions of such an agent would be necessary and foreseen, because forefixed. They would not be free, but in violation of the law of liberty."

He further says, pages 52, 53:

"Prophecies are certain; human actions, when free, are contingent. The reader, however, may reply that God foresees, with certainty, the future free actions of his prophetic instruments. If this be so, it must be either by looking directly at the human will, or at the objective attractions which may be presented to that will. But if you affirm that God foreknows future actions by knowing the objective attractions which may be presented to that will, you annihilate at once the distinction between the law of liberty and the law of cause and effect. The moment a future act is perceived only through the objective, in lieu of the subjective; the moment its securative cause is discovered and located in the objective surroundings, or in the motives addressed to either the reason or the sensibilities, in place of discovering and locating its incipiency in the subjective self, in the free causative will, that moment you inevitably sink human freedom into necessity, and make man a mere creature of circumstances. For, under such conditions, you are compelled to regard the will as acting under the constraint of the law of cause and effect, and not under the law of liberty; and you infer with certainty its action upon knowing merely the occasions of its acting. This mental proceeding is inevitable in regard to all events in the realm of material forces, of cause and effect. And this was precisely Jonathan Edwards's procedure when he bound fast the human will under the strongest motive. And after doing that, all the liberty he could claim for man was only the semblance of liberty, an irritating mockery of freedom—a will with the incipiency of all its volitions located in the objective. The uniform testimony of the philosophy of the current age supports our position.

"If it be possible for God to previse and to declare with certainty the future volitions of a free spirit, while acting under the law of liberty, it can only be by looking not at the occasions of the will's action, but at the source where alone its certainty can originate; namely, at the human will itself. But the free will of a future free spirit has as yet no existence whatever. Its future free choices are bound up in no existing causes. No existing causes can now give the slightest indication of what those future choices will be."

There is much truth in this statement, but we think that it is made to do more service than the element of truth in it warrants. That there may be an element of providential control in bringing about the fulfillment of some of the prophecies may be admitted; but that it overrides freedom is certainly not allowable. The scheme of prophecy is so broad as to cover almost the entire history of events, and to imagine that it involves an interference with the freedom of human agency in every case is an impossible conception, without endangering the doctrine of freedom itself, and introducing the idea of divine efficiency into almost the entire realm of human action. But its chief fault is the assumption on which it is based, namely, that it is impossible that free acts should be known, and therefore this explanation. Take that assumption away, and the whole ground for the theory is taken from under it. That assumption is without warrant. It is often alleged by Calvinists in the assertion that God knows the future because he has decreed it, and his power is pledged to effectuate it. The principle is precisely the same, only where Calvinism applies it to all events this theory only applies it to some. The principle, we think, is false, whether applied universally or limitedly. It is an infringement of Omniscience in either case. He may know events because he has predetermined them; he may know them because he purposes to bring them about by overpowering freedom, and by bringing human wills thus under the law of necessitation; but that he cannot otherwise know them is a restriction which is hazardous in the extreme, and which lacks convincing proof. The reason given in the closing sentences of the above extract is that future volitions are nonexistent, and therefore cannot be objects of knowledge. "No existing causes can now give the slightest indication of what their future choices will be." It is true that future choices of minds which at present do not exist cannot be known to finite mind, but to a Mind whose eternity lifts him above the limitations of time, who embraces the entire future in his existence, to whom the limitations of time do not apply, there is no future. God is not to be—he is. Things are to be—they are not; that is, those which are to exist hereafter. The future of things is present with him and in him, because he is in the future now as really as when it arrives. He does not wait for it to make revelations; to him it is here and now. It will give him nothing which he does not already possess. It cannot enlarge him. To suppose that it can is to make him finite and dependent, like one of us. In what respect does his knowledge differ from ours, if it bring him under the conditions of acquisition and growth?

On the principle on which the theory is built, that the free acts of wills cannot be known, that only those acts can be known or become matters of prophecy and promise in which he interferes and overpowers wills to secure their fulfillment, how are we to understand such promises as these: "I shall give thee the heathen for thine inheritance, and the uttermost parts of the earth for thy possession," and all such passages as predict the universal prevalence and triumph of the Gospel?*

In all these predictive promises the event was in the remote future. There were no existing facts upon which they were based, or from which they could be deduced as conclusions. The Scriptures are replete with explicit affirmations and implicit teachings which necessitate the belief that God knows the future as the past; that thoughts and interior secrets of minds are known to him as things are; that his knowledge is forever perfect; and that in this respect, as in all other respects, he differs from all finite intelligences as infinitude differs from finitude.

Are we to suppose that these predicted results are to be brought about by coercion of human wills? Calvinists might consistently take that position. It harmonizes perfectly with their system, or with any system of necessarianism. It explains perfectly how God could be prescient of the results. He need only know his own eternal decrees and his own efficiency to their realization to foreknow the fulfillment. In effect it is the doctrine of predestination in its worst form, including both election and reprobation as inevitable sequences.

But if we discard the doctrine how are we to interpret these promises? Must we suppose that they are mere guesses or sanguine conjectures? Either that or we must accept them as

* See Psalm ii, 8; Gen. xlix, 10; John xi, 52; xii, 32; Isa. xi, 10; liv, 3; lx, 3, 5; Jer. xvi, 19; Mal. i, 11.

the utterances of real knowledge—real prescience. If we accept them as such, then it follows that God is prescient of the actions of free causes; he sees with absolute certainty what distant generations of free beings will do. That he did so is in proof in the progressing fulfillment. The assertion that prescience in such cases is impossible is shown not to be true by the facts. It signifies nothing that we cannot understand how prescience is possible. The difficulty is not at all peculiar.

Most certainly Dr. McCabe is confused in his use of the word contingent when he criticises Mr. Watson and attributes confusion to him in his use of the term.* Mr. Watson correctly uses the word, not in the sense of doubtful or uncertain, but to describe a free, and not a necessitated, action. That is its philosophical use. To say that a thing could be known as certain which is not certain is absurd. Mr. Watson was guilty of no such absurdity. What he asserted, and what all respectable writers on the subject have held and do hold, is, that a free action may be known to be as certain of occurrence as if it were a necessitated action. The question is upon that point. The word contingent is used as synonymous of free or unnecessitated action. It is unfortunate that it should have been introduced, as it has two meanings running so nearly together that it is sometimes by even careful and usually clear writers and thinkers used interchangeably, and confusion is introduced.

A free action to be may be this or that. When the word contingent is used with respect to it, it means precisely that. How—that is, which way—a free mind will act is not determined by necessity, but is contingent on his self-determination. In fact, he will act one way or the other, and whichever way he will act, it was eternally certain to the divine mind that he would act that way; but if, as was postulated, he was free to either, it was as eternally certain that he might have acted the other

* See *Foreknowledge of God*, pp. 301, 302.

way. Now, what is affirmed is, that the divine mind is eternally prescient of which way he will act, when he had the power to act otherwise. If we use the word contingent to describe the act, we mean by it that it was not necessitated, that is, that it was free, and not to imply that it was doubtful. The predication would then be that God is prescient of free, that is, non-necessitated, actions. Dr. McCabe affirms that such prescience is impossible, and therefore introduces his argument on the subject of prophecies. These do not imply prescience of free actions, he says, for in such cases God overpowers the will, that is, destroys its freedom and necessitates its action. Mr. Watson affirms the very opposite, and is consistent in the affirmation. Contingency is not opposed to certainty, but is opposed to necessity.

But, once more, Dr. McCabe objects to prescience of free acts that the terms are contradictory; that is, that the foreknowledge or prescience of an act fixes it in necessity, makes it impossible that it should be otherwise. Here, again, we think, he falls into confusion, but the point is one of great difficulty. This is what he says:

"Richard Watson pronounces with much confidence that the argument that 'certain prescience destroys contingencies' is a mere sophism, and that 'the conclusion is connected with the premise by a confused use of terms.' 'The great fallacy in this argument lies,' he says, 'in supposing that contingency and certainty are the opposites of each other. If the term contingent has any definite meaning at all, as applied to the moral actions of men, it must mean their freedom, and stands opposed, not to certainty, but to necessity. The question is not about the certainty of moral actions—that is, whether they will or will not happen—but about the nature of them, whether they be free or constrained. The opponents of foreknowledge care not about the certainty of actions, whether they will take place or not, but they object to certain prescience of moral actions, because they think such prescience renders these actions necessary.' [1]

"And this is the best reply that one of the ablest of our theologians can give in answer to the argument that certain prescience destroys contingency. He charges 'confusion in the use of terms;' but in his refutation he himself is full of the same kind of confusion. His argument is not only a sophism, but it is one of the least reputable. It is a plain case of irrelevant conclusion. For, when we affirm that certain prescience destroys contingency, we are not then looking at the nature of the future act, whether it be a free or whether it be a necessitated act. A certain event is an event that will come to pass. That event may be in its nature either free or necessary. It may be the act of the Creator or the act of some one of his creatures. In this place, and in proving the proposition that prescience annihilates the distinction between certainty and contingency, we refer not to the nature of the future act nor inquire by whom it shall be performed, whether God, angel, man, or demon. We are simply looking at it as a *certainty*. If foreknowledge be true, every future event is now certain in the divine mind, and if certain in the divine mind it must be certain in itself. For perfect knowledge of a thing must correspond to the nature of that thing; and the thing must correspond to the perfect knowledge of it. [2] If I have a perfect knowledge of a reality, there must be a perfect correspondence between the reality and my knowledge of it.

"A contingent event is defined by all authorities to be one that may or may not come to pass. [3] Now, if God foreknows that such an event will be, how can that event ever be different from his present knowledge of it?"

The statement of Mr. Watson (see 1, above) is strictly correct. He is arguing for the freedom of events, and against the idea that prescience of the certainty of their occurrence is opposed thereto; and he properly says that certainty does not involve necessity; that is, that they may be certain and yet not necessary, but contingent, that is, free. It is perfectly apparent that he does not use contingent in the sense of not certain or doubtful, but in the sense of not necessitated, and in this he is exactly right.

Dr. McCabe's statement, that "For perfect knowledge of a thing must correspond to the nature of that thing; and the thing must correspond to the perfect knowledge of it" (see 2, on page 212), is perfectly correct—it is simply the equivalent that knowledge must accord with truth. But the question is, What is the knowledge in the case of a free act of a free being? and the answer to it is precisely that; that is, it is the knowledge that the free being *will* act precisely as prescience sees he will act; but the knowledge in the case is not that he had not the power to act otherwise, but is the very opposite of that.

The next statement made by Dr. McCabe (see 3) is not strictly correct. It would improve the statement to say, A contingent event is one which is not necessitated, and therefore that might have been otherwise. This correction entirely destroys the force of the statement which follows: "Now, if God foreknows that such an event will be, how can that event ever be different from his present knowledge of it?" The answer is the simplest possible: When God foreknows that an event will be, his knowledge cannot be different from what it is; but his knowledge in the case is that the event itself might have been otherwise, and then his knowledge would have conformed to that fact. The knowledge of it does not in the slightest degree make it necessary, but does show that it *will*, not that it *must*, take place.

"A contingency is a thing that may or may not be. But

can there be any 'may or may not be' between a perfect knowledge of a thing and that thing itself? God cannot know anything contrary to the fact; and a fact, when once a matter of certain knowledge, is unchangeable by any power, human or divine. If the treachery of Judas was foreknown it was certain; and if it was certain it could at no period be uncertain as to its coming to pass. Thus we see that one of the ablest of thinkers cannot rescue contingency from destruction, if certain prescience be maintained.

"And here we must be careful to distinguish between contingency as to the nature of an event and contingency as to its coming to pass. An event that is necessary in its nature may be contingent as to its happening. If I take forty grains of morphine my death will ensue necessarily. But there is a contingency as to the happening of my death as the result of taking morphine, because there is a contingency as to my taking the morphine; that is, my taking the morphine is an event that may or may not be. But as soon as my death, as the necessary result of my taking the morphine, is foreknown by Omniscience, there is no longer any contingency as to the happening of the latter event, nor as to my death coming to pass. An event, therefore, that is necessary in its nature may be contingent as to its happening. Moreover, an event that is contingent in its nature is contingent also as to its happening. A choice of my will is an event that is either free or necessary in its nature. We readily admit that the event is free in its nature; but the question is as to the happening of the event. We have no question as to the contingent nature of the event should it ever occur.

"If God foresees that A will forge a check to-morrow, while there will be a freedom in the nature of the act when it occurs, there is now no contingency as to its happening. If that choice of A be now foreknown, there is no contingency in the mind of God as to its happening. Its happening is a certainty to him. Even if the oft-repeated affirmation that foreknowledge can have no influence over the exercise of our freedom were true, it has not the slightest pertinence as to the question now before us. Even supposing that that knowledge has no influence over, nor any connection with, the freedom of the creature, with the free nature of his actions, it has all influence over, and a perfect connection with, the contingency of the happening of those actions, if they are foreknown. If God foreknows our choices, there is now no contingency as to their happening. The event will be free in its nature, but there can be now no contingency as to its coming to pass."

The whole of this reasoning, we think, evinces confusion on the subject of contingency, and loses sight of the real question. The assertion that "God cannot know anything contrary to the fact; and a fact, when once a matter of certain knowledge, is unchangeable by any power, human or divine," is perfectly true; but the question is precisely that we have just stated: What is the knowledge? It is not simply that an event will occur, but that when it does occur it might have been otherwise, and then the knowledge would not be what it now is, but different. The time of the possible other was when the event occurred, not afterward.

But then, it is said, the knowledge of it necessitates it; it must now be. Why must it now be? Because of the prescience of it? It has no connection with it to make it necessary. It does not at all affect the question of its existence. It is simple cognition. That which exact truth warrants us in saying is: It will be; it might have been otherwise.

The thing to be remembered is this: There is a perfect distinction between a free event and a necessitated event. Either may be foreknown, but the foreknowledge does not and never can obliterate the distinction between certainty and necessity.

When an event that might have been otherwise is known to be as it is or will be, it will certainly come to pass; but it will always be true that it might not have been. If we suppose a mind that was prescient of it a thousand years before, but who had no connection whatever with its occurrence except to foresee it, it remains and must remain a fact forever that it is not an event that might not have been otherwise. God's knowledge of what will be may be a knowledge that he will cause it to be. In that case the knowledge involves the fact not only that it will be, but must be—he will cause it to be; or it may be a knowledge that some other being who had power to cause or not to cause it will cause it. In this case the event is not, and cannot be, necessary, and his knowledge will always correspond with that fact. It is, therefore, not true that foreknowledge or prescience of an event makes it *necessary* that it should occur, but it is true that it makes it certain that it *will* occur. If it will occur, it will occur, and it was forever certain that it would, whether known or unknown, in the one case just as much as in the other. If at the time of its occurrence it was possible for the cause of it not to have caused it, it will forever remain true, whether known or unknown, in the one case as much as in the other, that it was not a necessary event, but might have been otherwise.

We now come to examine directly what has been supposed to be the real difficulty in the way of this doctrine. It is supposed to interfere with the doctrine of human freedom. The difficulty is to reconcile the two ideas of *prescience* in God and *freedom* in man. It might not be possible for us to reconcile them, and yet they might both be true. Our inability alone would not, therefore, be a sufficient ground of denial, unless we make our ability to harmonize truth the measure of truth, which it is presumed we are not vain enough to pretend. The two ideas may be respectively supported by such indubitable proof that we could not rationally reject either, and yet to our faculties they might seem to be irreconcilable. We should in that case be compelled to accept them, confessing at the same time that they seemed to be inharmonious. This is precisely the state of fact with regard to the doctrine of the omnipresence of God, and yet his non-relations to space; the infinite love of God, and yet the certainty that he will punish some souls that he has made to all eternity—the eternal certainty of acts which are contingent. The difficulty lies not in the facts themselves, but in the limitations of our faculties. In such cases we are not at liberty to deduce conclusions from our infirmities. Any system that predicates foreknowledge of the actions of human wills on the ground that they are causationally determined beforehand is inconsistent with the doctrine of human freedom; but that is not so of simple prescience. Knowledge is not causation, and has in it nothing of the nature of causation. The whole supposed difficulty arises from confounding certainty with necessity. The two terms are not equations, having nothing in common. *Any* future event is certain in precisely the same manner and degree, whether known or unknown. No event has ever occurred, or ever will, that it was not certain from eternity would occur, irrespective of its being known or unknown. An act or event perfectly free in itself is as certain as if caused by absolute necessity—certain, in the one case, as emanating from freedom; in the other, as caused by necessity; but in both cases always certain. The Infinite knows necessary things as necessary, free things as free. The knowledge of an event has nothing whatever to do with its occurrence; whether it be foreknowledge in no way affects it. The act is the act of one mind; the cognition is the perception of another mind; and the two minds are wholly disconnected, or individual units, persons, in their respective acts. Nothing is more certain than this, and nothing more important. It is said : Yes, but if an event or act of one mind is foreseen by another mind, it must necessarily come to pass. We answer : No, that does not follow. It follows that it will certainly come to pass, but that is not the same as saying it must necessarily come to pass. It may come to pass freely, and be just as certain as if it came to pass necessarily; and in that case, if the foreknowledge were perfect, it would embrace precisely this state of facts. The event will certainly come to pass freely, and not necessarily. Being free, it might not have come to pass, and prescience would then be precisely opposite to what it is—would be that the event will not come to pass. If the event is a necessary event, the prescience would be the event will certainly come to pass, and necessarily. But in either case the knowledge would have no influence whatever on its contingency or necessity. The sources of contingency or necessity are wholly independent of the fact of knowledge. Knowledge simply sees what is—causes nothing. Place an eye up in heaven, and let it look down upon the earth, and it, if open, will behold what is going on among men; but the transaction will go on all the same if it be shut; its being open or shut causes nothing. It is precisely so of the omniscient eye of God. What is free it sees as free; what is necessary, as necessary.

Certain events are *not inevitable*, if free. They might be otherwise—there is nothing to hinder or prevent that they should be; there is power sufficient to have made them so, and if that power had been used differently from what it is, and it might have been, there being nothing to hinder, the certainty would have been different, and prescience would have seen it otherwise. There is not, therefore, the slightest difficulty in reconciling the foreknowledge, or, better, the simple knowledge, of God and the freedom of man. There may be other difficulties growing out of the doctrine of prescience. This is not one. Is it said that what is foreknown as certain *cannot* be changed—men cannot make things different from what they will certainly be? We answer: This implies, if it mean anything, that men are not able to make their acts different from what they are. This we deny. They freely make things as they are, and they could make them otherwise; and they are conscious of that fact. They make the certainty, and they have the power, in every case in which they make it as it is, to have made it different from what it is. That it is as it is is their fault or praise, and not the fault or praise of some necessitating power that dominates them.

GOODNESS OF GOD.

THE question arises, How could a good and merciful God not simply permit evils, but, what is infinitely more inconceivable, organize a universe with the foresight of them? Foreseeing them, why did he not estop their occurrence by withholding existence in all such cases? How could he impose existence when he knew, whether necessary or not, it would in fact be only curse? There is no escaping the feeling that at a superficial view it seems discreditable and impossible—a procedure which we would condemn as abhorrent in a creature such as we are, much more in a Being of infinite resources. We shall not pretend that we do not feel the difficulty, or that any explanation of which we know is perfectly satisfactory; but we see no way of escaping the belief of the apparently conflicting doctrines, and must therefore offer such relief as is possible, which, if it do not satisfy, may nevertheless mitigate in some degree; assured, meanwhile, that ultimately, whatever be the fate of the doctrines, infinite goodness will be vindicated. But before passing we assert that the difficulty is not relieved by denying prescience, but is rather increased. To create beings who might become exposed to eternal evil is the real difficulty. The knowledge that they would adds nothing to it. Take that away, and then it would remain that he created with the possibility that every soul would be lost. It is a relief that, being prescient, he knew that the large majority would be saved.

The first method of reconciliation offered is that the divine goodness is in no way responsible for the evil in question, since the creature incurs it by his own voluntary misdeeds—it simply declares his own ill-deserts. Being was conferred for a benevolent end; his endowments were bestowed as means to utmost good; the scheme was fitted with infinite pains and perfect adaptation to the ends of well-being. That evil ensues is because of voluntary abuse of goodness for which the sufferer is alone responsible. Suffering never exists for itself's sake, but as unavoidable incident or possibility of the good, and in that case it becomes a possible concomitant of good, though not a good in itself. If, for example, it should be a fact that, incident to the creation of a universe in which a vast amount of happiness should be secured, some suffering would be certain, it might not only not be cruel to create, but it might be cruelty not to create. If it were certain that a moral creation would be on the whole productive of the greatest possible amount of good, and also perfectly certain that some beings would abuse their freedom and come to utmost evil, the question then would be, Would goodness demand that the certain happiness of the virtuous and deserving should be prevented, in order to prevent the self-superinduced evil of the vicious? It is doubtful whether any consciousness would so affirm, and especially if the creation, on the whole, to a vast portion should be a good, and to a small part only be made a curse by their own wickedness. It must be apparent that in such a case creation would be the imperative dictate of love, since it would be the best thing possible to infinite wisdom and power, and since the attendant evil would be not attributable to the Creator, but to the sinning and consequently suffering creature. The utmost demand that can be made on goodness is that it should secure the greatest possible good with the least possible evil. This we cannot doubt is the precise case. Foreseen evil is permitted on no other ground than that it cannot be hindered under a system which assures the greatest amount and highest quality of possible good, and is also not a part of the system itself, but the result of its wicked abuse, and so not chargeable to the Author of the system.

But the remaining difficulty seems still more embarrassing. It is the difficulty of explaining the conduct of the divine Being, as described in the Scriptures; namely, in employing means and methods to dissuade men from the acts which he eternally knows they will certainly commit, and then charging the failure of the means against them as crimes, and making it the ground of deeper punishment. This, it is alleged, is not only inconsistent, but is a species of disingenuousness unworthy of a great and holy Being. At first view it must be confessed that it has that appearance. But is it so? What is the real case? It is this: A soul is created and placed under law to God, which law prescribes right conduct, to which the soul is bound. It promises good to the obedient and threatens evil to the disobedient. It is within the power of the soul put under law to obey or disobey, as it may freely choose. It is so constituted that it can be influenced. Is it not the duty of God to employ all suitable influences to secure obedience? Could he be excused for neglect? Would the fact that he foresees failure in some cases excuse him for not making use of every proper influence, and thus relieving himself of the otherwise inevitable charge of criminal indifference? In other words, is not the only ground on which failure could be permitted precisely the ground on which he places it, that he did all in his power to prevent it? He tried his utmost to save, and the sinner would not permit him. Must he not, as the infinitely good, employ all means proper to induce the free being to pursue such a course as would insure his well-being, and must not failure be permitted only when it could not be hindered? That the blame of failure may rest with the culprit all possible opportunities must be furnished him. He can have no fair trial without this; and the fact that the Sovereign knows that he will not be influenced does not excuse him from furnishing the opportunity of giving proof thereof. Nor does the knowledge that efforts will fail imply disingenuousness in using them. The knowledge is that they ought not to fail, and that their failure is crime. The invitation and entreaty are not rendered insincere because they are rejected.

Foreknowledge or ignorance of the result determines nothing as to the sincerity or insincerity of the invitation. The case is this: The thing required is a thing right in itself—a thing that must be required. The party on whom the requisition is made is perfectly able to comply. The party making the requisition sincerely desires compliance. Influences are employed which ought to prevail with the responsible party. The influences ought to be used. This is the whole case. The moral government of the world must proceed on principles of righteousness, precisely as if the issue were wholly unknown. The knowledge of the outcome has no connection whatever with the case, and cannot in justice influence the relation of the parties. These are determined on other grounds. The case is not the same as is often assumed—that in which the result is fixed by decree. In that case there would be manifest insincerity in the use of means and persuasions to the contrary, since the decree makes the contrary impossible. The Author of the decree could not be sincere in employing means to induce acts which he himself by sovereign decree rendered impossible.

Fundamentally, moral being must be put on trial. The trial, to be fair, must be under the best and most favorable circumstances. Some will fail. They must incur punishment. The Infinite from eternity is cognizant of all the facts as they are— the fact of his own desires, his elations to the subject, his gracious helps furnished, the subject's circumstances in minutiæ, his temptations and ability to resist them, his willful and persistent sin, his consequent ruin. We may not suppose that his certain ruin being foreseen all the antecedents are useless and might be omitted. The destiny of a moral being cannot be separated from all the antecedents that contribute to it. The knowledge that a given case will eventuate in a given way, favorably or unfavorably, does not furnish a reason why the destiny should be fixed without the antecedents.

Here we rest the doctrine of divine omniscience. It is clearly the teaching of revelation. It is not in conflict with the freedom of created moral beings. It is not inconsistent with the goodness of God. It is not inharmonious with his conduct in the administration of moral affairs. It is exhibited in the permanence and accuracy of all laws in the natural and moral realms. It is indispensable to the righteous government of the universe. No moral being can be justly judged and recompensed without it. Each thought and motive and feeling and deed, together with the modifying circumstances of natural organization, association, education, amount of faculty, opportunities of knowledge, with all other things of every kind that influence character and action, of each of all the million souls whom he shall judge, must be perfectly known, in order to a just and righteous decision. Nothing short of absolute omniscience will be equal to the mighty task. And as all things are in him and of him forever and forever we may be assured that not the slightest defect or failure can occur in his administration throughout eternity. If the thought be bewildering to us we have only to reflect that we are dealing with the Infinite—the actual Author of all being—the eternal Spirit, of whose power and wisdom the universe itself is but a feeble reflection. Mites that we are, we can but worship with speechless wonder, evermore rejoicing that He whom we adore so transcends our utmost thought, and yet so shelters us in the bosom of his love, and so guards us with the overshadowing and encircling ægis of his power and omniscience.

In conclusion, we recapitulate what seem to us the conclusions fairly reached on the subject of divine omniscience:
1. That it includes the knowledge of all events from before the beginning of creation. 2. That its source is in the eternal self-consciousness of God, which possesses him of a perfect knowledge : (*a*) Of himself as to nature and attributes from eternity; in this respect and so far forth his perfect knowledge is complete and also eternal; that is, there never was a time when he did not possess it; it is an inherent and essential attribute of his being. (*b*) In the same eternal self-consciousness is also a complete and perfect knowledge of his purpose with respect to his own acts which will occur in time or under conditions of succession, and of all the effects that will flow from his acts in their exact order and content in the endless future; which, in effect, is simply the knowledge of his purpose and acts in perpetuation or continuance. (*c*) In the same eternal self-consciousness is also a complete and perfect knowledge, but arising from observation, of all events brought into existence by the action of free beings other than himself; which, together with the knowledge of his own acts, embraces the knowledge of all events that ever have occurred in all past time, and also events that ever will occur in all future time.

Thus his knowledge of himself as to his being and included attributes is simple self-consciousness of what is immutably permanent, and is not in any sense prescience, or knowledge of what will be; but his knowledge of what he will do is eternal prescience of his own acts as they will arise in time, but which are not existent from eternity, as his being is.

His eternal knowledge of other creatures and of their acts is primarily prescience, as to themselves; that is, it is a knowledge of what will be and not what is, which changes its mode as the events come to realization, and becomes the knowledge of what is, and when past becomes the knowledge of what has been, but in substance is identical, conforming to the order of events. There is no defect in his knowledge, and no addition to it; but its mode changes as events change from what at first was knowledge of what will be to what is or what has been. The power thus to become possessed of prescience of events from all eternity, brought about by creatures in time, is by simple observation, and not by causation of them, and arises from the peculiar mode of his existence, which is eternal and not successional. He eternally possesses the entire of his existence—a perfect sphere—in which there is no past or future. All events of time which exist successively exist within this all-encompassing sphere, and so are forever present, or in observation, with him, even when, as to themselves, nonexistent. In a deep and true sense things that are not are—are in his knowledge. With respect to themselves he knows them as not being, but to be, or as being, or as having been, as the fact is, when the predication is made.

For illustration : Suppose an eye endowed with intelligence, possessed with a power to observe all time, and to be forever open and observant of all that is in time, we should have as the result in permanent open vision and cognition all events included in time's history. The vision would have no past or future, but would be simple permanent vision, from which nothing ever escaped. Now, suppose that in fact there was in the events themselves an order of succession, some events being present in time, some past, some future. And suppose the intelligence of the observing eye to be such as to know this time or successional order of events in themselves, we should then have all the events permanently present to the observing eye, but in themselves some as past, some as present, some as future, and known so to be by the observer. In the intelligent observing eye the whole scheme of events would have existence in their order, but in themselves they would be coming and vanishing.

Now, as nearly as possible, this is what we suppose to be true of the mode of divine Omniscience and of the mode of God's relation to events of time. But you are, or some one is, ready to say that the supposition is that of an impossibility. How do you know that? That is precisely what God says is true: "All things are naked and opened unto the eyes of him with whom we have to do" (Heb. iv, 13). "Hell and destruction are before the Lord: how much more then the hearts of the children of men?" (Prov. xv, 11; Isa. xlvi, 9, 10.)

We can think of but one thing more that needs relief: The idea of the existence of all events in the divine knowledge each moment of time seems to involve this consequence, that all contradictory emotions with respect to the same being must exist in the divine mind at the same time. This was evidently Dorner's trouble. But does this follow? The case is put thus: At the same moment and forever is the observation of A, and all the events of history. But at a time (*a*) A is an innocent and lovely child, and as such must be beloved of the Lord; at time (*b*) he is a prodigal youth, guilty of all evil and sin; at time (*c*) he is a penitent seeking forgiveness; and at time (*d*) he is an eminent saint. What must be the feeling of God toward A? As a guilty prodigal he must be angry with him; as a penitent he must pity and forgive him; as a saint he must love him; and as he is seen to be all these all the time these contradictory feelings must coexist at the same moment with regard to him. Is this a fair or necessary putting of the case? If so, it must be fatal to the theory.

To our mind it seems this way: While all events are present in the divine knowledge at the same moment the events themselves do not coexist in the same moment; and the divine knowledge of them is according to the order in which they exist; that is, it is conformable to the facts. A is not at the same time all of these. God's emotions or feelings with regard to A do not exist from eternity, but exist when the occasions exist to call them forth. When A is an innocent child God loves him. A becomes an outcast, a guilty sinner. God is angry with him. A repents. God forgives him. A becomes an eminent saint. God communes with him in holiest love. There is not a saved soul that was not once under condemnation. The feelings or emotions of God, on immutable ethical grounds, must be appropriate to their occasions, and must therefore vary with the occasions. Both his knowledge of events caused by free beings and his feelings toward free beings arise from their acts and agree with their acts. The knowledge is observation of what is, but may be prevision, and is never causation. The feeling exists when the occasion exists, and not before. His feelings are as variable as the causes. Thus God has a true life with the creature of successive emotional experiences and of successive activity toward the creature. These are not immutable states, as his nature and attributes are, nor do they imply any changeableness in God as to his knowledge and immutable principles. Against this view it is alleged (*a*) that it makes God changeable in his emotional states—that it is anthropomorphic, imputing to God feelings and passions like our own; (*b*) that it raises the question, Why, with such an impulse to create, did he delay creation so long? (*c*) that it is inconsistent with that absolute self-sufficiency which must be found in the Eternal.

We answer by asking, Is sensibility to the good a defect, or is it a defect in an infinite Spirit that he should be supposed to have attributes analogous to those with which he clothes a finite spirit made in his own image? Would he be more or less perfect were he a being of infinite love? Does the implication help or hinder the problem of existence? The answer to these questions can only be one, and it relieves the first ground of objection.

With reference to the second we ask, Does the implication of benevolence in the Creator as an internal impulse to create add anything to the difficulty of accounting for the delay? Could the finite be brought into existence at all without leaving the question in its full force? Would any sooner be really sooner to the Eternal? If these are answered as they must be it will be seen that the objection implied is only seeming, not real.

To the third we answer by asking, If God was self-sufficient in the sense in which the questions imply, how can we account for creation at all? There must have been something in his own nature which demanded it, or it could not be. But if there must be something, what better than a benevolent impulse or an eternal prompting of love?

The only alternative is to depersonalize the world ground and assume either the materialistic theory or its twin absurdity of pantheism. The impossibility of these solutions of the world problem has already been shown. There is nothing, then, in the idea itself which can be ground of rational rejection. Its possibility is indisputable, and as it furnishes the only rational solution it becomes a necessity of thought. When we add to this that it is the uniform and unequivocal teaching of revelation itself it becomes an essential doctrine of Christian faith and sound philosophy alike. The world ground is neither the material mass, nor an impersonal force, nor the all in a process of necessary unfolding, but is an eternal free personal Cause, who contains in himself the power, wisdom, and motive by which all things exist. As his wisdom is forever seen *in* things revealing its existence in him, so his power is forever pervasive of them, asserting his perpetual presence *with* them; and his love is forever declared by them, as sole ground *why* he caused them to be. One no more than the other is thus seen to be an eternal inherence of his essential and ineffable nature.

But, it is said, there are facts which are irreconcilable with this view, and that the contradiction offsets the instinctive and apparently rational conclusion. The objection rests upon the implied assumption that a true theory must be able to account for all the facts, or at least must not be in contradiction of the facts. The principle must be accepted. It is undoubtedly true. But it is not true that the reconciliation must always be possible to us before we can accept the theory. The evidence may be clear and conclusive, despite remaining obscurities. A sufficiency of facts may be present to compel faith, while for want of others, or for the want of deeper insight, there may be real embarrassment to a complete understanding. The obscurity does not arise from a contradiction, but for the want of understanding, or for the want of a knowledge of all the elements of the solution. Larger time and a broader view may be all that are needed to a complete clearing up of perplexities. The function of rational thought is to determine in any case whether the known grounds are sufficient to warrant the conviction that higher knowledge and further developments will establish existing conclusions and remove apparent contradictions. But what, then, are the alleged facts which are irreconcilable with the doctrine that "God is love," or that essential goodness reigns in and over the universe. Whether explicable or not they should be examined. It is answered, There are evils in the system which contradict the idea.

In order to compare a fact with the good of being, so as to be able to know whether it is itself a good, or, if not a good in itself, condition of a good, and if condition of a good, the best condition possible, it is necessary that we should have a definite idea of the *good*. If evil is a something which is opposed to the good of being, which hinders or hurts it, to know that we must know what the good of being is, and know that the given fact is harmful thereto. And yet further, in order to determine whether the cause of a fact is himself good, whether the fact be a good in itself, or condition of an ultimate good, we must be able to know how the fact stands related to the cause. The quality of goodness in the cause is not determined simply by goodness in the effect either as ultimate or conditional, but in the fact of the freedom of the cause, and the motive to the effect. Though there be a good, if the cause did not freely produce it, and intend it as a good, it does not show the cause to be good; and *vice versâ*, though there be evil in the effect, if it be not a freely chosen effect, it does not show want of goodness in the cause. A cause working to an end which is good or productive of well-being is good as so working; that is, it actually produces good as well-being, and so must be accounted good; but if it be merely a blind power working under the law of necessity, however beneficent the effect, the cause itself can have no quality of ethical goodness in it. To have this quality it must have personality; that is, it must be a cause that perceives an end of good, and freely chooses it and then produces it.

What, then, do we mean by a good? A good implies existence of some kind. It is impossible to predicate good of non-being or nonexistence. It may be better that a given thing should not be than be, but the good in the case is a good only for that which is, and not for that which is not. Good must be the good of some being. But while there can be no good without a being of some kind, mere existence or being is not itself a good necessarily. When we predicate of a given thing that it is good the question immediately emerges, How good —good for what? and the explanation points out precisely what we mean by a good—or good. A thing is good as means to an end when it serves the end; if it minister to the end in the best way and the highest degree possible, it is good as a means in a superlative degree—the best possible. A thing is good as an end when there is good in itself, not as a means to an end, but as an end; and in this case the term is equivalent to realized welfare—happiness—perfect content of being. The different degrees of which good in this sense can be predicated of created being depends on the different degrees of capacity for welfare. Some beings have more capacity for good than others. Thus things are to be viewed as good when they are means to welfare, or realized welfare, and as subordinate and ultimate. Subordinate goods are goods in themselves, but not of the highest kind. Subordinate goods may give way when ultimate goods are attained. It is not necessary that that which is a good should be permanent. It may be necessary that a subordinate good for the time should be repressed or even entirely abolished, in order to ultimate welfare. Its continuance might become an obstruction, and it would cease to be a good and become an evil. The result is that the essence of the idea of a good or the good is that which is valuable to the enjoyment of sensitive existence, or that which is welfare or makes for welfare. Goodness in God implies that he who is the cause of all with unmixed intent works for the welfare of being.

What, then, are the facts in the light of which we are to determine whether goodness is an attribute of the world ground, which must be considered in the solution of the great problem? It might be deemed sufficient to rest it entirely on the instinctive conviction, without any attempt at explanation. Or it might be solved simply in the light of revelation. In either case the difficulties, if there be any, would be left unexplained and ignored on the ground that whatever they are, explicable or inexplicable, they are sufficiently answered in the positive teaching of instinctive reason or authoritative revelation, and therefore require no further attention. To justify this proceeding it might be said that, owing to the limitations of our powers and the inadequacy of our circumstances, we are not competent to judge in the premises, and therefore that it is the better wisdom not to meddle with questions which are too high for us—that we but increase our embarrassments by attempting to relieve them. There is plausibility in this view. There can be no doubt that a sufficient ground for faith is laid in the instinctive reason conformed with the divine testimony, though there should be difficulties which we cannot wholly remove. We may have adequate ground for faith, even when the understanding is insufficient to a perfect comprehension; and there may be difficulties which for the present cannot be fully removed. Belief in such a case is not irrational, necessarily. It is also a conceivable thing that difficulties may be so insoluble that the attempt would only engender doubt and discouragement, and might, therefore, be better omitted. But how shall we know the true state of the case without thorough examination? It would seem to be the wiser course for the theologian to take the full measure of all the possible embarrassments of his positions, and, if need be, confess his inadequacy to meet them, and then point out the grounds on which, notwithstanding, he demands faith. The question will then turn on the sufficiency of the grounds, and reason will have fair play. Possibly, after all, the facts may be explained, at least so far as to show that they would be found illustrative, rather than destructive.

There is a theodicy. God is not at variance with himself. No facts are at war with his goodness. Assured of this, it becomes us to look the difficulties squarely in the face, and find their real significance as far as possible, without doubt of the outcome. In this way only can we be self-respecting as rational beings.

The facts which bear on the problem are few and simple, and can be stated with perfect clearness:

First fact. The universe is God's product. Such as it is he made it. There is no being or force or law in it that is not from him as source. There never can be in it any being or force or law of which he will not be the source. There is no self-created and self-existing thing or force or law. No creature has any more being or power or law than it has got from its creator. There is no side door by which, in these respects, more has got into the universe than God puts in it, that is, more of being, power, law.

Second fact. There are no limitations which are not imposed by the Creator. He gives so much; he gives no more. This determines the limit. Why he fixes the limits as he does; why he makes as he does; why he makes no more, no less; why the peculiar forces, powers, laws, are points which at present we do not consider. The fact we posit is simply this one: He limits himself. He determines what he will put in, what he will leave out, what the content of the work shall be. He might have put more; he might have put less; he might have made differently; he might not have made at all. That he made at all, and made as he did, is of his own motion purely.

Third fact. A large part of what he has made has no enjoyable existence whatever. From it, for some reason, the capacity of enjoyment of any kind has been excluded. The entire insensate universe comes under this class. As to bulk, it is infinite as compared to sensate existence.

Fourth fact. To a small fraction of what he has made he has given a *limited* capacity of enjoyment of one kind or another. To the larger part, as to number and extent quantitively considered, the power of enjoyment seems to be merely sensational, and is wholly limited to the physical; it is a good of physical enjoyment—the healthy exercise of physical functions. Whether there is any self-conscious subject, that is, a subject knowing itself and knowing its enjoyments, is indeterminable by any light we have. There are sensations, without doubt. There are appetites, and pleasurable delights in their gratification. They must be viewed both as means and ends—means to the development of the economy of life. Without them life itself would lapse, or, in any event, would not propagate itself. As an end they give a measure of zest and enjoyment to life, and have in them a good, though of an inferior order.

The smaller fraction, as to number, has a higher capacity, or capacity for higher forms of enjoyment. To the enjoyment of sensational pleasures or physical delights they add the delights of reason and of conscience. Even the lower forms are taken up in self-consciousness, and acquire more than mere sensational character; but while means to an end of physical good, and in themselves a certain form of good or enjoyableness, they have their chief value in their higher relations, and the subject of them, in them and through them, finds more than mere sensational delight. But that which especially characterizes this smaller fraction of enjoying and enjoyable existence is the capacity for a good of happiness which transcends the physical—the delight of conscious knowledge and righteousness. The subject knows himself, perceives good, knows it as such, appreciates the good as an end, pursues it, finds in it satisfaction.

Fifth fact. Along with the capacity for enjoyment he has incorporated a capacity of suffering, and has placed the beings so capacitated in such conditions and environments of exposure that they are always in peril of more or less distress, and do many times come into extreme suffering.

Sixth fact. The higher the capacity for enjoyment the

greater the capacity for suffering, and the greater the liability and peril. That the suffering incident to mere sensational being is apparently great often cannot be disputed, but that it is really great cannot be known. That there is no such suffering with merely brute life as there is in the higher form of self-conscious life is most evident.

These facts must all be taken into account in framing a theodicy, or in any attempt to reconcile God's dealings with the universe to the principle of absolute goodness in him. It must be shown how, that is, on what principle, a being of infinite goodness, wisdom, and power could make such a universe; why so large a part of being should exist without capacity for good of any kind, absolutely without any enjoyment; why so large a fraction should have mere sensational life; why there should be such susceptibility to suffering in it; why there should be suffering at all; why, especially, in ascending into the highest forms of all, there should be found here the greatest amount of suffering.

It is assumed that the facts are such as to render a theodicy impossible. The ground of the assumption is that there are admitted evils. It is argued that if God is a being of infinite knowledge he knows how to prevent evil, and if he has infinite power he is able to prevent it, and if he is a being of infinite love he would have prevented it; but since, by admission, it exists, therefore he is destitute of either the requisite knowledge or power or goodness to prevent it. Or, again, it is argued that as all things are his free product, and evil is a fact, therefore he must have chosen its existence, and so he cannot be good, or evil itself is an inclusion of good. It must be obvious that the argument thus formulated depends for its force on the meaning of the term evil, and on the validity of the implications that evil exists, and on the relation which God sustains to its existence causationally or permissively. If that which is denominated evil be not so in fact, or if it be a necessary incident in attaining a good, or if it be wholly independent of God, or if it be something which he will finally eliminate, the argument would wholly lose its force.

It may be proper to indicate what facts of the system seem to show that goodness does preside over the universe. These may be grouped under the following heads: (*a*) The adjustment of means to ends of good; (*b*) the creation of beings capable of enjoying good; (*c*) the changeless law in the conservation of means and ends; (*d*) the infinite patience and long-sufferingness of God with transgressors; (*e*) the gift of himself in sacrifice for sin; (*f*) his readiness to forgive; (*g*) the eternal happiness he has promised for them who will accept it.

Let us assume, for the present, the truth of the doctrine that infinite benevolence underlies all the divine movement—an assumption everywhere honorable to the Infinite. How, might we suppose, under the operation of such a principle, would he proceed? By supposition he possesses all wisdom and all power. What would pure benevolence move him to do? It is plain that, actuated by that principle, he would carefully consider all possibilities; that from among them he would select those, to be made real, which would most adequately satisfy his benevolent wish. It is certain that he would exclude all things which imply malevolence; for the infinitely Benevolent could not be malevolent. He could not be cruel or unjust. He could not make suffering an aim. He could not permit suffering, except as means to a beneficent end or as an unavoidable incident in the best plan for reaching the most beneficent ends. The aim and outcome of his movement must be the attainment of the greatest possible good with the least possible evil—the greatest possible happiness with the least possible suffering.

It will be observed that the argument rests upon the assumption that infinite goodness could not create a universe in which evil should find place; that, therefore, either there is no evil or there is a lack of goodness in the Cause.

The difficulty has been met in various ways. It has been argued by some that what is called evil is not so in fact; that whatever is is best—is an element of good. It has been argued that if there is evil God is not the cause, and so its existence does not bear against either his power, wisdom, or love. It has been argued that though his love is opposed to it it is not possible for wisdom and power combined to prevent it, and so its existence does not imply either lack of love, wisdom, or power. None of the answers have given complete satisfaction, and it may be that no future attempt will be more successful. It may forever remain impossible for the finite so to comprehend the plan and purpose of the Infinite as to understand how it is that he has permitted evil to invade his system; and the whole problem may continue to be shrouded in impenetrable mystery, to be accepted by faith, rather than be construed by reason.

It is certain that in some way evil has gained a foothold in the universe. It is here by the permission of God, or despite him. Permission does not mean acquiescence or consent, necessarily, but may mean simply nonhindrance. The facts are as they are, and we cannot ignore them if we would.

Either he is their source or he is not. They are reconcilable with his goodness or they are not. If we must take the ground that he is sole Author of the universe we must seek to determine his relations to evils which are in it. If they are not reconcilable to his love, then they prove that he is malevolent. This alternative is one which the human mind will never admit.

The implication underlying the objection is that a universe emanating from a being of infinite power, wisdom, and love should be free from evil. That is by no means as clear as at first sight it appears. Suppose it should turn out that things which viewed in themselves are evil nevertheless are incidents of a progress to an end that is infinitely good, not otherwise to be realized, is it clear that such evils might not exist by the immediate act of an infinitely good being—much more, might be permitted to invade his system temporarily or permanently? Is there no way to vindicate the goodness of God except that his universe be absolutely free from evil? Must the actual be the realization of the absolutely best to rescue his attributes of love, wisdom, and power? Can nothing fall below his ideal without clouding his perfections? We must think the assumption cannot be sustained.

Can we assert with the confidence of certainty more than this: Given a God of infinite wisdom, power, and love: (*a*) If he create other beings he must not create unwisely or unlovingly; that is, he must not dishonor either his wisdom or his love. (*b*) To avoid this the thing created must be for an end of goodness, and must be well adapted to attain the end— he must purpose the highest good which his wisdom can discern, and he must put into operation the best possible means to attain the end. These conditions being met, would not the result be a complete vindication of himself as infinitely wise and good? (*c*) If it should so be that the highest possible good would include some possible evil, which it was foreseen would become actual, in the realization of the good, would the existence of some evil necessarily cloud the divine goodness? We must think not. The actual best thing possible may not be the ideal best, and if the ideal best should be for any cause unrealizable might not goodness accept the best possible, even if it involved some actual evil?

The things which we complain of as evil are suffering and sin. They have been classified as natural and moral evils. By natural evils is meant defects, pains, and sufferings of every description which pervade sentient existence, which seem to have no moral cause. By moral evil is meant sin, with its attendants of guilt and punishment.

Let us look them up in their order, and endeavor to see what lessons they will teach us: First, let us look at the fact of natural evil. There should be no attempt to change the fact itself. We must endeavor to see it just as it is, neither diminishing nor exaggerating it. And in order to keep things apart which are dissimilar let us first consider the sufferings of the unmoral world. This comprises all the realm of life below man which has sensibility. The problem is to reconcile God's dealings with this great department to the idea of his absolute goodness. That there is suffering here cannot be disputed, but it is also impossible that we should know the measure of the suffering. The precise nature of brute consciousness is an impenetrable mystery. It doubtless excludes all properly æsthetical, rational, and moral elements. The sufferings which come from these causes cannot be supposed to exist here. This is an important fact, which should never, for a moment, be lost sight of in discussing the problem of natural evil. The sufferings which remain are reduced to the two classes of physical and emotional distresses. But here, again, we have no means of knowing, even proximately, their degree, or the nature of the consciousness of them. If there be no evidence that brutes, or mere sensate life, have any proper self or self-consciousness, suffering may be reduced to mere automatism, mere physical motion, or if not to this it passes into a grade of intensity infinitely below what, interpreting it from our self-consciousness, we suppose it to be. It may, like the satisfactions of such a form of life, be simply functional to the continuance and preservation of the organism, and so be classed with the appetites which simply conserve existence. It is highly probable that real suffering and real enjoyment are capabilities only of a self-conscious subject, and so are to be found in a rational and moral nature exclusively. It is certain that in lower natures they can only exist in such modified form as to essentially change their character. Each form of life has its law. The insensate vegetable automatically or mechanically follows its tendencies and develops according to its law without feeling of any kind. Animal life in its lowest types can scarcely be distinguished in any respect, except as to functional arrangements of the parts and outcomes of the organism, from the insensate plant. The higher forms of animal life develop under a law in which sensation plays an important part, but it is impossible to know how real the sensations are, or whether they are anything else than mere physical and organic changes, working to the ends of developed existence—the exuberance of the life principle. That there is any proper feeling, any consciousness of suffering or enjoyment, any proper ego to realize such experiences, lies beyond our knowledge. As there is in every atom a tendency which we call gravitation, and in some atoms affinities for other atoms, but without any feeling or consciousness of such tendencies, so it is possible that in that obscure principle which we call life, which constructs this or that organism, under this or that set of laws, and with or without signs of sensation, there may be the same absence of any proper feeling, but only tendencies and movements which simulate sensations, all having a relation to the building of the structure and its uses and ends. In any event, the absence of a self-conscious knowing subject must differentiate any feeling that may exist from feeling as it exists in a self-conscious, knowing subject.

But, if it should be known to him that the greatest possible good could be attained only by executing a plan that would involve the evil of suffering to some degree of every being in it capable of suffering, then infinite benevolence might prompt him to execute that plan, and the sufferings themselves, though brought about immediately by his own agency, would not cloud his goodness. They would be chosen and caused, not for themselves, not because he took pleasure in them, for that would be contrary to goodness, but because, by introducing them, he could attain that which benevolence desired—the greatest good. It is plain that the least possible suffering would be accepted that the aim might be reached, for that which is not desirable in itself to benevolence could only be allowed in order to the ends of benevolence, and in the smallest degree possible.

Again, if it should be known to God that the greatest possible good would be secured by creating beings who would all of them suffer in some degree forever, but the good of whose being would vastly transcend their suffering and be somehow conditioned by it, infinite benevolence might prompt him to create them. But the suffering, not being chosen for its own sake, could only be introduced in the smallest possible degree, and for the sake of a transcendent good. The attainment of the good would be the only aim of benevolence, but suffering would be accepted by it as an unavoidable incident.

Again, if it should be known to God that the greatest possible good of some beings could be promoted by some sufferings of some other beings, infinite benevolence might proceed upon a plan that would involve the suffering of some for the sake of the good of others. Thus the good of the infant might be conditioned on the suffering of the mother.

Again, if the Infinite saw that for the attainment of the highest possible good of any being it was necessary that he should be so constituted and so posited that he might possibly by a free act of his own miss of his good and incur great misery, and if he should know that out of a vast number of such beings some would plunge themselves into misery, he might be compelled on the principle of pure benevolence to create such beings; nor would the misery of those who had equal chances with the others cloud his benevolence, even if the misery should be unmitigated and should last forever.

Again, infinite benevolence might create beings whose good should be an attainable prize, and who, to reach it, would have to undergo some suffering.

Again, infinite goodness might create beings who, by wickedly refusing to attain their good by submitting to some suffering, should be punished with the loss of the good which was in their reach, and with greater suffering than would have been required to reach it. If, for the interests of the ultimate greatest good of the whole, such infliction of suffering on the incorrigibly rebellious should need to be perpetual, it would not be inconsistent with infinite benevolence that it should be so, only so that the sufferings were not greater in measure than the interests of good required.

Again, infinite love is not inconsistent with infinite displeasure against acts and beings who interfere with the attainment of its ends—it might exist. The principle of wrath is a modification of the principle of love. The same impulse which makes good a cherished end makes that which prevents it an object of resentment in the same degree—it is energetic action in two directions, for the good and against the evil.

Again, it is not contrary to infinite benevolence that some beings should have capacities and opportunities for good which others do not enjoy, or that some should have peculiar liabilities or experiences. Such a circumstance does not imply more love in the one case than in the other. Such a difference, either in races or individuals, may be necessary integers in a universal economy of infinite love. The only requisite is that no individual or race shall be unduly limited or exposed, and that such good as they are made capable of be secured to them in the best possible manner, and that each in its place have the measure of good which universal benevolence allots it. It is not a partiality inconsistent with love that some creatures are beasts, some men, some angels, though thereby some have a capacity of good which others do not have, and that some are exposed to evil from which the others are secured. It cannot be shown that love requires a dead-level uniformity or shuts up the Infinite to a single allotment for every being. Precisely the same measure of love may place two beings in different conditions.

Again, infinite benevolence does not require that all races should be regarded with the same kind of affection. He may love men more than he does beasts, as he may feel toward one man differently from the feeling which he has for another, the difference being caused by the freely chosen characters of the men themselves. In the former case he makes the difference himself by creating the grounds of it in making beings of different capacities. In the latter case the creature makes the difference by himself creating the grounds of it. Thus love may originally discriminate in the matter of its favors without ceasing to be love, and it may subsequently discriminate by reason of a free creature's action without ceasing to be love.

But infinite benevolence could not arrange a system to produce suffering as an ultimate end. It could not create any being simply that it might suffer. It could not *inflict* sufferings on some beings for the wrongs of others, though it might permit the wrongdoing of one to bring suffering on the other. It could not inflict sufferings on a being for his own wrongs with undue measure and severity. It could not perpetuate an existence simply for the purpose of inflicting suffering upon it. Suffering must, if it exist at all, be means to good, and to a good not otherwise attainable; or it must be the outcome of abuse of good; or it must be inflicted as penalty for wrong, to maintain an economy which has good at its end.

These principles we believe to be all maintainable and sound, and they show how suffering may be corporate in a system of love without fault of any kind, anywhere, and how other forms of suffering may be interjected into an economy of infinite love, without detriment to the love which establishes the economy itself, so that sufferings in the universe are not, in themselves considered, any proof that the Founder is not infinitely benevolent.

There are forms of good which the infinite wisdom and power of God can infallibly secure. They are wholly within his immediate control. If these stood alone any failure would imply want of benevolent purpose on his part, and were such failure discovered it might justly cloud his love. It is possible that he could have made beings capable of a degree of enjoyment and without any liability to suffering whatever; at least it would seem possible; we do not know that it is impossible; but such a creation could only be on the plane of sensational enjoyment and under the conditions of necessity. The system might have been so organized, so perfectly adjusted, that every object would please and the enjoyment be perpetual, and, so far as we see, eternal. If such a form of good would have met the highest ideal of his love, then might there never have been pain or suffering of any kind. The earth might have been so adjusted that it would have been eternal summer, and living things might have been so constituted and environed that they would have drunk in only ecstasy and exuberance of life, and the anthem of peace and content might have rolled on forever. There need have been no births, no deaths, no hunger, no want, no care, no fear, no unsatisfied desire, no freezing cold, no scorching heat, no desert wastes, no destructive tempests or desolating earthquakes, no subtle poisons, no disturbing humors or fretting nerves or ferocious tempers. For aught that we can see He who had power to create might have spread forth creation over the same wide areas of space as he has chosen to occupy with just such conditions of universal enjoyment.

But if his benevolence should demand a higher type of good, the happiness which springs of virtue, then he must create a different kind of beings, free, intelligent, self-conscious persons. And if he create these he must put from himself the power of excluding suffering. The necessities which accompany this new form of existence may not only make it possible for it to suffer, but may even require that, for its development and discipline, by which alone its end may be reached, a general order or economy of suffering, extending through all creation, for a time may be necessary. Thus suffering, in some degree and form, extending from and including the Creator himself, down through all ranks of being, may be a necessary concomitant of any moral creation whatever. Having determined that benevolence demands the good of moral beings—the happiness which springs from virtue—the means thereto must be provided; that is, a universe constructed, in its inanimate parts, such that sensate existence within it, and under its order, may be in a degree of suffering, liable to want, and under the law of a transitory existence, having in it some pain and ultimate death.

If the discipline requisite to establish a commonwealth of such virtuous beings demanded this as the only method, then benevolence would require that it should be adopted. If the end might be reached by adopting several methods, and this among them, then still there would have to be some world where this method would be tried.

It is not impossible that infinite wisdom discerns that several methods are required by which to attain the ultimate end of the highest good for universal consciousness or welfare. The history enacting on our planet may be but one among many ways in actual operation by which the end is being reached. And by possibility it may be influential and conservative over vast realms where the economy is different. There may be orders untouched by moral defection, because of sin and suffering and redemption, which broke forth under the system of probation here enacted. If infinite benevolence demanded a moral realm, and the peculiar good which it makes possible, and if to secure that a probation similar to that here initiated, with its foreseen outcome, was necessary as a possibility and certain as a fact, then infinite goodness would dictate that the plan should be adopted.

The only thing necessary to infinite goodness is that it propose to itself the highest ultimate good possible, and that it freely adopt the wisest way or ways by which to reach it. This will preclude all needless sufferings of any kind, and it will reduce all suffering to the minimum, and carry all welfare to the maximum of possibility.

There can be no doubt, there is no doubt, that the bliss of holy virtue is the highest conceivable good, and that the effort to attain it is the highest possible aim and expression of goodness. Let us suppose that this is the ultimate aim of God, that all things are in order to it, is it possible to conceive any greater reach of love? To this end he creates spirits, who may know him, who may love him, who may be conscious of his love, who may by a free election obey him, who in obedience may forever grow in power and worthiness, who may enter into his plans and emulate his goodness, who may in the fellowship of his life and mutual fellowship of good will and holy offices of affection among themselves to all eternity grow in happiness. Suppose that in order to this he places them in a probation of temporary struggle, in which they must suffer some, but with the hope and promise of a blessed outcome ; suppose that the general economy of such a probation should involve just such a world as this, with inferior races conditioned just as those are about us; suppose that some should be ungrateful and abuse their great opportunity, would the immeasurable greatness of his love be any the less conspicuous? Would not the idea and effort be worthy of infinite benevolence? This is precisely what we understand to be the fact in the case. The effort costs suffering, it may be, and possibly the greatest of all to the infinite heart which makes it. The sufferings prove the love, for they are only permitted and endured for the sake of the end.

It remains that we examine the facts in the light of these principles and see if there be anything known which absolutely contradicts the idea of the infinite benevolence of God, or if it is possible for us to think him in any other or different view.

Beginning with the inanimate creation, do we find any light shed from hence on the problem? It must be answered without hesitation that, in itself considered, if there were nothing else, it reveals nothing but power guided by ingenuity; there is neither wisdom nor goodness in the display if it serve no end of good. There is no wisdom in it if it be sole, since, considered simply in itself, it serves no useful end; and there can be no kindness in that which is not profitable to a useful end. There is no goodness manifested, since there is no good secured, and that which has no good in it cannot manifest goodness in its cause. If there be any good, therefore, in the existence of the vast inanimate universe it must be in that it serves some end of good out of and beyond itself; and that end of good beyond itself displays the goodness of its Cause, since it supposes him to create it for the sake of the good to which it is meant. Its adaptation to the end proclaims his wisdom, as the end itself proclaims his goodness. Thus both wisdom and goodness are revealed in the inanimate creation as a system of means to wise and beneficent ends.

Three points immediately emerge: (*a*) What are the ends for which the inanimate creation exists? (*b*) Are the ends beneficial? (*c*) Are the means well adapted?

The end for which the inanimate creation exists is apparent

in the end it serves. It exists not simply as a mass of inorganic matter, but a mass ingeniously arranged into a system. The arrangement displays marvelous skill as well as power. It is pervaded by forces which act according to fixed and permanent laws—electrical, magnetic, thermal, luminiferous, chemical. These, together with the all-pervading laws of cohesive attraction and gravitation, give it form, order, beauty, and regularity of motion and position—stable and permanent harmony. The vast worlds float in an infinite ocean of impalpable ether; radiant and tempered atmospheres fan their surfaces; central suns lighten and warm dependent planets; aqueous floods pour from their caverns and run along their valleys and gather into seas and oceans in their broad basins; solar fervors vaporize them, and the winds carry the fleecy clouds again over the continents, and they return in showers over the wide surfaces of the thirsty land. Nothing could exceed the magnificence of the spectacle, but it is lifeless. Is it also meaningless? So it would have been had there been nothing more. But we soon discern that all its deft arrangements are prophecies of yet higher wonders. It is not an end. Every atom and each force point onward. Life stirs in it. The inorganic furnishes the condition for the organic. It covers itself with verdure as with a garment. Still, were this all we should have but meaningless display. We have reached no end of good—it reveals no adequate purpose. There is proof of power, skill, taste, adaptation, order, harmony, but absence of any good. It is impossible that it should rest here. These succulent compounds do not grow for nothing. The prophecy is soon explained. The air and earth and seas teem with hungry life. The earth has been spreading a table for them. They are ecstatic. The mystery of the inorganic mass is cleared up. It was for the support of exultant life. Had the program ended here it would have intimated something more than mere artistic inspiration.

In the Cause we should detect some generous impulse. He must have meant some good when he planted such ecstasy. But the revelation is still unsatisfactory. There is too much expenditure for such an end. The portico is disproportioned to the building. There has been too much preparation for the outcome. There is more display than value. It could not be that the ultimate end should be reached at such a point, but it does appear that the entire inorganic creation was a complex of means to an end, and well and wisely adapted to it; it was not meaningless, therefore. We advance one step further. A new type of life appears. In some respects it is not new. It has a general resemblance to the life which has flourished for ages. But in fact it is radically different. *It owns everything.* Its first act is to lay claim to the universe. It says, "*My Father made all these things for me.*" We have unmistakably reached the end of all inferior life and the whole inanimate structure. Throughout it is a system of means to the development and welfare of this crowning work. It is the regal heir —the child. From it we must interpret all. There is no instinct deeper or wider than this. The universe was made for man and beings of his type. He stands forth as lord. The regnant qualities are in him. He has dominion. He subdues and subjugates all things to his service. He commands, regulates, and possesses all. For him the sun shines. For him life flourishes. For him the mines are stored. For him are the gems and precious metals and ores. For him are the lessons of wisdom, beauty, love. For him is the consciousness of dignity, worth, responsibility. For him is the power of knowledge, virtue, freedom. For him is hope, foresight, wisdom. For him is the power to transcend his present surroundings in time and space, to live in the past and future and distant. For him is insight into the causes, nature, and purpose of things. For him is the invisible and intangible. For him are endless progress and immortal growth. For him is the power to know and worship and love the infinite Father, and enter into the fellowship of his thoughts and feeling and life. It is impossible that there should be any more ultimate end. We have reached in the child the grand climax of infinite power, wisdom, and love. The infinite Father can propose nothing beyond this. The training, complete development, and highest welfare of his princely offspring must henceforth be the ultimate object of all his activity forever and ever. He will do nothing contrary to it. He will order all things to its accomplishment. Therein shall be seen the measure of the Father's love, and it shall appear forever and ever that creation is a simple expression of love.

But the movement is eternal. The end is not reached *per saltum*. To attain the complete possession of his inheritance the child must pass through a period of training. His faculties must be matured and developed by hardy exercise. His virtues must ripen by trial. His good of happiness must spring from worthiness. He must win his crown to enjoy it. He could not else deserve his Father's approval or his own. The way to his ultimate throne is dutiful obedience. To reign he must serve. To enjoy he must first suffer.

This fact will explain the circumstances of his earthly condition —both of his own suffering and the suffering creation about him. The earth was fitted up, not as his ultimate home, but as his training school, the gymnasium of his probation. Nothing of it enters into his final life but the results in his character. Nothing of it was designed for permanence, but simply as means to an end. Everything in it is transient, destined to serve an end and pass away. If this view be correct the suffering and death of the inferior races are to be viewed as corporate parts of the benevolent system. They are not accidents, but original provisions, justified by the end they serve. It is impossible to show that they are in any proper sense evils, that is, that a higher good could be secured to the universe if they were abolished. No reason can be assigned why immortality of the inferior races would be a boon, why death to them should be considered a calamity. No one can show that it is not a good that of such races one should subsist upon another; that one generation should be removed to make way for another. No one can show that the plan adopted for their propagation and destruction is not on the whole the best possible. No one can show that the plan under which they exist implies any malevolence toward them, or any want of benevolent regard for them, in the degree in which they are proper objects of benevolence.

Suffering and pain are incidents of arrangements for happiness. Happiness was the object, pain is the incident. The provision for happiness is at its maximum, the liability to pain at its minimum. Death is not less benignant than life. The same love that devised the former appointed the latter. It is impossible to find a single arrangement in the whole realm of life which does not have for its primary end the good of the organism in which it is found. That the incidental suffering might have been avoided, and the sum total of good increased, no one is able to prove. On the contrary, it is certain that the fact of suffering, in many cases, conduces to the greatest good as means to ends. Famines and pestilences and earthquakes are not proofs of malice, nor yet of impotence. They are increments of an economy which in the sum total is indicative of measureless power and measureless love. Neither the liability nor the fact of either could be eliminated and the proof of goodness thereby be strengthened or increased. The abolishment of death and attendant pains would not necessarily heighten the proof of love; nor does it appear that the method could be changed in any way to the advantage of the creature. To a mind capable of taking in the whole case of life and sentient existence it does not appear probable a change in any respect could be suggested that would improve the evidence that love presides over all. There may be benefits accompanying the economy of pain in all the forms in which it exists, and death itself, among mere sentient creatures, which could not be equaled were they excluded. It must be remembered that mere power is not the only attribute exercised in conditioning good. There are forms of good which no amount of abstract power or power alone can secure, and this may be true of mere sentient enjoyment as really as of moral delights. To enjoy, sentient creatures must exist, and under certain conditions. There is no reason to doubt that the actual conditions are not selected and determined because they are the very best possible. That in them which works limitation and interruption is not proof of either defect of love or wisdom or power. If the Infinite were adequate to devise a universe in which neither pain nor death could exist, and unceasing enjoyment would result from the permanence of life, and if infinite power could make the device a reality, which may or may not be true, it is not perfectly certain that infinite love could choose it in preference to the present order. The outcome of infinite ages might show the method actually adopted the best. We do not doubt it will so appear.

When, now, we turn from the inferior races to man, the problem becomes still more involved. Here we encounter the same evils as are found in the inferior races, but also others of much more serious nature. How can this be explained? We have reached a realm now where we can speak much more understandingly of what suffering is, and how it stands related to God, than we were able to do when we were considering the case of the inferior races. The sufferer here is of a very different being from the sufferer there. The sufferings are of a very different kind. The problem takes on new elements.

Mere pain to a man is more than it is to a beast. The *great* evil that happened is sin, and the sufferings which spring from it. It is common to connect all human suffering with sin, and on that ground to explain the problem of suffering. It assumes that had there been no sin there would have been no suffering. Man is made the sole source of his own suffering, and God is exculpated. It is assumed that his benevolent plan for man entirely excluded suffering of every kind. We do not believe that truth lies in the direction of this theory, or that it has any warrant whatever, either from reason or revelation. Into human life has come two kinds of suffering, and their sources are different—one class corporate with the nature of man emanating directly from God in creation or constitution; another class issuing from man's sin, and of which he alone is the guilty cause, but both arising under the government of God, though in different ways.

Would there have been any suffering for man had he not sinned, and if so, what? And how would such suffering affect the question of the infinite benevolence of God?

That man, in common with all sentient life, would have been liable to, and would actually have experienced, the forms of suffering incident to such natures, we do not for a moment doubt; and that he would have experienced some higher forms of suffering we find it as little possible to disbelieve. He was connected with, and part of, a suffering system. The body with which he was clothed was not simply an instrument for use and help, to the development of his deeper self, but it ministered to that end by opening to him certain avenues of suffering. It prompted to pleasures and awakened desires which must be repressed. It was thus that he came under the conditions of probation, and was enabled to realize personal worthiness, or virtue, or righteousness, or holiness, and the ultimate high bliss which constitutes his real good as a moral being. His body was an instrument by which, being sensitive, he was able to avoid things harmful to his life; but that it might accomplish that end its sensitivity must take on suffering. It is in its very nature an open avenue to pain. It exists under conditions in which pain is inevitable. Its pains are part of a system of means to higher ends. Mere pain is not in itself necessarily an evil. It may be conservative of good. It is a vain thing to attempt to extricate man from the physical system of which he is a part, so far forth as he is a part.

No more, we think, can it be reasonably doubted that there are forms of suffering to which his higher nature is open, such as an uneasy sense of limitations, unrealized and at present unrealizable desires, possible forms of emotion; all of which were incidents of a probationary state and occasions of good.

That unsinning humanity would have been wholly free, therefore, from the common sufferings of sentient existence in the instrumental organism, and even in the higher nature, does not appear probable to reason, and is nowhere implied in revelation. Nor is there any occasion of doubt of the infinite benevolence of God on account of the fact of such suffering. There is no occasion to attempt to find any reason for it apart from his direct and simple purpose. There is no such evil in it as to reflect upon his goodness. It needs no apology. But there are aggravations of suffering which are penal, and these must be ascribed to abuse of good for which the Author of nature cannot in justice be held responsible, except as providing for their possibility and as not preventing them. The justification must take into account the full extent of the evil. There are those who look upon sin as a trivial thing—a mistake of erring creatures whose evils are small and transient, mere incidents in the progress from lower to higher stages of existence. The outcome, they believe, will be a permanently holy and perfectly happy universe. To such the reconciliation is not difficult. The whole is resolved into the discipline of love, as means to ends. The end justifies the means, on the ground that the end can be reached in no other way. If the outcome could be admitted the justification would be complete. But it does not appear that such will be the outcome. Sin, in fact, to the view of reason and revelation both, seems to be a deadly evil, not only blighting this world by spreading temporary ruin and woe over the hearts and hopes of men, but also projecting its fell shadow over eternity and desolating many souls with final and eternal curse. The evil is not temporary, but eternal—not disciplinary, but penal and destructive. Its hell is not a reformatory prison, from which its unfortunate wards are to come forth purified by wholesome cultus into the estate and happiness of virtue, but a dungeon whose doors never open and whose victims have no prospect of release. The problem must be as it is—a universe with an eternal heaven for some souls, and an eternal hell for others. How can such a state of facts be reconciled to the idea that its Author is an infinitely benevolent being to all his creatures alike, and without respect of persons? It must be confessed that the problem is difficult of solution. It is not diminished when it is viewed in the light of prescience, as a well-known and certain result when the scheme was projected. The theory that it was not only foreknown, but foreappointed, makes it appalling. What is the defense? In general it is that sin and all concomitant curse is an evil which God did not desire, did in no sense cause, did in every proper way strive to prevent. It is here not by his consent, but against his positive prohibition. It is not of his origination, but an inimical and alien force. It is not a part of his scheme, but an enemy to it. It is neither an end nor means of his. His universe did not include it, as a necessary or desirable part. It serves no purpose of his, and is in no proper sense of him. The only sense in which he is responsible for it is that he created beings with such powers that they might produce it, and with the knowledge that they would, at the same time that it was declared to be against his will that they should do so. Why did he, then, create them? If he did not desire sin why did he give existence to creatures whom he knew would cause it and its train of evils? Does he not thereby become the *de facto* author of it, despite his protests to the contrary? We do not desire to evade the difficulty if we cannot relieve it. It is one which we are all equally interested to study with honest candor and humble self-distrust. We have no other desire than to get at the truth, or as nearly as is possible to our finite faculties.

We know that he did create the universe, and that sin has smitten it. These are facts, and must be accepted as such by all. We cannot doubt his love or mistrust his wisdom and power. Its presence, therefore, must be reconcilable to these perfections, and all are alike interested to work out the reconciliation. He either did, or did not, desire it; did, or did not, cause it. That he did in any proper sense cause or wish it we find it on all accounts impossible to believe. Could he not, then, have prevented it? We are constrained to believe that he could. He might have created just such a universe as now exists, moral beings excepted. In that event sin would have had no existence. He might have varied creation so as to include other orders and kinds of being, capable of high degrees of good, and still have left out the possibility of sin from his plan. Possibly he might have made a moral universe on such a plan that sin would not have arisen. We cannot fix metes and bounds to possibilities with him. In determining on a plan of creation all possible concepts were present with him, however, and that which he did choose was chosen, we must believe, because his love accepted it as the best. That which he did choose had the possibility and foreknown certainty of sin in it, which to him was an objection to it, but he preferred it, despite the objectionable portion, to any other possible plan that did not include sin ; and the reason that his love preferred it was that it was less objectionable, or more desirable, with sin included, than any other *possible* plan was with sin excluded—more acceptable to love with sin, because it would reach a greater good, despite it, than could be reached in any other system excluding it. If it were possible to make moral beings who would certainly never sin, it would seem to be best to make some who certainly would sin, not because it was better they should sin than not sin—this we are certain is not the case—but because he saw that it would be better they should exist, even though they would sin than that they should not exist to prevent them from sinning. Sin was not desired, but their existence with attendant good was the thing desired, even though to give it sin must be possible.

Having admitted that possibly a moral universe might have been projected under such conditions that sin never would arise, we desire now to call attention to the fact that no such creation could be projected without the *possibility* of sin ; and we add further, without the probability and *de facto* certainty of sin, unless the conditions should be such as greatly to limit its extent and the degree and kind of its virtues.

This must appear if we consider what idea we attach to the term moral being. A moral being is one who is endowed with intelligence, conscience, and free will ; who knows a law ; who perceives its authority, and who has power to obey or disobey it. It is impossible to have a moral being without these constituent elements. Wherever moral beings are found, therefore, the *possibility* of recreance to law, or of sin, must exist. A moral nature might be so constituted and posited as to make the chances as a thousand to one that it would pursue a course of unvarying rectitude, and, *vice versâ*, a thousand to one that it would go astray. What would be the relative degree of virtue or sin we may not be able to determine. Infinite wisdom and love, if they exist in the Creator, must adjust the plan, in view of the single question, What, on the whole, taking the scale of eternity and the greatest number of moral consciousnesses, is the best? It might be best that the relative security of moral races should differ ; that some should be so circumstanced as to make the chances greatly in favor of their standing, and others so circumstanced as to be more in danger of falling ; but in no case could love permit the necessity of wrong-going, or the trial to integrity to be out of proportion to the power invested in the subject to withstand any possible temptation. The self-super-induced ruin of one might be the occasion of the safety of a thousand. That being a possibility, love might dictate the acceptance of that plan as preferable to any other. Nor let it be said that the supposition is equivalent to the supposition that sin is itself chosen, or a good. The plan provides for its nonexistence. The Author of the plan would prefer its nonexistence. It, under the plan, might not exist. That it does exist is fault of a free being, who was obliged by provision of law against it. He is its guilty author. He breaks his Maker's law and brings curse that but for him would have no existence. But now that he sins and evokes curse his Maker will extract from his crime a virtue of influence which will fix the allegiance of a thousand worlds. The walls of his prison shutting him in shall be converted into walls of defense against others coming to the same fate. Not a particle more love in the case is shown to the saved than lost. The same love gave being to each—planned in the same manner for the good of each—desired in the same measure the good of each. That one is destroyed is his own fault, when his opportunity to escape destruction differed in no respect from that of him who did escape. If his voluntary ruin is subordinated by love to purposes of defense and protection, that circumstance would furnish only another proof that love works to the uttermost against evil of every kind. The result of all that we can know in the premises is that love dictated the creation as it is; that not to have created, or to have created something else, would have been adverse to its dictate. The universe may not be, presumably is not, the best conceivable to infinite wisdom, but the best possible. It would have been better, we cannot doubt, the best conceivable, projected on the present plan, if the necessarily included possible sin had never become actual; but it is better with sin than any other possible would be without it. And though sin is an evil, fearful and great, infinite love and wisdom offset it, to as great an extent as possible, by making it the occasion of a manifestation of most glorious attributes which possibly might else have not found expression in the same degree. It is possible that out of evil, which the Infinite never could have desired, or caused as means, and which exists against his will, he may yet adduce a good more than counterbalancing. It is certain that the result will be so glorious, despite the foil, that it will reflect infinite honor on every attribute of the infinitely perfect Author. The evil itself, in his relations to it, will praise rather than dishonor him. By being shown to be an abuse of his love it will be an eternal witness to it. The infinite glory and happiness of those who reach the end his love devised will forever testify to the love he bore for all, even the lost, since it was his plan that all should attain to the same bliss, and since he made it as possible for those who fail as for those who succeed, furnishing them the same means, and discriminating in nothing against them. Their failure will recoil upon their own head, and it will be seen that for their ruin they are themselves the only and guilty cause. They will feel, and the universe will know, that their hapless lot is not for that they were unloved, but that they crucified love. Love opened heaven to them, invited them, died in sacrifice to win them. They spurned the offer and, self-doomed, are excluded. Love crowned them with blessings; they turned the blessings into curses.

But it is said since it was preknown that they would so destroy themselves love should have withheld the boon of existence from any ; that it would have been better there should have been no heaven than that *any* should be excluded from it; that, if in order to secure the happiness of many, some must be permitted to destroy themselves, it would have been better that the many should not have been created ; that heaven might better be blotted out than hell be a possibility ; that the raptures of millions of angels had better be hushed than that one should wail amid shades of woe. Who dare say that reason and conscience so affirm? Must love extinguish the bliss of myriads of holy and noble spirits, who might enrich eternity with their raptures, because it is powerless, with all its ministries, to rescue some from self-superinduced destruction? Would it be love that should do such a deed?

But is it said that in any event love should have withheld being from such as it was foreknown would prove unworthy of the boon, and have conferred it only where it would certainly be rightly used? If that were possible we do not doubt its preferableness; love would have been moved thereto ; but what if it were known to God that the very system which he has adopted contains in it the minimum of failures and the maximum of successes? What then would have been the dictates of love? Who dare say that it is not so? Does not the manifest love everywhere displayed warrant the belief that it is so? If, under any system, some will be lost, may we not reasonably suppose that the accepted system is that which contains the smallest number?

But is it said that at least those who show themselves unworthy should be extinguished and their sin and woes terminate at once and forever? Who is capable to determine that such a course would be productive of greater good than that they should continue to exist, as monuments of evil and sin? May we not reasonably believe that He who can only be actuated by love will use utmost influence to limit the evils of sin and suffering to the smallest extent possible, so that not a single pang will be allowed to remain that by any possibility of love might have been excluded? Surely all that can be known of Jehovah warrants this assuring belief.

There are peculiar phases of God's lovingness which merit especial mention. If, primarily and generically, it is universal good will and unchanging disposition to promote welfare it assumes special forms according as its objects vary in character and condition.

For the good and deserving it adds to the desire of welfare, and as a special means thereto, the manifestations of complaisancy and delight. It flows forth in benedictions. It admits to fellowship. It communicates joy. It warms and vivifies and exalts and ennobles its object. It feels and expresses affection. Such is God's love for all pure and holy beings. They are his " beloved," dear as the " apple of his eye," " engraved on his hands," " precious in his sight," his " friends," " his delights are with them," " he dwells with them ; " he uses all terms of endearment and approval and confidence, and fills them with exalting and rapturous sense of his regard for them ; they are always in his thought, and are his dear children ; he guards and watches them, and when sorrows and trials menace them he sends his angels to camp about them and comes himself to comfort and support them; he is tender of them and bears them in his bosom ; he has built a beautiful heaven for them, and will bring them away from all griefs and hardships to live with himself forever and ever. So his love is for the good. In the Scripture it is called grace—gracious favor, as importing its freeness and fullness and spontaneity—the overflow of infinite love to a finite creature—condescension.

For the undeserving and wicked who must always necessarily, to an infinitely holy God, be objects of disfavor and wrath, paradoxical as it may seem, love assumes another form. It cannot be complaisant; it is impossible it should approve; it is grieved and wounded. It assumes the form of pity and compassion. It entreats. It seeks. It longs to save and secure. It is fecund of arts to win. It restrains wrath. It stays the blow of punishment. "It is long-suffering and kind." It is willing to forgive slights and injuries. It is a father waiting at the gate for the returning prodigal.

For the penitent it is "joy among the angels of God;" it is the smile of acceptance, the balm of forgiveness; its hands hold out pardons; its tongue pronounces peace; it kisses the prodigal; its name is Mercy; it spreads a feast of rejoicing; it puts a ring on the hand and robes on the person of the returned prodigal, and says to him, "Thy sins, which were many, are all forgiven. Go in peace."

Such is God's love through earth and sky: approval and benedictions for the good; compassion for the suffering; patience and long-suffering for the wicked; mercy and pardon for the penitent. "God is love." But these are not the only forms of infinite love. There are that will not hear the pleadings of love; that grow more wicked because of its tenderness; that glory in their sin; that, living and dying, will never repent. Compassion fails, patience waits in vain, long-suffering is of no avail; all means are abortive, and it becomes evident that repentance is clear gone forever. What shall love do now?

There is but one thing left; it must give place to retribution. Nor does it cease to be love in doing this. It cannot longer prevent punishment, but the stroke is permitted and administered by love. The good of being at large prompts the individual retribution. To withhold the blow would be recreance to love. Hell itself is a monument of love. It is the prison house love builds for the protection of those who deserve the shelter. A father is none the less a loving father when his kisses turn to blows if the blows are administered in the interests of good. Just wrath is but incensed love.

JUSTICE OF GOD.

AKIN to the goodness of God is his justice. In the last analysis they are one. Justice is but a modification of love— love in one of its primitive and most fundamental aspects. It is that form of love which respects rights. In God it is that disposition which makes it impossible that he should be reconciled to wrong, or fail to punish it, or exact the equivalent of punishment, and which makes it impossible that he should not love right and defend and recompense it. It involves the perfect concept of right, and so is akin to wisdom. Love and wisdom are the primaries. Justice is the union of the two. It binds the divine nature to allegiance to their joint dictates, and is the realized essence of his righteousness. It is impossible that, being absolutely wise, knowing all things, and absolutely good, having in his essential being nothing contrary to love, he should not be absolutely just. Many brief definitions have been attempted; as Stapfer defines it, "Goodness directed by wisdom." The idea could not be better compendiously expressed. That is as nearly as possible its essence—the last thought of goodness regulated by wisdom, with respect to rights and welfare. The definition of Cudworth, expanded, is its exact equivalent, "Goodness administered by law;" law being the embodiment of wisdom. Knapp reaches the same in substance: "That attribute by which God actively exhibits his approbation of what is good, and his disapprobation of what is evil." Justice in essence is thus the approval of what love and wisdom determine ought to be, and in administration it is the unchangeable and perfect application of the principle.

Dr. Lord succinctly states the more common distinctions,

which ages of discussion have elicited on the subject. He says:

"The two most general distinctions which have been made touching the justice of God are those which resolve it into the absolute and the relative. (*a*) By the absolute justice of God is meant the perfect rectitude of his own infinite nature, or of all that is in himself. (*b*) By his relative justice is meant the perfect rectitude of all the actings of his nature with reference to creatures and events throughout the universe.

"Theologians have divided the relative justice of God into the rectoral, distributive, commutative, retributive, and punitive.

"(*a*) The rectoral justice of God is his justice viewed as that of the moral Governor of the universe, enacting righteous laws and righteously executing them.

"(*b*) His distributive justice is his justice viewed as bearing on individuals and communities, with rewards and punishments, according to their deserts. He distributes these on this ground.

"(*c*) His commutative justice is his justice viewed as changing the ground of his action in any particular case, but still maintaining every principle and claim of righteousness, as, for instance, when God justifies the ungodly. In this case the ground of action is not the personal righteousness of the sinner; it is the righteousness of Christ imputed to the sinner. [This Calvinistic tenet we reject.]

"(*d*) His retributive justice is that which dispenses rewards and punishments. This is essentially the same with that justice noted as distributive.

"(*e*) His punitive justice is that which inflicts punishment on sinners."

These distinctions are not without reason as noting the various aspects of the one principle of justice in its subjective essence and objective expression. They all point to the one essential idea of rights—the rules determinative of them, and an administration enforcing them.

The summation of which is that, such is the nature of God that he cannot himself do or tolerate wrong or fail to do right; that his nature is the perfect standard of right. There has sometimes been a bootless controversy carried on as to whether there is a standard of right to which God conforms or whether his will creates the standard. The answer must always be that there is no reality of any kind apart from God; nothing which dominates him; but, also, that right is eternal in him, and could not be different from what it is by any arbitrary act of will. He no more creates it than he creates his eternity. He has no power to change it. Were it possible for him to reverse his own nature he would not any more be the righteous God that he is. Righteousness dominates him as it does every moral creature. And this is only saying that his eternal nature is law to him, changeless and eternal.

This eternal inhering principle of justice in the divine nature makes it impossible, except by self-renunciation, that he should become or be unjust. Its imperative holds him immutably. It determines his will with relation to other beings whom he creates or might create. But since he determines himself, and is not determined by external agency, his justice is the free movement of an infinitely free nature—utmost spontaneity. That he cannot be different from what he is does not rise from want of freedom, but from the inevitability that an infinitely perfect being should act perfectly by spontaneity.

As the sole Author of the universe, his own essential nature holds him to strict responsibility for it. His justice as a form of love was a factor in deciding him to create. It is an eternal factor in deciding what he will do in the government of his creation. It determines the fact that he must govern. It determines the rules and regulations of his government. It makes it impossible without self-renunciation that he should require either too much or too little of his creatures; that the rules which he prescribes touching their relations to himself, or touching their relations to their own personality, and to other persons and things, should be faulty in any way, excessive, or defective. It necessitates a perfect law as to its requirements, for it is perfect justice—the legislation of infinite wisdom and goodness, neither requiring too much nor too little. It requires that the perfect rules and regulations should have suitable sanctions, neither excessive nor defective; that rewards and penalties should be in due measure, and be faithfully and effectively administered. It will neither allow of excuses nor escapes, but it will take exact account of all modifying circumstances. Its judgment will be exactly according to truth. It will in no wise clear the guilty. It will not be partial. It will be uniform, universal, and eternal. Such, we must believe, is the infinite justice of God, which is but another name for infinite love in one of its fundamental aspects and infinite wisdom in another. The anger ascribed to God as inspiring punishment is not of the nature of hate or evil animus. He punishes, not because he delights in the suffering inflicted, but because righteousness, which is but the principle which determines and maintains right, or but the assertion of the good—for the good is the right, and the right is the good, and that which maintains the good is goodness—demands it. Any other treatment would make him recreant to goodness. There is a necessity in his nature, if he remain the loving and wise, that he should render according to deserts; not to do it would be to deny his Godhead. Sin is of such a nature that not to punish, except for such reasons as would be the equivalents of punishment, answering the same ends and revealing the same character, would be to be partaker of its evil. We shall find in another part of this discussion the circumstances under which justice will allow of pardon.

The sum of which is that the infinite God infinitely and perfectly discerns what is right, and will eternally love the right, and administer according to the right in every case in the entire universe forever, without flaw or possibility of mistake, punishing where, all interests duly considered, punishment is for the good of being; rewarding where it is right to reward; and in no case violating the principle; the right being precisely as the good, as infinite wisdom discerns it and infinite love ordains it.

It is an essential element of justice, as love regulated by wisdom, that it should not tolerate suffering inflicted for no end of love or in excess of the demands of love. It may be perpetual, but it cannot be excessive, that is, more than love requires. That in the nature of God which requires him to resent whatever infringes the good of being does not move him to infringe the good of being himself, but it does require him to maintain it. The bestowment of good may be in excess of merit—may transcend any claim of right, may emanate from mere goodness; but the infliction of suffering can never be in excess of, or in opposition to, goodness.

There are bearings of the principles of justice, in relation to the treatment of sin, which will emerge when we come to the doctrine of atonement, which cannot be properly treated apart from that subject.

Under the general idea of goodness, as an attribute of God, we have found, are included the following: (*a*) That it denotes an eternal affection of his nature which seeks the greatest good of being, moving him to create and regulate the universe to that end; (*b*) that in the case of moral beings it assumes the form of complaisancy and esteem for those who conform to the order which works out the good of being, or the laws which are to that end, itself being the active principle which determines the laws; and it assumes the form of resentment against those who maliciously violate the same laws, thereby infringing the good of being; (*c*) in the case of those who suffer from any cause it assumes the form of compassion and pity, rendering the helps of support and comfort when possible ; (*d*) in the case of the willfully evil, along with resentment against their sin, it assumes the form of desire to reclaim them, and induces all possible methods of redeeming agency, forbearance, long-suffering, patience, entreaty, chastisements, sacrifice, showing that he is unwilling that any should destroy themselves ; (*e*) in the case of repentance assuming the form of forgiving mercy and regenerating grace; (*f*) in the case of the finally incorrigible assuming the form of punishment, administered by love for the protection of the universe ; (*g*) in the case of the obedient working out for them the most exalted character and bestowing upon them the rewards of immortal blessedness. Throughout he shows himself a God of infinite and impartial love. If whatever is is not best, this is not so of anything he has done, or ordered, or purposed. It is neither defect of his plan nor fault of his disposition. Flawless, ceaseless, infinite love sits upon the throne of the universe. "*God is love.*" "His mercy endureth forever." "His tender mercies are over all his works." "Justice and judgment are the habitation of his throne," but it is justice and judgment against evil. "He is a consuming fire," but it is only against evil. "He is angry," but his wrath kindles only against the wicked. He condemns and banishes and destroys, but only the workers of iniquity. He will forever hate sin, but his hate is but the intensity of his love of good. He enforces love, he pronounces blessings on every act of love, he inspires love, he is himself the eternal fountain of love. It is because he is love that he is an avenger, that evil trembles at the thought of him.

His love is not a mawkish sentiment against suffering. He does not account mere suffering an evil ; he ennobles it. His love does not shrink from pain; if need be he exalts it. It is heroic; it hurls wrath against evil. It makes no compromises. It hews to pieces its enemies. It is "slow to anger," but when it rises to judgment there is no escape. It waits long and patiently, but in the last it is a terrible avenger.

As justice is love protecting and regulating rights, so mercy is justice tempered to the feeble and erring and suffering, or a form of love which pities and under all possible circumstances forgives. It has relations to weakness and guilt. To the weak it is compassionate tenderness and helpfulness; in kind what the pitying mother feels for the suffering and helpless child. That such tenderness is a mode of infinite love is a most consolatory truth. "His tender mercies are over all his works." In ways past finding out he ministers to the broken in spirit. He tenderly carries them in his arms. He is the gentle Shepherd. In all their afflictions he is afflicted. He maketh all things work together for their good. He binds up their wounds and soothes their sorrows. He supports them with hope. When he ministers suffering, or bruises them with sorrow, it is not that he is hard and cruel, or unfeeling and unsympathetic, but it is as a father chastiseth his own son. All his discipline of reproof and suffering is that of compassionate love, that it may bring forth fruits unto holiness and life. He woos and entreats and comforts. He is a Father in his holy habitation. His tenderness and delicacy are seen in all the arrangements of nature, even among dumb things, in his care of maternity for the helpless young. It is he who coos and flutters in the dependent nest; hovers with sleepless vigils around the infant's cradle; softens the voice into soothing sweetness, and stills the footsteps into gentleness, and draws the curtain, and smoothes the pillow, and laves the aching temple and fevered brow in the chamber of sickness and death; gives to the eye tenderness and to the hand and tongue holy ministries in the presence of sorrow and misfortune. "A Father of the fatherless and husband of the widow" is God in his holy habitation.

To the guilty it is a disposition to forgive, expressed in long-suffering patience, in persuasions to penitence, in awakening reproofs, in provisions of grace, in atoning sacrifice. In this case it takes the name of mercy. Mercy is not unjust, and justice is not unmerciful. They are but reverse phases of the same attribute. An unmerciful God would be an unjust God, and an unjust God would be an unmerciful God. Redemption by the gift unto suffering and death of his only Son is an eternal monument of infinite mercy and also of his justice. He proclaims himself, as his dearest name, "the Lord God gracious and merciful, keeping mercy for thousands, forgiving iniquity and transgression and sin." He inspires the faith of this in every human heart. Alarmed guilt flies to him with confident hope of pardon. Only obduracy and impenitence dread his blow. He takes to himself the name Jesus, that is "above every name," because he will save. Judgment is a strange work with him. He delights not in the death of him that dieth, but would have all men turn to him and live. Punishment is his last resort. Whatever the severity of final retribution, it can never be unmerciful. It will still be a merciful but just Judge in the person of a loving Father, measuring punishment to an incorrigible child, whom not to punish would be both unmerciful and unjust. It is the universal consciousness of this that must forever compel the moral universe to reverence his righteous and holy throne. "Keeping mercy for thousands, forgiving iniquity and transgression and sin, and that will by no means clear the guilty," is the mystery of his reign of coequal justice and mercy, or perfect love to all being.

Van Oosterzee says: " It must not be passed over unobserved that this great saying ['God is love'] is met with in the utterance of an apostle who certainly penetrated more deeply than any other into the spirit of his Master; even the form of the expression shows more than that God may be spoken of as loving and kind. Kindness and love are certainly not convertible terms, although the expressions are constantly interchanged. Kindness may be shown to irrational creatures, animals, for instance; love can be shown only to rational beings. Kindness has reference to well-being in general ; love, on the other hand, has a higher aim, the development of the rational creature to its highest good. We may be kind even to the man whom we heartily despise ; love to such a one is possible only in so far as we still recognize and respect human nature in him. In a word, kindness is one of God's attributes; but love is, properly speaking, the nature of him who unites all these attributes in himself; he is love himself. All his properties must be regarded as the attributes of love, as adjectives of this peerless substantive. God's power is thus the power of love ; God's knowledge is the intelligence of love ; God's righteousness is the righteousness of love, and in its manifestation simply a means to attain to the exalted aim his love has in view. God is himself love, and his nature is nothing but pure love, so that if anyone would paint and set forth God he must draw such an image as should be pure love, representing the divine nature as the furnace and burning point of that love which fills heaven and earth (Luther)."

TRUTH A DIVINE ATTRIBUTE.

TRUTH is an attribute of God. He is himself the true God and the only, in contradistinction to all idols and false gods. The essence of all deific qualities is in him. He is real and personal, not a mere fancy or product of human thought. He is the most real of all beings, having the sole essence of eternal and and necessary existence exclusively in himself. All other being once had no existence, and might again become nonexistent. He always was, and never can cease to be. Other beings have no ground of existence in themselves—are but projected shadows, of which he is the substance and cause. If they should vanish he would abide—the " I am." In the deepest sense he is reality itself. As in his being he is real, so he is incapable of shams or dissimulations or falsities of expression. He will not deceive or fail. "His words stand fast forever, and his counsels to all generations." "He changes not." He is immutably sincere. His promises and threatenings will all be fulfilled to the last minutiæ. Implicit trust may be placed in him. No circumstance can ever arise which might make it desirable in him to alter his purpose or deviate from the straight line of his preconceived plan. The notable instances in which he seems to have altered his purpose, and to have failed in his promises and threatenings, are not exceptions in fact.

The summation of these ineffable moral perfections is absolute holiness. They interblend like prismatic hues in the solar ray, or as primary colors in the rainbow, to constitute one faultless whole—a pure and flawless unity. In him these perfections rise to such height that no defect or dimness blurs his glory. Nothing can be added. Nothing is wanting. "Holy, holy, holy, Lord

God of hosts: heaven and earth are full of thy glory," will be the shout of all exalted intelligences forever and ever. The higher they rise in faculty, and the more they become cognizant of his thought, and the deeper becomes their experience of his plans and ways, the more they will see that in him are the rounded and inexhaustible splendors of all perfections to utmost eternity.

Wardlaw beautifully says: "The different perfections of the divine nature might be likened to the seven primary colors of light, brought out as splendidly to the charmed eye when the solar rays, refracted by the intervening shower, paint a rainbow on the opposite clouds. Each of the colors is capable of distinct contemplations, like each of the perfections of God. But as all blended together constitute the pure, colorless, white light, so do all the divine excellences, combining in lovely, harmonious, and inseparable union, constitute his holiness."

Dr. Lord says: "Though usually treated as a distinct attribute, the holiness of God is, in fact, the result and sum of all the divine attributes, that is, the moral. It is God's moral perfection, the absolute conformity of his whole being and expression of being to that which is right, true, and good. Not only is he free from all moral imperfection, but he also possesses all moral excellence in an infinite degree."

Universal, absolute, and eternal sovereignty are prerogatives resulting from these infinite perfections. The universe belongs to God absolutely. No being possesses anything, not existence itself, except as a loan. The primary right is in God. The creature holds possession simply of grace. The being conferred is upheld by God from moment to moment. If he should withdraw his hand for an instant being itself must of necessity sink back to nothingness—nonexistence. The question has indeed sometimes been mooted whether existence, once conferred, has not a standing in itself, whether continuity of support is necessary. It has been assumed that it might and certainly would remain if the creative power were withdrawn; that, in fact, it would require an omnipotent fiat to abolish it, as much as it did to create. The controversy is to some extent a logomachy—a wordy dispute. The universe exists by the will of God—the reversal or abatement of his will would remove its foundations, and it would as necessarily perish as motion would cease when impelling force is withdrawn. As existence is evolved by volition, so its continuance is determined by volition and coextensive with it. Being is not only of him, but in him. All things are thus in his hands. He is sovereign over all, and renders no account of himself to any. He has neither counselors nor partners of his throne. "He does always and in all things what seemeth good in his own sight." All spirits and all atoms and forces bow to him. The entire creation is as nothing, and less than nothing, and vanity before him. Nothing can be more certain than this absolute supremacy of the Almighty. Nothing of being or power can stand against his will or out of his will. But for the ægis of his love it would excite dismay to think of the utter helplessness of all being—how with a single volition in a moment of time the pillars of heaven would crumble and all created being fade away, and only silence and emptiness reign where worlds and angels were.

But let us not mistake the nature of God's sovereignty, as is sometimes done. The fact of absolute sovereignty and consequent nonamenability to any other being does not imply nonrestraint of law. If he imposes law upon all creatures his own nature imposes law upon himself. The perfections which determine the metes and bounds of created things govern the uncreated as well. His sovereignty is that of the infinitely perfect. The power that sways him is subjective, immanent, moral, the last dictate of unerring wisdom and limitless love. Absolutely free in its obedience, it nevertheless leads his activities unerringly as gravitation determines the marches of the universe. Freedom with God is not freedom of imperfection, but freedom of perfection. He has absolute power over his own acts, as well as over the things which he creates, but his freedom will not do violence to his wisdom and goodness. He will forever do right. Nor let us imagine that his absolute sovereignty implies that he reigns over persons as he reigns over things. There his rule is of necessity; here it is that of liberty. There he governs by force; here by law over free beings and moral influence. In the realm of force his will is necessity. In the realm of mind his will is law, but not causation. His sovereignty consists in this, that he alone gives law and he alone administers law. Of his own will here he gives freedom to the subject to break or keep the law which he appoints. He acts as a sovereign in bestowing the liberty. It is a sovereign act by which he creates a being who shall be free from necessity, who shall have power to be a cause himself. His sovereignty will not interfere with the liberty it bestows. He, by an act of sovereignty, puts from himself the determination what the creature's act shall be, but he does not therefore put away his sovereignty or release the creature from subjection and responsibility. He may do as he lists, and he will not fetter him, but he will call him to account. The sovereignty that will not override liberty will demand an account of its use. The laws of the two realms differ—the subjects differ, the modes of administration differ; liberty reigns here, necessity there, but the same sovereign holds the reins of universal dominion, alike in regions where atoms form necessitated compacts and in the realms where spirits, self-determined, select their own pursuits and elect their own destinies.

Nor does this idea of sovereignty imply that there is any uncertainty in events—any unforeseen exigencies—any possibilities of facts not anticipated and arranged for at the beginning. The facts of freedom, as much as those of necessity, are perfectly under the governance of law and sovereign control, the difference being that in the one case the Sovereign exerts his power to cause the immediate event, which is to express his will; in the other he permits a power which he has created to act from itself, foreseeing how it will act, and from eternity adjusting his administration accordingly. In the latter case, when the free power expresses itself freely, without causation from him, it is acting as he created it to act—freely; when it disobeys his command, it is acting contrary to his law, as to the use of power, but in accordance with the power he bestows; foreseeing that it would so act, he holds it under government, by subjecting it to punishment. The sovereignty over it is strict and perfect, but it is the sovereignty of law for free beings, and not of force for necessary beings.

It must be obvious that so soon as we depart from this idea of sovereignty, and adopt the idea that sovereignty implies the sway of absolute causational force, directing all events, we abolish freedom from the universe.

The sum of our conclusions thus reached shows that there is perfect harmony between the teachings of the Bible and the deepest reaches of human reason. The God set forth in the former is the God demanded by the latter. There is no break in the harmony—neither defect nor excess nor contradiction. Reason has nothing to allege which revelation has omitted, and will permit nothing to be removed which it has affirmed. Neither science nor philosophy brings forward any facts or principles which call for a modification of the divine statement. The wonderful fact is that after all the improvements in knowledge, and growth of the power of expression, we still are compelled to go to the ancient Scriptures for the truest and richest delineation of the divine character. Neither reason nor fancy can improve the picture, by addition or subtraction. What poet or sage has ever surpassed or equaled the sublime predications of Moses, David, Isaiah, and others of the ancient prophets, not to mention the more simple teachings of Him in whom all the matchless attributes were incarnated? Astronomy has brought treasures of knowledge from the stars; geology has quarried into the bowels of the earth; metaphysics has searched the deepest secrets of mind itself. Has any light come from any quarter which has corrected any teaching of the holy books? We challenge the learning of the world to furnish the proof. There it stands, and must forever stand, as impregnable as the geometric axioms, unchangeable and unmodifiable. God is a spirit, eternal, absolute, unconditioned, infinite, immutable, sole self-existing; a person, intelligent, self-conscious and self-determining; omniscient, omnipotent, omnipresent, the sole Creator in and of the universe; absolutely good, just, and holy in all his principles, laws, and administrative acts; who doeth according to his own pleasure forever and ever; whose sovereignty is, and forever must be, one of absolute regnancy, but regulated by love and wisdom; whom no one hath seen, or can see, but in whom all have their being. In comparison with him all things are as nothing—less than nothing—and vanity.

No thoughtful mind can think of the Almighty without awe. The prophet of Uz well exclaimed, "When I consider, I am afraid of him"—I stand in awe of him. "He spreadeth out the heavens as a tent to dwell in" (Job xxiii, 15; Isa. xl, 22). In vain we strive to reach the height of the great theme; words and even thought fail us. The awful solitude and majesty of his being overwhelm us. We cannot but find relief in adoring wonder, and in the more comforting thought that his majesty is our unfailing strength. The ultimate conclusion of reason is that God is, and in the universe is eternally at his best. It is in its progress forever the best universe possible to omnipotent power, infinite wisdom, and holy love.

In our helplessness we take refuge in the almost inspired words of the German hymnist, Ernest Lauge:

> "O God, thou bottomless abyss!
> Thee to perfection who can know?
> O height immense! what words suffice
> Thy countless attributes to show?
>
> "Greatness unspeakable is thine;
> Greatness, whose undiminished ray,
> When short-lived worlds are lost, shall shine,
> When earth and heaven are fled away.
>
> "Unchangeable, all-perfect Lord,
> Essential life's unbounded sea,
> What lives and moves, lives by thy word;
> It lives, and moves, and is, from thee.
>
> "High is thy power above all height;
> Whate'er thy will decrees is done;
> Thy wisdom, equal to thy might,
> Only to thee, O God, is known!"

THE END.

www.ingramcontent.com/pod-product-compliance
Lightning Source LLC
Chambersburg PA
CBHW022023240426
43667CB00042B/1066